Speaking Truth to Power

Speaking Truth to Power

CONFIDENTIAL INFORMANTS AND
POLICE INVESTIGATIONS

Dean A. Dabney and
Richard Tewksbury

UNIVERSITY OF CALIFORNIA PRESS

University of California Press, one of the most distinguished university presses in the United States, enriches lives around the world by advancing scholarship in the humanities, social sciences, and natural sciences. Its activities are supported by the UC Press Foundation and by philanthropic contributions from individuals and institutions. For more information, visit www.ucpress.edu.

University of California Press
Oakland, California

Library of Congress Cataloging-in-Publication Data

Names: Dabney, Dean A., author. | Tewksbury, Richard A., author.
Title: Speaking truth to power : confidential informants and police
    investigations / Dean A. Dabney and Richard Tewksbury.
Description: Oakland, California : University of California Press, [2016] |
    Includes bibliographical references and index. | Description based on print
    version record and CIP data provided by publisher; resource not viewed.
Identifiers: LCCN 2016018678 (print) | LCCN 2016018070 (ebook) |
    ISBN 9780520964624 (Epub) | ISBN 9780520290464 (cloth : alk. paper) |
    ISBN 9780520290488 (pbk. : alk. paper)
Subjects: LCSH: Informers—United States. | Drug control—United States.
Classification: LCC HV8141 (print) | LCC HV8141 .D33 2016 (ebook) |
    DDC 363.25/4—dc23
LC record available at https://lccn.loc.gov/2016018678

Manufactured in the United States of America

25 24 23 22 21 20 19 18 17 16
10 9 8 7 6 5 4 3 2 1

*To our families: Lisa and Wyn, as well as Carmen,
Tate, Addie, and Tate*

CONTENTS

ACKNOWLEDGMENTS

We want to thank the Andrew Young School of Policy Studies at Georgia State University for funding our visiting scholar proposal, which allowed for critical data collection and collaborative writing trips that would have been otherwise impossible. We are also grateful to colleagues at Georgia State, specifically Don Hunt and Shila Hawk, who assisted with data collection, coding, and library work; Lou Arcangeli, who assisted with interview recruitment and insightful feedback on the project's direction; and Richard Wright, who provided invaluable feedback on draft materials. At the University of Louisville, we are thankful for the excellent transcription work of Sandra Wade. We also appreciate the support and assistance that we received from the staff of the University of California Press, including Maura Roessner and Jack Young, who oversaw the editorial process; Chris Loomis, Dore Brown, and Jessica Ling, who oversaw various stages of the marketing and production process; and Genevieve Thurston, who copyedited the manuscript. Finally, this project would not have been possible were it not for the officers of the two unnamed metropolitan police departments that boldly opened their doors to our wide-ranging ethnographic work and the many law enforcement officers from the more than a dozen local, state, and federal agencies who took time out of their busy lives to participate in our lengthy interviews.

ONE

Police and Confidential Informants

For the past forty years, the American criminal justice system has been at the forefront of a war on drugs. Law enforcement authorities have served as the front line in this battle, heading up a wide-ranging array of domestic interdiction operations. Budgetary data speak to the breadth and depth of this prolonged intervention. According to a recent Rand Corporation study, police have spent an estimated $600 billion on domestic interdiction operations since the early 1980s (Chalk 2011). In fiscal year 2015 alone, federal and state authorities budgeted nearly $10 billion for local, state, and federal drug enforcement operations; an additional $5 billion was requested to fund domestic and international interdiction efforts (Office of National Drug Control Policy 2015).* Moreover, government and private funding entities allocate hundreds of millions of dollars for research, training, and technical assistance grants to agencies, universities, and nonprofit organizations.

Domestic drug enforcement takes many forms, from the rural patrol officer who happens on a small-scale mobile "shake-and-bake" methamphetamine lab during a routine traffic stop, to the city narcotics detective who initiates a low-level buy-bust operation that nets a few hits of crack cocaine on the street corner, to the local, state, and federal agents working in multiagency taskforces that coordinate large-scale sting operations that net thousands of kilo bricks of near-pure cocaine being transported by tractor-trailer. Regardless of the form, there is a high probability that the precursor or aftermath of each of these scenarios will involve law enforcement authorities exploiting access to known offenders and exerting pressure on them to gather

---

*In fiscal year 2015, supply-side spending came to $14.8 billion, or roughly 56 percent of the total $26.3 billion allocated to the US war on drugs.

inside information about active illicit drug markets. "Confidential informant" is the common label affixed to those individuals who provide intelligence on the inner workings of an illicit drug operation in exchange for leniency or remuneration. Given the heightened enforcement efforts and heavy legal penalties associated with drug crime, persons who sell drugs often find it in their best interests to conceal their activities from law enforcement agents and diversify operations so as to minimize their exposure to the threat of apprehension and escalating sanctions. Concomitantly, harsh formal responses have led to the development of a sophisticated and hierarchical structure to deal with the manufacture, transportation, and distribution of illicit drugs, with many players serving many different roles within a clandestine system that necessitates deliberate means of intelligence and infiltration. While police enlist the intelligence of confidential informants to advance their criminal investigation efforts into most every type of offending, it is within the context of narcotics enforcement that this practice most frequently comes to our attention.

PUSHES AND PULLS OF CONFIDENTIAL INFORMANT USAGE

The above-mentioned multilayered reality both pushes and pulls law enforcement authorities toward the use of confidential informants. The secretive, wide-ranging, and hierarchical nature of illicit criminal enterprises pushes law enforcement authorities to use confidential informants. In the case of the illegal drug market, all players—from street level dealers to cartel chieftains—methodically conceal their identities from law enforcement as a means of mitigating negative consequences. Narcotics investigators have come to rely on insiders, from witnesses to drug users to street hustlers, as a means of revealing the identities of the persons who manufacture, traffic, and distribute illegal drugs. Once the identities of drug dealers are known, police must discern the nature of the drug operation and catch the participants engaging in an illegal transaction. Here, again, police are pushed to rely on participants in the drug market (e.g., users, lower-level dealers, etc.) as a means of setting up and participating in the transaction under the watchful eye of fellow law enforcement authorities (Worrall 2001; Wisotsky 1986).

Not only are officers pushed toward the use of confidential informants due to the outsider status of police in criminal enterprises but they are also pulled toward it by the internal workings of modern police agencies and by their own self-interests. Today, police officers are routinely evaluated based on their success in disrupting criminal activity. Law enforcement agencies have grown increasingly accustomed to systematically counting arrests, showcasing significant disruptions of criminal enterprises via the media, and documenting changes in crime rates within their jurisdiction. This is especially true when it comes to drug crime, as the aforementioned massive budgetary commitments and high-profile nature of the problem ratchet up expectations to impact drug crime in a measurable and meaningful way. At the most mundane level, especially in the growing number of local police departments that have adopted a Compstat management system, the meticulous tracking of the number and location of calls for drug-related service and arrests has become an institutionalized practice.* The officers account for their existence and present their work outputs in the form of weekly briefings, annual reports, and web platforms that afford near real-time access to crime statistics (Weisburd et al. 2004). This produces various forms of internal pressure within police agencies, which in turn leads to competition among officers and across units for the glory that goes along with changes in arrest numbers and high-profile drug busts (Dabney 2010). The use of confidential informants is a proven means through which to clear drug crimes. In fact, Roger Billingsley, Teresa Nemitz, and Philip Bean estimate that "about one third of all crimes cleared up by police involve the use of informers [broadly defined to include citizens who provide tips, paid informants, and apprehended criminals seeking to work off charges]" (2001, 5). Thinking more proactively, police agencies have come to appreciate that the threat of sanctions for drug crimes serves as a valuable tool to compel persons to provide actionable information on any unsolved crime. Investigators routinely pry information pertaining to open burglary, robbery, rape, or murder cases from offenders who are faced with the threat of heavy charges and sentences for drug offenses. It is on this basis that former director of the FBI William Webster is credited with stating: "The informant is the single most important tool in law enforcement" (cited in Bloom 2002, 158).

At a more bureaucratic level, Kraska (2001) observes that police agencies have grown increasingly specialized in their structures, instituting myriad

---

*A national survey effort led Weisburd, Mastrofski, Greenspan, and Willis (2004) to estimate that more than half of all local police departments were employing a Compstat-based system at the turn of the twenty-first century.

specialty units dedicated to drug interdiction, violent crime, and any number of other proactive investigative entities. With the creation of these units comes a heightened expectation for results. Once again, unit competition for resources, accolades, and promotions prompts officers to increase their arrest numbers. Confidential informants have become a primary means through which to achieve this goal, and thus specialty units are pulled toward using them. Alexandra Natapoff observes that, "especially in the expansive arena of drug enforcement, turning suspects into so-called snitches has become a central feature of the way America manages crime" (2009, 2). Here, again, the pull of confidential informant usage is readily apparent.

At the officer level, be it the patrol officer who happens on a drug offense during routine 911-driven activities or the tactical officer charged with full-time drug interdiction work, the use of confidential informants represents an efficient and effective means of generating arrests. This is not a new development in law enforcement. A full 44 percent of patrol officers in Arthur Niederhoffer's 1969 sample of metropolitan police officers claimed that the best arrests come, "as a result of good information from an informer" (1969, 218). This longstanding pull has been exacerbated greatly by the aggressive war on drugs, in which the officer is the cat and the offender is the mouse. The mouse knows where all the other mice play and the cat wants in on the game. The most expedient way to find more mice is enlist the help of those mice that are at your disposal. Peter Manning's ethnography of the inner workings of metropolitan narcotics units illustrates this point well. Referring to detectives' views of informants, he observes that "officers had learned to see their possibilities for success as dependent on identifying, cultivating, working, and maintaining their informants. They assumed that this was the most fruitful way of working in large part because they had never done anything else, had received little or no formal training, had not seen other modes used, and because it was seen as an almost standard mode of working" (Manning 2004, 149). Simply stated, officers are pulled toward using confidential informants because doing so feeds the officers' occupational self-interest; informants represent the path of least resistance in the war on crime in general and on drugs in particular.

Although it has been thrust into the public eye in recent decades due to heightened media coverage and the war on drugs, the phenomenon of confidential informant usage has a long and storied tradition in law enforcement. Clifford Zimmerman (1994) and James Morton (1995) provide the most in-depth and far-reaching historical accounts of the practice. Focusing globally,

Morton finds evidence of government officials coercing information from at-risk citizens dating as far back as ancient Greece. Zimmerman concentrates his historical account on the development of informant practices in England and the United States. He documents the British use of an "approver system" as far back as the late thirteenth century whereby entities of the state offered reduced sentences to convicted criminals in exchange for information that led to the conviction of a set number of their criminal counterparts. Zimmerman also documents the emergence, in the sixteenth century, of a "common informer system," wherein state officials paid common citizens in exchange for information about ongoing wrongdoing in the community. Both Zimmerman and Morton provide detailed historical analyses of legal and bureaucratic history of informant use in twentieth century Britain and America.* Clearly, the United States and Britain are not the only countries to rely on confidential informants to advance the investigative efforts of law enforcement. *Undercover: Police Surveillance in Comparative Perspective,* edited by Cyrille Fijnaut and Gary Marx (1996), provides additional historical details as they relate to the phenomenon in France, Germany, Holland, Belgium, Britain, Iceland, Sweden, Canada, and the United States.

APPLIED LITERATURE ON INFORMANTS

Given the long tradition of reliance on confidential sources of information and the prominence of these sources in the daily operations of law enforcement, it should come as no surprise that there exists a wide body of literature on the topic. What is somewhat surprising is the limited depth associated with this body of published work. Generally speaking, the literature on confidential informants can be divided into two categories: training materials that provide pragmatic insight to law enforcement officers and scholarly works that apply a social science lens to the confidential informant phenomenon. The former category is comprised largely of book-length instructional treatises (Billingsley 2001b, 2003, 2009; Billingsley, Nemitz, and Bean 2001; E. Brown 2007; Cloyd 1982; Fitzgerald 2007; Harney and Cross 1960; Hanvey 1995; Madinger 1999; Mallory 2000; Motto and June 2000;

---

*See also Billingsley (2001a) for a complete history of confidential informant usage in Britain; and Natapoff (2009), Marx (1988), and Harney and Cross (1960) for parallel accounts within the American experience.

Palmiotto 1984), government reports or agency manuals (Federal Bureau of Investigations 2005; Gardiner 2002; International Association of Chiefs of Police 1990; Janzen 1990; H. Katz 1990; Newburn and Merry 1990; Nugent, Leahy, and Connors 1991; U.S. Department of Justice 2005), and articles published in law enforcement trade journals, such as *The Police Chief, FBI Law Enforcement Bulletin,* and *Law and Order* (M. F. Brown 1985; Geberth 1979; Hamilton and Smykla 1994; Lee 1981; Kleinman 1980; Mount 1991; Rees 1980; Vasquez and Kelly 1980). Collectively, these works outline best practices in informant usage, provide a cursory overview of the legal landscape associated with informant usage, and draw attention to a host of potential pitfalls that are associated with the involvement of informants in police operations.

Two seasoned state and federal narcotics investigators, John Harney and Malachi Cross, got the ball rolling with their 1960 book, *The Informer in Law Enforcement.* Designed as both a descriptive treatise and an effort to dispel misconceptions about the role of informants in the criminal investigation process, the book advocates for a host of informant roles within the investigative process, details the various motives that lead persons to serve as informants, provides guidance on how to handle informants, and proffers a summary of the legal landscape of informant usage. A decade later, Carmine Motto (1971), a former Secret Service agent, presented *Undercover,* a trade book designed to outline the interrelated relationships between investigators, informants, and suspects. Based on years of experience and personal insights, Motto's book (which was updated and released in a second edition in 2000) sought to both inform law enforcement officers and provide the public with a look inside such relationships.

In the modern era, retired British police commander Roger Billingsley has been at the forefront of the applied literature on confidential informants (Billingsley 2001a, 2001b, 2003, 2009; Billingsley Nemitz, and Bean 2001). The books that he and other seasoned practitioners have published (Alvarez 1993; Cloyd 1982; Fitzgerald 2007, Grimes 2009; Hanvey 1995; Lyman 1987; Madinger 1999; Mallory 2000) provide a wealth of useful background information on different types of informants, their practical use in modern criminal investigations, and operational insights on how to most effectively nurture these intelligence assets. Designed principally for a practitioner audience, these training resources are descriptive and instructive in nature, intended to cover all the relevant topics that an in-service reader would need to maximize his or her agency's efforts to use covert intelligence sources, which include goodwilled citizens reporting on isolated crime incidents, apprehended criminals seeking to curry leniency in charges, and paid informants. In this context, enlisting the assistance of known criminals to further criminal investigations is generally framed as a necessary evil, especially when dealing with hidden and/or networked criminality, such as narcotics distribution, gunrunning, or transactional property crime. Common chapter headings in these books include "types of informants," "recruitment," "handling informants," "compensation options," "communication strategies," "risk management strategies," "ethical considerations," and "legal issues." The books are written from the viewpoint of seasoned insiders, and the authors are all current or retired police officers who draw on personal experiences to assist their law enforcement colleagues in navigating the trials and tribulations that go along with informant usage.

Primarily as a result of the centrality of informants within narcotics and organized crime investigations, numerous large law enforcement agencies and justice support organizations have published manuals or reports that add to the literature on confidential informants. For example, government agencies in the United States (H. Katz 1990; Nugent, Leahy, and Connors 1991; U.S. Department of Justice 2005) and the United Kingdom (Newburn and Merry 1990) have produced full-length reports outlining the legal landscape of informant usage, listing steps that can be taken to effectively utilize these assets within the context of various types of criminal investigations, and recommending structures and processes that have yielded the best results in this regard. In a similar vein, law enforcement support organizations such as the International Association of Chiefs of Police (1990) and the Police Executive Research Forum (Janzen 1990) have published resource manuals designed to provide actionable guidance on various aspects of confidential informant usage.

Not surprisingly, as criticism and scandal have beset agency reliance on confidential informants, oversight entities have conducted formal inquiries at the micro or macro level to remedy past transgressions and forge a path forward in the way of best practice articulation. Reports such as those issued by the Federal Bureau of Investigation (2005) or the U.S. Department of Justice (Gardiner 2002) stand as obvious examples in this respect. The practitioner-oriented literature is also interspersed with short articles in trade journals that amount to agency retrospectives or targeted practical guidance on various aspects of confidential informant usage (M. F. Brown 1985; Geberth 1979; Hight 1998; Kleinman 1980; Lee 1981; Mount 1991; Rees 1980; Vasquez and Kelly 1980).

Much can be learned from the practitioner literature about the bureaucratic realities and logistical considerations that come with the use of confidential informants. It is important to note that these sources emphasize policy and practice over issues such as theory development and thick description of social phenomena, which guide the present research monograph. Therefore, we turn to the scholarly literature at this point to provide a better context for the current project.

SCHOLARLY LITERATURE ON INFORMANTS

The informant literature targeting academic audiences is partitioned into two broad categories: (1) legal analyses intended to systematically articulate and assess the legal landscape of informant usage in law enforcement and (2) social science scholarship designed to describe, contextualize, and/or theorize the nature of the informant-police relationship in various ways. Legal scholars have provided detailed analyses of the existing case law relevant to confidential informant usage (Glover 2001; Leson 2012; Mauet 1995; Natapoff 2004; Neyroud and Beckley 2001; Rich 2010; Sobczak 2009; Weinstein 1999; Zimmerman 1994). These works detail and theorize the legal landscape related to informant usage in what is generally a critical tone. For example, Rod Settle notes: "When it comes to the use of informers, many basic legal principles concerning admissibility of evidence, disclosure of sources and even, to some degree, the use of agent provocateur, are explained away in the interest of 'serving the public good' by obtaining convictions for breaches of the law" (1995, 5). By highlighting precedent-setting cases, these legal treatises articulate the steps needed to establish informant reliability, protection of informant identity, the application of entrapment issues, liability issues surrounding informant acts and payment, applications of the Thirteenth Amendment ban on involuntary servitude as it applies to coerced informants, administrative transparency issues, due process protections expected in informant-involved cases, and how informant cooperation can be incorporated in negotiated plea agreements. As is customary in the law review format, scholars such as Michael Rich (2010), Thomas Mauet (1995), and Tim Sobczak (2009) conclude their articles by articulating and proposing theoretically informed revisions to the system of confidential informant usage. These proposed changes amount to recommended system improvements, in that extrapolations of precedent and legal theory aim to make modest changes to the structure and process through which police recruit and manage informants as well as how the courts incorporate the resultant information into the adjudication process. Legal scholars such as Natapoff (2004) and Zimmerman (1994), however, raise more serious concerns about the use of confidential informants and call for system redesign, proposing broad sweeping revisions. Referring to the current system, Natapoff notes: "Characterized by secrecy, unfettered law enforcement discretion, and informal negotiations with criminal suspects, the informant institution both embodies and exacerbates some of the most problematic features of the criminal justice process" (2004, 645). Calling into question the fundamental legitimacy and ethical foundation of turning a blind eye on known criminal activity and pitting criminals against criminals, Natapoff (2004) and Zimmerman (1994) draw heavily on the principles of due process and governmental openness and call for heightened transparency and accountability for law enforcement agencies using informants and dramatic restrictions on informant reward structures. Several other scholars have expanded on the ethics of confidential informant use (Clark 2001; Cooper and Murphy 1997; Dunningham and Norris 1999; Langworthy 1989; Schoeman 1986; Westmarland 2013; Westley 1956; Williams and Guess 1981; Williamson and Bagshaw 2001).

In addition to the legal analyses above, which adopt a broad sweeping focus and provide survey coverage on a host of issues, there also exist law review articles that are narrower in focus and provide in-depth analysis on informant usage in specific contexts. For example, there are articles that detail the special circumstances and precedents that apply to informant usage in cases involving juveniles (Herbert and Sinclair 1977; Osther 1999); informant usage within specific agencies, such as the FBI (Schreiber 2001); and informant usage linked to wrongful convictions (Natapoff 2006). For sure, the extant legal scholarship illuminates a host of due process and evidentiary issues and raises important questions about the consequences of informant usage in criminal investigations. However, with the exception of Natapoff's work, this body of literature does little to delve into the lived experiences of the law enforcement officers and suspects who proffer and extract the sensitive information that makes its way into the official record. This endeavor is reserved for sociologists and criminologists who engage the subject matter on the ground level. Given the hidden and stigmatized nature of this behavior, it is not surprising that these sociological and criminological inquiries have relied on convenience samples and pursued face-to-face interviewing and/or observational data collection techniques.

The majority of the ground-level work has explored the informant phenomenon from the law enforcement agents' perspective (Dodge 2006; Dorn, Karim, and South 1992; Ericson 1981; Jacobs 1992, 1996, 1997; Leo 2008; Manning 1980; Marx 1974, 1981, 1985, 1988; Morton 1995; Niederhoffer 1969; Pogrebin and Poole 1993; Skolnick 1966; Wilson 1978), while only a select few studies have undertaken the difficult task of exploring the topic from the perpetrators' vantage point by assembling a sample of offenders. Under the broad rubric of offender-based research, there is work (e.g., Miller 2011) that seeks to articulate the behavior and cognitions of those who provide inside information on criminal behavior (i.e., the snitches). Other studies seek to shed light on the way the criminal operators (i.e., the snitched on) seek to protect themselves from being exposed or how they respond to those suspected of snitching (Fleisher 1995; Jacobs 1993a, 1993b; Murphy, Waldorf and Reinarman 1990; Pfuhl 1992; Rosenfeld, Jacobs, and Wright 2003; Tewksbury and Mustaine 1998; Topalli 2005; Tunnell 1992).

Agent-Based Research

Initial empirical insights about the nature and dynamic of confidential informant usage came from organizational ethnographies of criminal investigation efforts in large metropolitan police departments. For example, *Justice without Trial: Law Enforcement in a Democratic Society,* Jerome Skolnick's 1966 classic research monograph on the culture within a large metropolitan police department, includes a chapter on the "informer system." Skolnick observed that police investigators were afforded high levels of discretion when dealing with drug offenders compared with when they dealt with the perpetrators of property crimes or violent crimes. He noted that investigators held generally negative views of drug offenders and sought to leverage the long criminal records of these offenders and the threat of severe sentences to generate leads on bigger and better cases. He went on to suggest that narcotics investigators were dependent on users and low-level dealers to generate inside information on the hierarchical and secretive narcotics market. In an article written two decades later, Skolnick (1982) described an acceptance of informant usage among police supervisors who were simultaneously frustrated by the complexity of the drug market hierarchy that they were tasked with cracking and encouraged by the ease with which actionable intelligence and solid case materials could be generated by exerting pressure on vulnerable drug offenders who found themselves caught up in the criminal justice system. Skolnick concluded his 1966 book with: "There can be no doubt that informants are essential for law enforcement, especially for narcotics control" (1966, 68).

James Q. Wilson's 1978 research monograph exploring the relationship between organizational structure and investigative processes of the FBI and DEA also includes a chapter dedicated to confidential informants. Here, again, the role of informants is characterized as being central to the goals of the organization, as evidenced by the following sentences that open up the chapter: "Having productive informants is essential to many FBI cases, indispensable in virtually all DEA cases. Differences in the ability to develop and utilize this vital resource accounts, more than any other factor, for the differences in the success of investigations" (Wilson 1978, 61). Wilson characterizes informants as serving three primary roles in federal law enforcement: generating leads, assisting undercover agents in infiltrating complex criminal organizations, and testifying in court about the misdeeds of criminal accomplices. He also provides systematic insight into informant recruitment, management, and motivation. He concludes by detailing the various benefits and pitfalls that come with the heavy reliance on confidential informants. These insights largely mirror the themes contained in the applied practitioner-authored literature but are delivered in a more sociological context. It is noteworthy that Wilson's (1968, 1978) work helped inform several other scholarly projects detailing the interplay between informants and police officers in various other aspect of criminal investigation (e.g., Leo 2008; Reuter 1982).

A more in-depth and theoretically centered discussion of confidential informants was provided by Peter Manning in his 1980 monograph, *The Narcs' Game: Organizational and Informational Limits on Drug Law Enforcement*. This organizational ethnography focuses on the narcotics units within two urban police departments, with several chapters dedicated to what the author terms the "agent-informant approach." These chapters detail the interplay between officers (i.e., agents) and the paid, civic-minded, or pressured citizens who provide leads or evidence that shape street-level drug policing efforts. The agent-informant approach, which is operationalized as a wide range of strategies and tactics specific to the intentional exchange of intelligence between officers and members of the criminal underworld, is theorized as being central to effective narcotics investigations. The text also sheds light on how investigators view and seek to manipulate sources of information to advance personal and unit-level goals. Manning's analysis is a largely cautionary assessment of the centrality of informant usage in narcotics enforcement, one that stresses the manner in which situated rationality leads detectives and the larger bureaucracy to embrace building drug cases based on information extracted from informants. He places confidential informants at the center of what he calls the "narcs' game," through which individual investigators and the larger department document and justify their efforts to systematically control illegal drug markets.

In 1988, Gary Marx published the book *Undercover: Police Surveillance in America*. The monograph is a critical assessment of undercover work in law enforcement and makes the case that the scope and complexity of covert policing expanded greatly during the post–World War II era. Marx observes that, up to that point, undercover police work had been restricted to "buy-busts" targeting the suppliers of sex and drugs. He reinforces that, from its inception, this approach to law enforcement was deemed a necessary evil due to the covert and consensual nature of vice crime transactions and the insulated hierarchies of the illicit organizations that supplied them. However, he argues that increasing complexity and aggressiveness in law enforcement, along with the perceived threat of organized crime syndicates, led to a considerable expansion in undercover operations. Marx notes that the investigation of property crimes and violent crimes slowly became laden with undercover operations as well. Buy-busts targeting the suppliers of illicit goods and services were expanded to include covert "sell-bust" operations targeting consumers. He contends that human surveillance derived from confidential informants and undercover officers eventually morphed into a host of technologically enhanced means of electronic surveillance. He concludes that law enforcement organizations, from small-scale local police departments to vast federal agencies, had grown to see undercover operations as a cornerstone of effective crime-fighting. In detailing this expansion in the scope and complexity of police surveillance, Marx adds considerably to our scholarly insight on confidential informants. Similar to those before him, he details the motivations and behaviors of officers and informants involved in covert police operations, the norms and policies of the agencies within which they take place, and the way in which they shape crime-fighting outcomes. However, he advances the argument that confidential informant usage has grown more central to the daily crime-fighting endeavors of law enforcement agencies and also experienced a heightened level of technical sophistication over time. He also details for the reader a host of intended and unintended consequences that these operations have on police and citizens.

Other researchers have used studies on undercover police operations as a means of informing the literature on police use of confidential informants (Girodo 1984, 1985, 1991; Jacobs 1994, 1996; G. I. Miller 1987; Pogrebin and Poole 1993). For example, building on the collective observations in Marx's (1974, 1981, 1985, 1988) work, Mark Pogrebin and Eric Poole (1993) interviewed several dozen local and federal law enforcement agents with experience working as undercover operatives. Entitled "Vice Isn't Nice: A Look at the Effects of Working Undercover," this work sheds considerable light on the personal stress and moral ambiguity that officers deal with when assuming false identities to infiltrate criminal operations. Given that undercover agents' entrée into and infiltration of criminal ranks is often facilitated by known criminals who are paid or excused of charges for their help, the Pogrebin and Poole inquiry includes rich insights on agent-informant relations. Similarly, George Miller (1987) draws on interviews with undercover police officers to detail the selection, training, work roles, and pitfalls that go along with covert police operations. He differentiates between "light-cover" operations, in which officers assume covert identities on a daily basis, and "deep-cover" operations, in which operatives totally relinquish their legitimate identity to infiltrate criminal enterprises for prolonged periods of time. In both cases, the officers' relationship with confidential informants is shown to play a key role in entrée and exit efforts.

Nearly a decade after his data-driven inquiry was first published, Marx partnered with Cyrille Fijnaut (Fijnaut and Marx 1996) to produce an anthology detailing police surveillance efforts in an international context. The book's chapters describe and contextualize undercover operations within nine different countries. Focused on the law enforcement experience, contributors shed light on the intents, methods, procedures, and legal landscapes that shape covert surveillance efforts across North America and Europe. Much consistency is observed in the behaviors and intentions of the persons who provide information to police agents. Conversely, diversity is observed in the motivations and practices of the various law enforcement jurisdictions under study, with variations in the bureaucratic structure and sociopolitical context leading police to pursue different forms of covert surveillance. Some level of confidential informant usage is observed in all jurisdictions.

Our understanding of confidential informant usage in an international context is further broadened by the work of Richard Ericson (1981) and Martin Innes (2000). Ericson's monograph on detective work in Canada focuses attention on how Canadian officials identify, use, and manage paid informants and accused suspects within a broad array of police units. Its focus is similar to that of the Peter Greenwood, Jan Chaiken, and Joan Petersilia (1975) study of detective work within U.S. police agencies in that it samples case work generated by detectives investigating property crimes, violent crimes, and vice crimes. That said, the chapter focusing on information provided by confidential informants deals almost exclusively with vice investigations and echoes many of the observations generated by previous studies. Two decades later, Innes (2000) published a work contextualizing informant usage within British law enforcement. He describes an increased reliance on confidential informants at the close of the twentieth century and attributes it to the rise in the "new managerial state," a system-wide emphasis on efficiency in case processing. His ethnographic work on British police agencies reveals a sense of urgency within modern law enforcement agencies as shrinking budgets, breakdowns in communication, and rising crime rates undermine police legitimacy in the eyes of community members and key stakeholders. He theorizes confidential informant usage as an efficient means of closing large numbers of cases, ranging from narcotics cases to property crime cases, and notes a trend of individual officers and supervisors placing added emphasis on covert police work. He cautions against a host of moral conundrums and practical problems that follow from this escalated use of informants in British policing. Perhaps most insightful is his observation that the increased reliance on informants might lead to a blurring of the "thin blue line" that separates police from criminals: "The trouble for the police is that if they admit to being overly reliant upon informants, then this has implicit connotations of the criminal community being effectively self-policing" (Innes 2000, 381).

Not surprisingly, as the war on drugs grew in prominence and priority within the broader context of law enforcement workload, sociologists and criminologists began to conduct inquiries that were more tightly focused on narcotics enforcement. Several works have placed the use of confidential informants in modern drug enforcement efforts center stage (e.g., Hess and Amir 2002; Wisotsky 1986). For example, Steven Wisotsky (1986) provides a wide-ranging and highly critical treatise on the war on drugs. Central to his argument is that U.S. and international law enforcement agents have become dependent on confidential informants and undercover police operations to infiltrate all levels of the illegal drug market. He points to a host of ethical and legal problems that emerge from this trajectory. More importantly, he observes that these supply-side investigation and interdiction efforts have produced very little change in the vitality of the illegal drug markets domestically or internationally. He questions the utility of covert policing efforts in light of this fact and calls for an emphasis on demand reduction and scaled back covert policing as a more practical and sustainable course of action. During the 1990s, Bruce Jacobs (1992, 1994, 1996) published a series of papers based on interviews with narcotics officers who had experience working undercover drug investigations within high school settings. While not centrally focused on confidential informant usage, this body of work provides valuable insight into the identity management exchanges that occur between officers and youthful drug market insiders and how these infiltration efforts force officers into moral and tactical choices to generate trust and access to information. Several years later, Alex Hess and Menachem Amir (2002) published an article based on ethnographic work on Israeli narcotics enforcement officers. They detail the various relationship and interactional complexities that exist between narcotics officers and the confidential informants on which they rely. Similar to Girodo (1984, 1985, 1991), Goddard (1988), and Pogrebin and Poole (1993), these authors document a host of negative life outcomes, including drug use, excessive drinking, and family stresses, that are commonly experienced by undercover agents and those who routinely handle confidential informants. Despite obvious access and trust concerns, several scholars have managed to gain access to samples of known offenders to shed light on the behaviors and perceptions of snitches and the snitched on.

Informant-Based Research

In the only systematic study of informants based on insights provided by persons with personal experience working with the police, Mitch Miller (2011) draws on interviews with eighty-four former informants in five states to shed light on the informant role. The confidential informants' perspective is used to detail how individuals entered the informant game, their motivations for snitching on other criminals, and how they managed and neutralized the underworld stigma associated with their behavior.

Offender-Based Research

Numerous studies have sought to capture the way that seasoned offenders manage the threat of confidential informants and of undercover officers exposing their misconduct. Given that the 1980s saw law enforcement agencies ratcheting up their reliance on confidential informants to crack complex drug and crime organizations, it should not be surprising that the 1990s saw a spate of offender-based research focused on how active drug dealers seek to conceal their criminal conduct from law enforcement (Jacobs 1993a, 1993b, 1999; Murphy, Waldorf, and Reinarman 1990; Tewksbury and Mustaine 1998). Dealers reveal that a central part of this equation is being able to identify undercover officers or confidential informants as they solicit drug exchanges. Various behavioral cues and approaches are detailed in these studies, along with the common negative appraisal of those deemed to be "narcs" (narcotics officers) or snitches.

Additional insight into the confidential informant game comes from offenders engaged in violent crimes (Laskey 1997; Rosenfeld, Jacobs, and Wright 2003; Topalli 2005) or property offending (Shover and Honaker 1992; Tunnell 1992; Wright and Decker 1996), who must deal with the threat of being exposed by confidential informants. Common themes running through these studies are the subjects' expressed distain for snitching and their contention that snitching runs contrary to the "code of the streets" (Anderson 1999). For example, Rosenfeld, Jacobs and Wright (2003) found that hardcore street offenders universally resent and debase the fact that some offenders either actively (for money) or passively (to work off charges or to stamp out competition) cooperate with police. Moreover, very few of the offenders interviewed were willing to own up to engaging in such behavior themselves and, consequently, accepting the stigma that follows from doing so. That said, the authors observe that offenders describe widespread snitching among street criminals, and they thus call into question the veracity of this general denial. They go on to detail neutralization techniques that appear to be used by offenders to manage involvement in snitching and also note that criminals view some reasons for snitching to be more acceptable than others. Finally, the authors identify snitching as a key ingredient in the contagion of violence that exists on the streets, as codes of the streets compel offenders to retaliate against individuals who they suspect or know have snitched.

SUMMARY AND CURRENT RESEARCH PLAN

Despite its central presence in past and present-day law enforcement, confidential informant usage is largely understudied and underappreciated. While there exists a substantial body of literature aimed at providing technical assistance and training to law enforcement officials who are inclined to enlist the aid of confidential informants in their policing efforts, much less attention has been focused on the sociological underpinnings of the phenomenon. The social context of confidential informant usage involves three broad categories of actors: police, individuals who provide information about criminal conduct and offenders, and individuals who are engaging in criminal behavior and are thus targeted for subsequent enforcement efforts. A thorough review of the scholarly literature reveals that no study seeks to bring together all three perspectives in one comprehensive inquiry and that each of these three perspectives has been subject to limited, structured inquiry in a standalone fashion. While it is safe to say that the existing tapestry of systematic inquiry paints a relatively consistent picture of the roles, behaviors, and motivations that apply to the various actors in the confidential informant game, there exists a need for current and far more detailed information about the nature and dynamics of the use of confidential informants in law enforcement operations.

This book seeks to advance our understanding of the confidential informant phenomenon by privileging the law enforcement perspective on it. Specifically, we draw on ethnographic data derived from three separate police-based fieldwork projects to provide a rich and detailed assessment of the nature and dynamics of confidential informant usage in modern-day American policing. Our aim here is to provide a "thick description" (Geertz 1973) of the confidential informant phenomenon through the eyes of the law enforcement officers who have come to so ardently rely on it. We seek first to theorize the nature of the citizen-agent information exchange and then to situate confidential informant usage within the broader context of contemporary law enforcement efforts, specifically the ongoing war on drugs. The hope is that this theoretical exercise will illuminate the potential ramifications that follow from the primacy of confidential informant usage in policing.

What follows are eight chapters of substantive content. Chapter 2 provides a thorough overview of the research design underlying this project. Details are provided about three separate fieldwork projects and subsequent interviews with law enforcement officers that formed the basis for our observations and conclusions. Chapter 3 provides a theoretical framework to organize the nature of the police-citizen exchange of intelligence information. This is followed by the presentation of a four-part typology of confidential informants. The typology stresses the varied motivations of law enforcement agents and information providers and situates the subsequent information exchange within the context of law enforcement and criminal enterprises. Chapter 4 considers the logistics of informant usage from the law enforcement perspective. Emphasis is placed on the intended roles of informants as well as on the common means through which informants are recruited and managed by officers. Chapter 5 explores in depth the community context of confidential informant usage. Information providers are situated within the urban drug markets and the neighborhoods in which these markets thrive. Chapter 6 details the nature of the officer-informant relationship and the personal and professional considerations that shape these interpersonal relationships. Chapter 7 delves into the organizational, professional, and personal benefits of using confidential informants, while chapter 8 explores the corresponding pitfalls connected with the work. In the concluding chapter, we step back from the confidential informant phenomenon and situate it within the broader context of contemporary law enforcement. We build on Natapoff's observation that, "pragmatically, snitching flows from two dominant characteristics of our criminal system: plea bargaining and a tolerance for a high level of law enforcement discretion," and thus, "banning snitching altogether would effectively require restructuring fundamental aspects of the American criminal process" (2009, 11). In this context, we seek to stimulate a policy discussion about the future of confidential informant usage in policing.

TWO

Study Methods

This book is based on multiple forms and sources of qualitative data. The data are drawn both from ethnographic fieldwork projects in two different law enforcement agencies and from a series of in-depth interviews with a diverse sample of law enforcement officials who were approached due to their known work experience with confidential informants. The ethnographic aspects of the study come from us both having spent extended periods of time working with and in investigative units of major metropolitan police departments, one located in what we call "Central City" and the other in what we call "River City."* In particular, the lead author conducted a ten-month ride-along project with officers tasked with narcotics enforcement in Central City and a similar eighteen-month project with the same department's homicide unit. The second author spent six months immersed in an ethnographic inquiry with members of a street-level vice unit in River City. All of the ethnographic work involved recording copious field notes while accompanying officers during their regular work activities as well as conducting loosely structured one-on-one interviews with the officers that were designed to flesh out observational data and query them on specific topics guiding the research.

RIVER CITY FIELDWORK

The first fieldwork case study contributing to our understanding of the role and function of informants in drug-crime policing is based on six months' worth of immersion in a drug and street-crime undercover investigative unit

---

*Pseudonyms are used for all organizations and individuals participating in this study.

of the large urban police department of River City. River City is one of the thirty largest cities in the United States, with a 2010 population of over 600,000, and it is the center of a metropolitan area with a population of more than 1.2 million. The population is 70 percent white, with a median household income of $43,000. Crime in the city is not a major problem. In 2012, the FBI's Uniform Crime Reports noted nearly four thousand violent crimes and more than twenty-eight thousand property crimes. The River City Police Department employs nearly 1,500 individuals, including more than 1,200 sworn officers. It is among the fifty largest local law enforcement agencies in the nation, with 1.9 sworn officers for every 1,000 residents.

The River City Police Department is organized into eight districts, or precincts. Each district has one undercover unit of five to seven officers whose responsibilities focus on street-level drug sales and prostitution. It is in one of these units that the fieldwork for this book was conducted. The specific investigative unit under study was comprised of a sergeant and five officers. Sergeant Perez had eight years of service but only five months experience as a sergeant at the time the fieldwork commenced. He was in his early thirties, was married, and had two elementary-school-age sons. Justin was the senior investigator assigned to the unit, with more than five years of experience in the unit. As senior officer, he was the acting sergeant when Sergeant Perez was not present. Justin was in his midthirties, was married, and had no children. Investigators George and Lucky were both in their late twenties, single, and from the same recruit class. Both of them spent most of their free time drinking, dating, and living a relatively carefree lifestyle. Mickey, another investigator, was in his early thirties, married, and the father of a two-year-old daughter. Mickey was the quietest member of the unit, rarely initiating conversation with anyone. The fifth investigator, Skye, was the unit's oldest member, at thirty-four. She was unmarried, had six years' tenure with the department, and had spent the past three years on the flex unit. Prior to joining the River City Police Department, Skye served as an enlisted member of a branch of the U.S. military. She was known to be very involved in local athletics leagues and rarely socialized with the other members of the unit outside of work. All of the unit's officers were Caucasian.

This ethnographic endeavor grew out of the second author's role as the River City Police Department's community policing consultant assigned to the district. Through meetings and ride-alongs with the flex unit, the researcher developed friendly relations with both the sergeant and the other members of the group. After several months of casual interactions, members of the unit began to invite the author to accompany them on occasions when they had "something good going on." After accompanying the unit on a couple of search warrants and periods of surveillance, the researcher approached the district's commanding officer, Major Button (who was a former student of the author and division supervisor of the flex unit's precinct), and Sergeant Perez about allowing a more structured and prolonged period of observation with the flex unit. Both readily agreed, although they qualified their endorsement with the requirement that the flex unit members had to be agreeable. After the sergeant talked with the other five, the author was invited to accompany the unit on their daily activities "whenever and as often as you want." Over the course of the next six months, the author spent an average of three days a week with the unit, usually arriving at the district when the unit members did and staying through the eight- to ten-hour work shift. He did an estimated five hundred hours of fieldwork with the unit.

After about a month, the researcher performed essentially all the activities that the unit members did. Although he was not permitted to drive any agency-owned vehicles, display any credentials, or carry a firearm, he was in most other respects integrated to the unit. He dressed and acted similarly to unit members and seemed to be perceived by community members as a true unit member. All members of the larger patrol district knew about the author's presence and the fact that he was conducting "some type of study where he hangs out with the flex unit." He openly took handwritten field notes using a pen and 3-by-5-inch paper notebook, and as time passed, unit members would remind him to record things: "Don't you think what just happened is important? Aren't you going to write that down?" The author "partnered" with different unit members on different days to assure broad exposure to unit activities and work styles and, throughout the course of the fieldwork, spent relatively equal amounts of time with each unit member.

During the fieldwork, the author accompanied officers—individually, in pairs, and as a group—on all types of unit activities. These included unit meetings, strategy sessions, interrogations, surveillance activities, court appearances, and downtime spent in the precinct, in vehicles, at meals, and simply patrolling the target areas. During daily activities, and especially during surveillance and downtime, the author probed the officers for their experiences, advice, perceptions and views of the community, offenders, other officers, and local political developments.

Data from the second fieldwork site comprises two separate ethnographic projects conducted in a large metropolitan police department located in Central City. The department is staffed by roughly two thousand sworn officers and is consistently ranked among the twenty-five largest municipal police departments in America. The department has jurisdiction over approximately 150 square miles of urban landscape with a population of over four hundred thousand. In 2010, the population was 53 percent African American, with a median household income of $52,000. The jurisdiction constitutes the heart of a metropolitan area that exceeds five million in population. The department confronts high levels of violent crime, property crime, and public order crime, and Central City's crime rates are consistently ranked in the top ten in the nation, according to the Uniform Crime Reports. In 2012, the Uniform Crime Reports noted more than six thousand violent crimes and over twenty-eight thousand property crimes. The department command is organized around a system of six geographic zones and driven by a Compstat management system. Separate but interdependent field operations, criminal investigations, community policing, and administrative services divisions make up the administrative structure of the organization.

The first fieldwork project in Central City was centered on ten months of ride-alongs with officers tasked with policing a residential area that, for several decades, had served as the home of an active and vibrant open-air drug market. The lead author was granted access to all officers and command staff responsible for conducting police operations in the targeted neighborhood, which had two motorized patrol beats, each covering less than a single square mile. The primary drugs sold in the area included heroin, cocaine, and marijuana. The researcher conducted roughly 350 hours of fieldwork over the course of the project. His activities included forty ride-alongs with patrol officers, line supervisors, investigators, and tactical units deployed to the geographic command. Participants were mostly males, of diverse ages, ethnicities, and ranks. The ride-alongs were coordinated across the three different shifts and included members of the patrol staff and each of the tactical units within the targeted geographic command. Each ride-along lasted the duration of an eight-hour shift and involved the lead author accompanying the officers as they conducted their determined work duties. The author dressed in street clothes and was not permitted to drive any agency-owned vehicles, display any credentials, or carry a firearm. However, in most other respects, the researcher was integrated into the daily activities of the officer he was accompanying and seemed to be welcomed by the officers. This arrangement afforded him near-unfettered access to all aspects of the policing that was occurring in the area, including mundane patrol operations, narcotics enforcement strategies similar to those in River City, and tactical raids of suspected drug dens. During these ride-along sessions, semistructured, face-to-face interviews were conducted with each officer. The interview content was shaped by an interview guide built around a dozen core topics. The goal of this exercise was to elicit a conversational dynamic that would encourage officers to provide insight about their work history, their interactions with and perceptions of persons present in the neighborhood (offenders, residents, and stakeholders), and the dynamics of the entrenched open-air drug market operating within the neighborhood. All interviews were recorded using a digital audio recorder. Interview conversations were supplemented with audio field notes that the researcher dictated into his voice recorder intermittently throughout the course of each ridealong session. This fieldwork project also included dozens of hours spent at the precinct house and police headquarters observing administrative activities (e.g., roll call, Compstat meetings, strategy briefings) and conducting interviews with middle- and upper-level commanders responsible for the administration of the geographic command in question as well as the central administration of the department. These activities were subject to the same data collection protocol detailed above.

The end result of this fieldwork project was a rich appreciation of all aspects of the narcotics enforcement strategies being directed toward this longstanding open-air drug market. The experience also gave the author considerable exposure to confidential informant practices, including opportunities to observe the development and use of paid informants and the on-the-fly recruitment of apprehended drug offenders who were cajoled into providing inside information on active drug operations or into helping set up subsequent drug deals in exchange for some sort of leniency.

The second Central City fieldwork project involved an eighteen-month stint with the department's homicide unit. Central City is a jurisdiction that faces an average of roughly one hundred homicides annually and relies on a twenty-six-member homicide unit to investigate these killings. At the time of the data collection effort, the unit was made up of mostly males, of varied ages, mixed on-the-job experience, diverse ethnicities, and different ranks. Roughly two-thirds of the staff members were investigators, and they were assigned to cases on a unit-rotation basis. Heavy caseloads are the norm in the unit, with each investigator shouldering lead responsibility for five to ten cases annually. The unit was partitioned into two shifts: a day watch and an evening watch. When a homicide occurred, all members of the shift, along with a team of civilian crime scene technicians and a medical examiner, responded to the call to assist the lead detective with evidence collection. The data collection protocol closely resembled that of the other fieldwork project. Namely, it involved the lead author conducting ride-alongs with each member of the unit, during which time unfettered access to all aspects of the individual's work duties was granted, affording the opportunity for a semi-structured interview effort. Just as when he was conducting the other fieldwork, the researcher was not permitted to drive any agency-owned vehicles, display any credentials, or carry a firearm. And again, in most other respects he was integrated to the unit, dressed and acted similarly to unit members, and seemed to be welcomed into the unit by investigators and supervisors alike.

The primary focus of this particular data collection effort was to shed light on the stress and coping experiences of homicide investigators. As was the case with the River City fieldwork, the Central City fieldwork activities granted the researcher repeated exposure to officers engaging confidential sources and suspects at crime scenes and during the investigation activities that followed. The interactions ranged from formal interviews conducted at police headquarters to back alley meetings or phone conversations conducted in speaker mode. Given the high incidence of drug-related homicide in Central City, the field notes and interview transcriptions resulting from this effort are rich with information on the police-citizen information exchange that occurs pursuant to a criminal investigation.

INTERVIEWS

The fieldwork projects in River City and Central City provided us with a rich source of information on how law enforcement officers use and interact with confidential informants. However, we deemed it necessary to supplement these data with additional interview data in order to reach data saturation on all aspects of the confidential informant phenomenon. Specifically, we further explored the insights and patterns that emerged from our fieldwork projects via a number of semi-structured interviews with active and retired law enforcement officers from a host of local, state, and federal agencies, all of whom were known to have substantial experience working with confidential informants. Participants were gathered using a snowball sampling technique whereby the researchers drew on their own professional contacts within law enforcement as well as the referrals of fieldwork participants to identify and approach law enforcement officers to be interviewed. Some officers and agencies insisted on reviewing our interview guide prior to agreeing to participate, while others graciously offered to allow us to "hang around" for a few days and ask questions as we shadowed investigators in their work. All referrals and contacts resulted in willing participation.

Based on our long-term immersion in the above-noted law enforcement organizations and our comprehensive review of the extant literature, a multi-topic interview guide was constructed to cover a range of structural, processual, and conceptual issues associated with law enforcement's use of confidential informants. Specifically, the means by which confidential informants are recruited and worked with and how law enforcement officers in these investigative units perceive their work and the war on drugs were explored in great detail as a result of the interview guide's topical prompts. Content was focused on the experiences of officers working with informants and of officers supervising other officers' work with informants. Flexibility was built into the interview format to allow for the topics on the interview guide to be covered in order or in a sequence that was amenable to the natural flow of the conversation. As a result, the interviews were sometimes very formal, structured interactions and were at other times rather informal, free-flowing conversations that ebbed and flowed across the topics represented on the interview guide. We found both approaches beneficial and altered our styles and the structure of interviews to fit the setting and interactional styles of interviewees.

The interviews were conducted by both of us and by a graduate student who had previously worked as an undercover narcotics officer. All interviews were audio-recorded. Interviews lasted, on average, approximately one hour, and they were completed in a variety of settings—including interviewees' places of employment, university offices, restaurants, and vehicles. As the snowball sample proceeded and we collected interview data, we relied on a process of analytic induction (Charmaz 1983, 2006) as well as focused review for insights regarding specific questions left unanswered by ethnographic observation and immersion to guide our decision of when data saturation was reached. On completion of fifteen interviews, we determined that we had exhausted the need for further interviews and proceeded to transcribe and analyze the totality of the data at our disposal.

All interview and field note data were transcribed verbatim, and they were subject to thematic content analysis and the constant comparative method of analysis with an eye toward identifying discernable and prominent themes in the data (Berg 2007). This involved several coding passes, whereby broad substantive themes were refined into more specific and theoretically refined ideas that emerged naturally from the data. Interview excerpts were marked with subject codes to allow them to be paraphrased or directly quoted in the presentation of the results in subsequent chapters.

Access to the day-to-day inner workings of law enforcement, particularly to specialized investigative units, and explicating sensitive topics such as the use of confidential informants, represent difficult and rarely achieved research tasks. The world of police activities is well recognized as being shielded from outside view and staunchly protected by insiders (Mastrofski and Parks 1990; G. I. Miller 1987; Worden 1986). Moreover, access to day-to-day and minute aspects of what police do, including how they conduct their relationships with confidential informants, is notoriously difficult to attain; G. I. Miller (1987) even says it is largely impossible. Breaking through this veil of secrecy and accessing the backstage realities of street-level investigators is a challenging, time-consuming, and sometimes dangerous endeavor. We believe we have permeated the barriers and shields of the agencies in which we worked, and, while we did not achieve full membership in these organizations, we did achieve sufficient entrée into them to allow understandings of the who, what, how, when, and where of the day-to-day criminal investigation work done by police.

As with nearly any qualitative endeavor, we acknowledge that our work reflects the specific organizational and procedural issues unique to the two agencies in which our fieldwork was conducted. As is always the case with such inquiries, generalizability may be limited, although our prolonged research experiences in the two agencies suggest consistencies in how informants are viewed, recruited, managed, and used in investigative police work, especially in drug-crime focused work. These consistencies were reinforced in the content of the follow-up interviews that we conducted with individuals who had work experiences in, collectively, over two dozen other law enforcement agencies. The sort of study that we have undertaken presents an important approach for generating theoretical and substantive contributions to developing bodies of literature (see Davies 2004). The goal of a study such as ours is to examine a "phenomenon within its real-life context" (Yin 1989, 23). As such, it is our contention that, in order for an inductively driven study to be maximally beneficial, it needs to rely on qualitative, preferably ethno-graphic, methods that yield both broad and deep data. This research is just that, drawing on data from four distinct data-collection endeavors.

As outlined in chapter 1, the literature on police informants, undercover police work, and the intersection of these issues is limited. It is typically based either on outsiders' views and interpretations of law enforcement activities or on practitioner-oriented how-to types of directives. True insider-based analytic studies, such as those carried out by Manning (1980), Marx (1988), and Pogrebin and Poole (1993), are available, but they are over two decades old. Others, such as Mitch Miller's (2011) study, have looked at informants themselves, but they acknowledge that the processes and actions of informants and their relationships with law enforcement officers remains largely unknown. Miller concedes: "Still to be addressed are the central issues of what informants actually do in the role to facilitate casework, the degree of their influence" (2011, 216). The literature lacks a contemporary insiders' view of how law enforcement and informants work collaboratively and coop-eratively on the front lines of the war on drugs. Our goal is to fill this gap in the literature.

THREE

Types of Informants

SOCIAL CONTEXT OF THE POLICE-CITIZEN
INFORMATION EXCHANGE

At its most basic level, this monograph focuses on information exchanges that serve to inform criminal investigations. There are two primary types of actors in these information exchanges: law enforcement officers who consume the information and citizens who provide it. The information that is provided and consumed focuses on the criminal wrongdoing of third-party actors (i.e., at-large offenders).

While there exists variation in the occupational roles and information-extraction skills of police officers, the same cannot be said for demand levels. Any competent law enforcement agent will acknowledge that there is no such thing as an investigation that cannot benefit from quality "inside information" provided by ground-level actors. This applies equally to the beat officer responding to a 911 call and to the narcotics or homicide detective trying to make or close a complex murder case. Whether they are dealing with public order offenses, such as prostitution or drug crimes that play out in underground markets, or violent or property offenses that occur outside the plain view of law enforcement, officers of all kinds are continually looking to tighten up their case files. This basic truism played a large part in our decision to turn to law enforcement officers to inform us about the dynamics of the information exchange and the persons who provide the intelligence. That said, the organizational position occupied by a law enforcement officer has an impact on how he or she is perceived by other players in the information exchange. This is driven partly by logistical realities and partly by street credibility. The practical reality is that patrol officers and street-level general

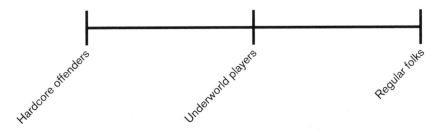

FIGURE 1. Criminal involvement continuum

investigators have little time to concentrate on any given criminal inquiry; they are predictably busy running from call to call or working their way through the thick stack of case files assigned to them. This time constraint is abundantly evident to residents in crime-ridden communities. Thus, low-level investigators and patrol officers are often devalued by citizens as potential partners in information exchanges. On the other hand, federal agents or members of high-status investigative units generally find themselves facing more focused and manageable caseloads. This translates into added discretionary time and autonomy, which allows them to repeatedly cajole citizens into cooperating. This reality does not escape the members of the community, who are thus more likely to take these agents seriously when they are queried for criminal intelligence.

The other set of primary actors in the information exchange are the citizens that offer up the criminal intelligence. Like their officer counterparts, citizens occupy diverse roles within the communities in which they reside and/or in which the crimes occur. These social roles can be situated on a continuum, ranging from very active members of the criminal subculture (i.e., hardcore players) to people who live largely law-abiding lives (i.e., regular folks). See figure 1 for a visual representation of this observation. An individual's location on this continuum plays an important role in how he or she is treated by other players in the exchange.

While the bulk of the text focuses on the subpopulation of offenders who are known commonly as confidential informants and located on the left side of the continuum, it is important to appreciate the broad range of intelligence sources that are critical to the work of law enforcement officers. Regardless of where a person stands on the criminal involvement continuum, within the context of the information exchange, he or she possesses firsthand or secondhand insight about criminal conduct occurring and agrees to share this information with members of law enforcement. When doing so, the information source engages the police with certain motivations in play and occupies a distinct role in the criminal justice process. The above set of observations begs the formation of a typology or conceptually grounded classification scheme to organize the playing field.

There are numerous examples in the scholarly and applied literature of experts providing classification schema to define and categorize the different ways in which police officers engage people to get actionable intelligence on criminal conduct (Bloom 2002; Fitzgerald 2007; Harney and Cross 1968; Madinger 1999; Mallory 2000; J. M. Miller 2011; Settle 1995). We will review some of those examples later. But first, we set forth our own typology to guide the heuristic exercise.

A TYPOLOGY APPROACH

Figure 2 shows the 2 × 2 typology matrix that we used to organize the subject matter of this book. The vertical axis of the table focuses attention on the motivation of the individual who is providing information to the police. Generally speaking, when engaging police, individuals are motivated either by self-preservation or by self-advancement. Informants are commonly motivated by self-preservation when they are providing information as a result of being engaged by criminal justice agents. These citizens are being pressed to provide some sort of privileged information to the police. This might manifest itself as a person being questioned as a victim, witness, involved party, or suspect at a crime scene. Regardless of the details, persons motivated by self-preservation are seeking to alleviate a strain placed on them by an unforeseen contact with the police. A victim or witness may partner with the police to provide details about a crime that has just been thrust into his or her world. Fitzgerald (2007) refers to these individuals as "citizen informants" or "walk-in informants." An involved party or suspect may seek to manage the potential negative consequences that police or prosecutors are holding over his or her head by incriminating fellow law violators. Dennis Fitzgerald (2007) and John Madinger (1999) call these individuals "jailhouse informants," as they are usually persons who reach out to police from the confines of jail after being charged with a criminal offense. In another variation, Harney and Cross (1968) and Settle (1995) observe that police often make contingency deals with the persons they bust on the street, outlining a short- or long-term arrangement wherein the officer will suspend an arrest in the moment in

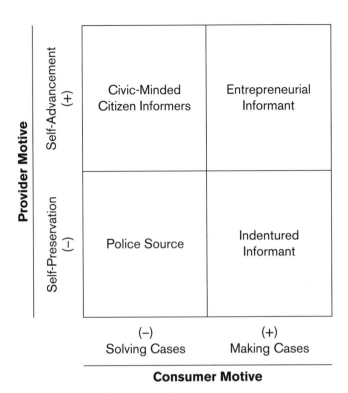

Provider Motive

Self-Advancement (+)

Self-Preservation (−)

	Solving Cases (−)	Making Cases (+)
Self-Advancement (+)	Civic-Minded Citizen Informers	Entrepreneurial Informant
Self-Preservation (−)	Police Source	Indentured Informant

Consumer Motive

FIGURE 2. Typology of the police-citizen information exchange.

exchange for information that will help in resolving open cases or generating new ones (through buy-bust operations). If the offender satisfies the arrangement, he or she is granted grace. If not, the original charges are filed. Regardless of the status that the police assign to an individual in the wake of a crime, the primary objective for an informant motivated by self-preservation is to restore balance or order in the wake of a negative life event.

Alternatively, some intelligence providers are motivated by self-advancement. These citizens tend to be proactive and deliberate in their mindset; they are bringing forward information to the police to achieve a desired outcome in their social world. Rarely does this sort of informant come forward in the immediate wake of a criminal event. Instead, the proactive thinking of these informants usually builds over time as an investigative process begins to unfold. There are three generic subtypes of these informants. The first are hardcore offenders who tip off the police about the criminal operations of a known rival or market competitor. The second are members of the criminal subculture who, taking on the role of what Harney and Cross (1968), Mallory

(2000), and J. M. Miller (2011) label the "mercenary informant," are motivated by the money they can make by providing leads to police. The third are largely law-abiding regular folks who, with the aim of reducing crime, operate as resident sleuths to direct police toward unknown criminal conduct or provide tips though a Crime Stoppers hotline. Stephen Mallory (2000) uses the term "civic-minded or altruistic" to identify these noble do-gooders.

The horizontal axis of figure 2 situates the exchange of criminal intelligence within the investigative process. It is well established that police adopt both passive and active roles as they engage crime. Passive policing is sometimes known as "911 policing," which is when patrol officers respond to crime reports generated by the citizenry and relayed to them via the 911 communications infrastructure. However, passive policing takes on a slightly different form when the lens is shifted away from the patrol division and toward the criminal investigation division of an agency. Criminal investigators, be they covert narcotics investigators, plainclothes property crime or violent crime detectives, or federal agents, rarely arrive immediately after a crime has been reported through the 911-notification system. Instead, they get dispatched shortly thereafter to relieve the patrol officers who have secured the crime scene, and they then launch an investigation into the events that produced the call. In this reactive capacity, the criminal investigator is trying to solve the case and effect an arrest on those responsible for a specific crime that has been reported to law enforcement authorities. The agents may go about this by extracting information from victims, witnesses, involved parties, or suspects at the scene of a crime. They may also carry out a follow-up investigation based on information from an altruistic citizen who flagged a detective down on the street, came to the precinct to provide information, or anonymously relayed leads through the Crime Stoppers program. In each of these scenarios, the investigator occupies a passive role in the law enforcement organization, solving open criminal cases.

This differs from those instances where criminal investigators generate or make new cases by adopting an active role in the investigative process. New cases get generated when crimes or criminals previously unknown to police come to light via information provided by persons situated somewhere on the criminal involvement continuum depicted in figure 1. Confidential informants are most frequently recently arrested individuals who are pressed by police to identify a fellow offender higher up in the criminal market in exchange for leniency. Sometimes, results are demanded quickly. For example, a low-level drug dealer might be pressed to set up a drug deal with one of his or her suppliers immediately or shortly after being apprehended by police. Other times, the delivery of new cases can be more time-fluid. In these cases, a detained prostitute, for example, might be given a week or two to provide one solid lead on violent crime occurring on the "track" she works, or a busted drug user might be told he has a month to produce three good leads on drug dealers.

Criminal investigators also proactively make cases when a person motivated out of self-advancement brings them valuable information about criminal enterprises that were previously off the officers' radar screen. Several scholars have used the term "revenge-oriented informant" to describe this sort of individual (Fitzgerald 2007; Mallory 2000; J. M. Miller 2011). For example, when a drug dealer provides insight on a competitor's nearby street-corner operation in an effort to expand his or her own market share, investigators will make a case. Similarly, when an informant comes forward with details on a new gun- or drug-smuggling operation that they wish to exchange for a defined level of personal compensation, investigators will proactively make a case.

The 2 × 2 layout of figure 2 is designed to organize the police-citizen exchange of criminal intelligence along two important dimensions: the motivation of the person providing the information and the motivation of the person consuming the information. Citizens, be they hardcore offenders or regular folks, are motivated out of self-preservation when they are responding to negative life events, such as when they seek to restore balance after a recent crime or try to wiggle their way out of pending charges. Conversely, citizens are motivated by self-advancement when they take charge of their situation and seek to alert police about the heretofore unknown criminal activities of a third-party, be it to improve their community, stamp out the competition, or put food on the table. On the police side of the equation, criminal investigators "solve open cases" when they respond to cases previously assigned to them, and they "make new cases" when they proactively take the fight to the criminal enterprise. Solving cases can involve developing a victim or offender who is responding in self-preservation mode into a source. It can also involve an officer getting a solid lead from an offender or law-abiding citizen acting out of self-advancement. How investigators make cases runs the gamut from pressuring arrestees to give up others in the criminal underworld to exhibiting a willingness to work with a greedy or vengeful criminal.

Figure 2 provides a four-part typology of the police-citizen information exchange. The bottom left quadrant of the figure is reserved for cases where the provider of the information (civilian) is motivated by self-preservation or by a desire to restore balance, and the consumer of the information (investigator) is striving to solve one or more open cases. Commonly associated with this mutually reactive dynamic are the police source and unwitting informant. We, like Hanvey (1995) and Madinger (1999), use the term "source" to characterize a person who is party to a criminal event—be he or she a victim, witness, involved party, or offender—who provides information to the police in the wake of a crime. In these situations, the information providers, whether they are regular folks who want to repair a perceived harm or members of the criminal subculture who wish to deflect attention from their own misdeeds, seek to restore balance to their lives or community. This category of information provider maps closely to what Steven Greer (1995) calls "casual observers." Greer, who emphasizes the level of stability of the information exchange relationship (i.e., single event versus multiple event sources of information) and the proximity to the criminal underworld (i.e., insiders versus outsiders) as the conceptual basis for his multipart taxonomy of informants, describes casual observers as outsiders to the criminal underworld who serve as one-time sources of intelligence to police. This type of information source includes a victim or witness to a crime who helps the police make an arrest and clear the open case. Greer differentiates between a casual observer and a "one-off accomplice/witness." The latter designation is reserved for members of the criminal subculture who assist police in solving a single case. In these cases, the information provider is akin to an involved party or offender who unwittingly or begrudgingly provides police with information on a criminal incident to which they were a party. George Miller (1987) assigns the term "informer" to individuals who simply transmit information to the police. He sees this as different from informants who seek out and cultivate criminal intelligence before relaying it to police.

In a police-citizen information exchange, a police source gets paired up with a passively oriented officer who is working an open investigation and is seeking to secure an arrest and conviction against the responsible parties. Under these circumstances, the officer is narrowly focused on the case at hand, methodically trying to piece together the events of the crime and prepare the case to be handed off to the prosecutor for presentation within the adjudication process. Officers respect that eyewitnesses or individuals who are party to firsthand conversations with a suspect can play a vital role in securing the desired juridical outcomes. Within the context of a police source exchange dynamic, the officer is apt to stay narrowly focused on what the citizen knows about the case at hand, do his or her best to corroborate this information using physical evidence or other testimony, and learn as much as he or she can about the background of the information provider in order to make a credibility determination. Information exchanges involving a police source require officers to do their homework to situate the evidence within the case file and assess the integrity of the information, but otherwise, these situations present themselves as relatively straightforward for the information consumer.

The top left quadrant of figure 2 is reserved for those police-citizen intelligence exchanges that come about from instances involving information providers motivated by self-advancement and information consumers driven to solve open cases. We assign the label "civic-minded citizen informers" to this category. Again, multiple manifestations of the civic-minded citizen informer can be realized and several of them overlap nicely with conceptual designations found in the literature. For example, George Miller (1987) described "citizen operatives" and "amateur police agents" as community members who routinely take the initiative to query fellow citizens about criminal activity in the neighborhood and relay the resultant intelligence to police. In effect, these persons serve as information conduits between the street and police. The literature gives various titles to this sort of arrangement, such as "cop wannabe" (J.M. Miller 2011), "snoop" (Greer 1995), and individual with a "detective complex" (Harney and Cross 1968). Mitch Miller uses the term "cop wannabe" for people who go out of their way to provide information to police due to their fascination and obsession with police work. He observes that these "police buffs" are often individuals who, for whatever reason, have not pursued or cannot pursue a legitimate career in law enforcement yet see themselves as valuable to crime fighting. Motivated by a desire to be near and work alongside real police officers, the police buff information provider presents as a concerned citizen offering both information about and (supposed) access to criminal offenders and activities. Settle (1995) used the label "anonymous grassing" to describe situations where citizens voluntarily come forward to provide anonymous tips about ongoing investigations.

Another variation of the information provider in the civic-minded citizen informant category is the Neighborhood Watch member who provides information to the police out of a sense of responsibility to the community well-being. Greer (1995) and Settle (1995) use the term "respectable grassing" to refer to the efforts of these individuals, who are quick to report criminal activity observed in the community or to follow up on unsolved past crimes. Persons who anonymously report information to police through the infrastructure of a Crime Stoppers hotline also fall into the civic-minded citizen category of information exchange. Erdwin Pfuhl (1992) and Dennis Rosenbaum (1989) document in depth the spread and utility of these pay-for-information exchanges that have been popularized across American police jurisdictions over the past forty years. At the core of these local programs are monetarily motivated citizens who anonymously call in information about ongoing police investigations. It is commonly understood that the callers come from all walks of life and span the continuum depicted above in figure 1. If an information provider offers up information that plays a central role in the conviction of the responsible party in a case, he or she gets paid a set reward amount.

Under the civic-minded citizen informant rubric, the information provider is motivated by self-advancement. He or she is privy to criminal intelligence and voluntarily comes forward to police with this information in exchange for some benefit to him- or herself. On the law enforcement officer side of the exchange, the agent is saddled with an open investigation and engages the information provider in hopes of solving the case. Focus and follow-through are key facets of the law enforcement officer's role in this scenario. He or she is most interested in keeping the conversation trained on the events of the crime under investigation and must be sure to probe as many links to existing evidence as possible. In these situations, the officer seeks to corroborate physical evidence at his or her disposal and also to substantiate the claims made by the witnesses, victims, and suspects already in play. What makes the civic-minded citizen informer situation dicey for the law enforcement officer is the fact that the information provider is motivated by self-advancement.

The bottom right quadrant of police-citizen information exchange depicted in figure 2 is designated for the indentured informant who is working off charges. In this case, the informant is motivated by self-preservation due to pending criminal charges. In essence, he or she is beholden to the law enforcement officer who can act on the pending charges or seek to introduce some measure of leniency into the formal proceedings against the offender should he or she cooperate with law enforcement. Under these circumstances, the law enforcement agent seizes on this power differential to enlist the apprehended person's role in the criminal subculture to develop additional cases against yet-to-be-identified offenders. It is commonly accepted in the literature that the variations in this broad category of indentured informants are shaped primarily by the informant position in the criminal market in question. For example, Greer (1995) differentiates between "pure informants," "agent provocateurs," and "supergrasses." He describes the pure informant as a low-level operative in the criminal pecking order who has limited knowledge of the illicit market's organization and corresponding players. Police can predictably rely on these individuals for identifying street-level offenders but not much more. Greer and others (Madinger 1999; Marx 1988) describe the agent provocateur as a knowledgeable and seasoned mid- to upper-level operator who, when faced with declining commitment to the game or heavy criminal charges, chooses to "flip" on the persons above and below him or her and help law enforcement officials start or close numerous criminal cases. Finally, Greer and others (Bloom 2002; Morton 1995; Settle 1995) describe supergrasses as high-level operatives who, due to their wide-ranging knowledge about criminal enterprises of their own and those of others, are afforded a protected status by law enforcement officials in exchange for repeated tip-offs and intelligence-providing efforts over time.

Indentured informants who are working off charges occupy a central presence in the current research monograph. These low-, mid-, and (less frequently) upper-level operatives provide law enforcement officers with a steady flow of information about covert criminal activity. The information is provided due to duress caused by pending charges being held over the head of the individual; self-preservation is the core motivation. Numerically, the low-level operatives far outnumber the persons who occupy mid- or upper-level positions within their respective criminal enterprises, regardless of whether these enterprises are centered on drugs, sex, or other criminal exchanges. There exists a long-standing tradition within modern policing, especially as it relates to vice enforcement, to nurture and expand the use of criminal informants who are pressured to help police initiate new cases both upward and downward within the market. Chapter 1 details the host of training manuals and bureaucratic policies that guide these tenuous coercive arrangements.

Mitch Miller (2011) interviewed an unprecedented snowball sample of eighty-four persons who self-identified as drug informants. He categorized informants using a four-part typology. The largest group, which he describes as "getting hammered," closely approximates our indentured informant category. The individuals in this group are offenders who are initially arrested for (usually) small drug offenses and are offered and accept opportunities to inform on (typically) other drug offenders in exchange for leniency or the dropping of charges against them. This same idea is conveyed by Peter Manning (2004), who argues that frequent drug violators are the easiest to turn into informers, as detection and arrest present a more serious threat to their freedom. Mitch Miller concludes that the drug informants in his study constitute "temporary workers" who provided actionable intelligence to police in an individual case or a small set of cases and then, on satisfying the demands of their handlers, moved on and away from informing. This short-term approach to informing, however, stands in contrast to what we observed in our study. We found that a number of informants were active and working for extended periods of time, not infrequently well beyond earning their initially motivating payoff or benefits. Vic, a retired detective who worked metropolitan narcotics for two decades and was one of our respondent officers, put it succinctly when he said: "Once you get a case [on a drug user], especially if they're on probation, then they are your bitch. . . . Work him like a borrowed mule." Later in the chapter, we will draw further on our interviews with local, state, and federal law enforcement officers to describe the logistics of the give-and-take relationship. Regardless of the short- or long-term nature of their obligation, the indentured informant exchange arrangement involves a citizen who provides intelligence out of a sense of self-preservation and an officer who consumes this information as a means of generating new cases to pursue.

The fourth and final category of criminal informant is the entrepreneur type, depicted in the upper right quadrant of figure 2. This category is reserved for those arrangements that involve a citizen who is motivated by self-advancement and a proactive law enforcement authority driven to make new cases. Criminal investigators looking to make new cases are rarely afforded the luxury of drawing intelligence from citizens located on the right side of the criminal continuum presented in figure 1. Given the covert and usually consensual nature of the criminal activity in question, persons occupying this category of confidential informant usually constitute active or previously active offenders, not law-abiding "regular folks." Numerous authors (Fitzgerald 2007; Greer 1995; Mallory 2000; Madinger 1999; G. I. Miller 1987; J. M. Miller 2011; Natapoff 2009) have operationalized this type of entrepreneurial agent, assigning these individuals labels such as "mercenary" (Harney and Cross 1968; Mallory 2000; J. M. Miller 2011), "active informant" (Hanvey 1995; G. I. Miller 1987), or "vengeful" (J. M. Miller 2011). These confidential informants are normally motivated by money or revenge when they seek out their entrepreneurial arrangement with law enforcement authorities. In this regard, Mitch Miller (2011) describes them as "mercenary informants" because, like for-hire soldiers in international conflicts, they enter into their work solely for financial benefit. Such informants are not interested in who else is involved in an investigation or what the final outcome of a situation may be. Instead, they approach their informant role merely as a job. Further, Miller (2011) uses the term "vengeful informants" to describe informants who turn to the police in an attempt to use the police as a tool for striking back at enemies, competitors, or merely others that they dislike. Often, a vengeful informant will provide information to the police—typically voluntarily and not as a result of any police-initiated contact—to get revenge on drug dealers whom the informant perceives as having either ripped him or her off or as being competition threatening his or her own illicit business. While initially appearing altruistic in their efforts, the vengeful informant is in fact seeking to manipulate the criminal justice process for his or her own interests (which are typically also criminal). Finally, Dennis Fitzgerald (2007) suggests that some informants are akin to a double-agent spy. These are the informants who find opportunities to make the acquaintance of and work alongside law enforcement not to benefit law enforcement efforts but rather to gain information about law enforcement activities, strategies, and personnel so as to further their own criminal enterprises. An example of this entrepreneurial actor would be a drug dealer who informs on his competition so that he can learn more about how the police operate and subsequently use this information to protect his own interests and activities. As Fitzgerald explains it, "the double agent, also known as the perversely motivated informant, begins his relationship with law enforcement to further his own criminal ambitions. In becoming an informant, it is his objective to learn how the agency conducts its investigations and to identify its undercover agents, informants, and targets" (2007, 36).

The entrepreneurial informant situation almost always generates new cases for law enforcement agents. On rare occasions, a vengeful or mercenary subtype will approach a member of law enforcement to assist in closing an open case. In these sorts of situations, the informant serves a more active role than the officer, bringing forth unsolicited information. Not surprisingly, whenever possible, criminal investigators prefer to be active rather than passive when engaging known criminals to provide case intelligence. As such, the entrepreneurial informant scenario also takes shape as an officer-initiated contact where the officer nurtures an ongoing fee-for-services model with dependable underworld insiders who agents can rely on to generate new case leads when the proverbial well is running dry.

Regardless of who initiates the contact, the entrepreneurial type involves an information provider motivated by self-advancement and an intelligence consumer who cautiously engages the source knowing that there are likely strings attached to the information. This signals to the officer that the information must be subject to follow-up vetting to determine its veracity. It is well known that these sorts of double agent, mercenary, and vengeful informants exist across the modern urban landscape. In an effort to simultaneously tap and insulate themselves from these persons, most local, state, and federal law enforcement agencies have tightly defined policies that govern how they are to interact with such individuals in their intelligence-gathering efforts. In the sections that follow, we draw on our interviews and ethnographic experiences with law enforcement officers to illustrate the four types of informants depicted in figure 2. Given that the data for this study was drawn from a diverse group of law enforcement officers working within largely metropolitan jurisdictions, the text below focuses considerable attention on the informants who are working off charges (indentured informants) and acting in an entrepreneurial capacity.

Police-Source Exchanges

As indicated above, there exist a variety of circumstances under which the police-citizen information exchange might manifest itself as a police-source event. In this section, we detail a host of these scenarios and draw on our interactions with law enforcement officials in River City and Central City to flesh out the dynamics involved in each.

Cooperating Sources. Citizens involved in the cooperating-source scenario provide information to law enforcement officers out of a sense of civic duty, a desire to see particular crimes or criminals addressed, and/or simply because they relate to and endorse the goals of law enforcement (or more frequently, of a particular officer). In these scenarios, the citizen generally initiates contact with a law enforcement authority that he or she knows and/or trusts and voluntarily provides information that she or he deems relevant to an open investigation. In many cases, the citizen's motives border on altruistic, as it is the community, not his or her own immediate self-interests, that the citizen seeks to preserve. Julius, a supervisory-level official within a federal law enforcement agency, sums this situation up as follows: "The best informants are the ones not motivated by personal gain. They're doing it because they see it as the right thing to do. You know, that's coming from more of a trust standpoint, and the ends, the end product there I guess."

While altruism is discernable in these cases, elements of self-preservation are often present as well, as the citizen will frequently seek anonymity in exchange for the case leads so as to avoid potential reprisals from members of the offender population or stigma from community members who adhere to the "no snitching" credo. Ranger, a seasoned investigator who has worked for several local law enforcement agencies, expounded on this scenario:

> There are a lot of people that prefer to remain anonymous, but they live in that high crime area, and so they will pick up the phone and dial it and they'll call you or they'll send information another way. In those cases, when you know it's a non-criminal [source], it's a resident who may be exactly the one to help us in the types of things like the YMCA, or Boys and Girls Clubs, or the Optimist Club, or anything. You know, they hear things too and are very happy to share that information. So, in that case, you don't have to worry so much about them lying, and you don't have to worry about the veracity of the information they are giving you.

This quote illustrates that police officers welcome and tend to hold in high regard these law-abiding members of the community who align their interests with the crime-fighting role of law enforcement authorities. Officers note that they are more than willing to keep a cooperating source's name out of the case file if at all possible. They are simply happy to have the information and expect that the pure motivations coming from an upstanding member of the community ensure that the information provided is true.

Cooperating sources are often regular folks who consistently do what they believe to be the right thing. These persons don't generally differentiate between the officers they provide information to. Members of the criminal subculture tend to be more selective about the officers with whom they choose to share privileged information. The sentiments of Miller, a longtime street-level investigator in Central City, are illustrative in this regard:

> Just being out there [working the streets] for many years, you talk with people and stuff like that; you just run into them. Or they hear about you, or they see you and decide, "He's a pretty good officer or detective." They say, "He's a pretty good dude to work with." It could be that these are the guys that are at the homicide scenes. You interviewed them, and they were cool with you. And they know stuff about other shootings and homicides too. . . . [Crime is] going to happen every weekend around them. It's going to happen all of the time, and there's going to be shootings or robberies or selling dope here and there, and they're going to know. I mean, they are the ears out there. That's what they hear all day since they're out in the middle of it.

In these cases, a savvy street-level operator is likely to harbor a healthy distain for the police in general but will selectively overcome this concern when presented the opportunity to put forward information to a particular officer or officers that the individual has deemed to be trustworthy and authentic. This positive assessment can come from personal experience or be the result of an endorsement from a fellow member of the street subculture. Alonzo, a longtime homicide detective in Central City, made the following observation about the street credibility that he has painstakingly nurtured over his decades on the streets: "My name recognition rings out as, 'Oh he's cool, you can fuck with him' [street slang for 'trust him'], . . . in terms of me never doing people wrong." As a general rule, seasoned criminal operators are also hyper selective about which acts they choose to discuss. Garden-variety offenses remain outside the prying eyes of law enforcement; only those offenses that are deemed transgressions against the predominant street code are open for potential information sharing.

Another important point warrants mention in this regard. Cooperating sources do what they believe is right or righteous, but they are most likely to cooperate if and when they know that the police are conscientious and committed to acting on the information that the source possesses to bring about swift justice. In short, cooperating sources are willing and wanting to help but only if and when they believe that the law enforcement agents they are helping are active and interested.

Unwitting Sources. Unwitting sources are individuals who unintentionally provide information to law enforcement officials. In other words, they disclose valuable street-level intelligence without realizing they are doing so. These exchanges often take the shape of "casual" conversations between police investigators and persons on the street. They can occur on the corner, in a convenience store, or in any host of other neutral locations. There is often a veiled one-way nature to these conversations, as the investigator is attempting to probe for information without appearing to do so. The savvy officer seeks to use what appears to be a nonthreatening chat to surreptitiously extract intelligence from a person on the street. This scenario plays itself out over and over again as seasoned investigators question citizens during the course of their workday. In other instances, an unwitting source exchange may fall into the lap of a police officer if a citizen provides unprompted intelligence during the course of a genuinely mundane conversation. For example, a citizen might comment that a friend just got a new fur coat, and an alert officer might make a connection to an open clothing heist.

Some unwitting informants may set out with the explicit purpose of providing information about a specific suspect and/or criminal offense but, in the course of providing that information, may inadvertently share intelligence regarding another suspect and/or crime. Kareem explained how he occasionally obtained valuable information this way: "Some informants are what we consider unwitting informants—they are informants, but they don't necessarily know that they're giving information. So of course those are not paid informants. Maybe they don't necessarily know what we know about them, but in the course of talking with them and working with them, maybe in another type of capacity, [they give] us information, but they're not actually documented informants."

A police investigator usually treats information that emerges from an unwitting or cooperating source as a solid starting point but not as a cornerstone of their investigative efforts. It is useful to think of the information as an initial lead or tip that points the investigator in a certain direction, and these tips require much more follow-up work than intelligence provided by a true confidential informant who participates in a staged drug buy or wears a wire during a conversation with a criminal associate.

Civic-Minded Citizen Informers

There exist in most communities individuals who actively seek opportunities to act like, be with, and try to make themselves indispensable to law enforcement agents and agencies. Alonzo detailed several ongoing relationships that he maintains with members of criminal subculture. He mentioned several prostitutes that regularly track him down when homicides occur in the neighborhoods where they work. He also noted an illegal gambling den operator who frequently volunteered case leads. Finally, he made mention of a female waitress who, on several occasions, helped connect him with key witnesses and case leads. In all of these instances, the community members willingly and voluntarily provided the detective with critical intelligence. They did not seek anything in the way of compensation, nor did Alonzo offer up any such reward. Instead, he said that he would proactively help them out from time to time by buying them cigarettes, getting them something to eat, or giving them generous tips when he engaged in legitimate transactions with them. As Alonzo saw it, being nice to people from the street was a tried and true way to gain their trust and respect, and doing so often turned out to have a convenient payoff down the road when he needed it. There was nothing nefarious about these relationships; rather, they were part and parcel of how Alonzo build informant relationships on the street.

Police Buffs. Citizen-police information exchanges of the civic-minded citizen variety also come in several subtypes. The police buff is one such subtype. Police buffs are individuals who frequently idolize police and police work but, for whatever reason, never realized a career in law enforcement. These individuals often come forward with information on nonexistent and manufactured criminal conduct solely to gain access to officers and their activities. Police perceive this sort of person as potentially dangerous, especially when these individuals have a history of interactions with law enforcement. With repeated exposure and involvement in investigative activities, police buffs are likely to blur the lines between real police and themselves and may be at risk of over-stepping authority. They seek relationships with investigators of a depth that is not reciprocated and consequently may end up feeling used and discarded by investigators when the relationships they desire are not realized. This variety of informant is not only potentially dangerous to work with due to their questionable reliability but also likely to consume large amounts of officers' time. Shawn, a street-level drug investigator, explained:

> I can name you a couple of guys that no one wants as CIs. . . . We have one guy who literally thinks he could become a police officer. So he has the holster-sniffer mentality that, "Hey, I'm working with these guys," and he probably goes out and tells his buddies or his family, "Hey, I'm working with this agency." Those are the guys that they're calling you all of the time, they're trying to get as much information out of us as they can because they want that whole aura of being a police officer. But they're the ones that can—man—they can nag you. Just really bug you.

Officers most often view these "cop wannabe" informants as a nuisance. Yet they can sometimes be among the most valuable and productive informants. As individuals who want to think of themselves as, or who truly desire to officially become, law enforcement officers, these men (no female cop wannabes were identified in our study) are rather easily motivated and rewarded. Ranger, a seasoned narcotics officer, recalled his experiences with this type of person: "You know, there are always those guys who want to be cops, and they think that [providing information to police] is the way to get in. I have, and know others who have said, 'Yeah, I can get you on the force. I'll put in a good word for you.' You know, 'I'll write a letter of recommendation' and all of that, right? Hell yeah, you do that, and I don't know how else to put it, . . . you lead them on and you know full well you're lying to them the whole time." Such an approach may not be nice, and it may even be deceitful, but it is also viewed as acceptable because it is productive.

In our research, we consistently heard officers explain that they knew of people who became informants in all varieties of ways. Knowing why a new informant is interested or willing to collaborate with law enforcement was deemed critical to understanding how to work with the informant, what to expect, and what problems might be encountered. As Miller explained: "The first thing you want to look at in an informant is what their agenda is, what they want out of it. Do they want money, are they working off a case, or do they want revenge? Do they want the competition knocked off? As an officer or a detective, you need to know that, and you've got to know what their intentions are because that's what they do, that's their game."

Indentured Informants

Police-citizen information exchanges regularly come about after a citizen is arrested and subsequently offered a "deal" by an officer. We liken the deal to a form of indentured servitude wherein the arrestee is pressed to provide information in exchange for either leniency in subsequent court proceedings or, sometimes, a complete dismissal and dropping of all criminal charges. This is a classic carrot-and-stick approach to turning an informant. The literature suggests that this approach (i.e., simultaneously threatening a negative consequence and offering an alternative positive outcome) is the most common means through which informants are recruited and developed by law enforcement.

Opportunistic Development. There is often an opportunistic dimension underlying the indentured informant scenario. Once arrested, typically for possession or sale of small amounts of drugs or involvement in prostitution, the accused individual faces the usually undesirable situation of being processed by the criminal justice system. This includes being booked into jail, awaiting court proceedings, and a high probability of being convicted and sentenced. This threat of sanctions provides an opportunity for savvy law enforcement officers. When trying to convince a potential informant that he or she should "work" with law enforcement, an officer typically offers an incentive (although not always a very attractive or large one) for choosing to work with the officer and a consequence for choosing not to work with the officer. Sometimes, the consequence is directly stated: "If you don't want to work with me, that's fine. Just know that that means you're going to go to jail and I will go forward with the charges." Other times, there is only an implied consequence communicated to the potential informant: "Hey, it's your choice, but if you don't work with me, I can't control what may happen to you." While varying in degree, the consequences of not cooperating are disruptive to daily life and to legitimate or illegitimate occupational activities. Hence, to an individual faced with the threat of some unpleasant potential outcome, the offer to "work off" his or her misdeeds and make them go away can be a very enticing temptation. A more critical take on this "opportunity" is that it amounts to coercion, whereby accused persons are deliberately pressured into the indentured role. In this view, the offer of reduced or forgotten charges is not such a grand enticement as it is a byproduct of avoiding other possible negative repercussions that may be implied or threated by arresting officers.

Our fieldwork revealed that the opportunistic indentured informant scenario is pervasive in modern law enforcement. Asked to estimate the percentage of informants that fit into this category, Kareem, a federal investigator, replied: "Of all the informants I've dealt with, I would say 98–99 percent have had criminal backgrounds. I'm guessing you know, but that's how we get them. There are places where they just come forward and say, 'Hey, I just want to do the right thing,' but the majority have a criminal background." In simple terms, individuals who were arrested on a variety of relatively small charges (such as possession of a few grams of marijuana or a few rocks of crack; selling a small amount of marijuana or crack or a few pills; offering a sex act for a price; or possessing a few stolen items) were typically offered the opportunity to work with the arresting officer in exchange for having the charges against them dismissed.

Most law enforcement officers do not consider arresting someone for these types of minor offenses worthy of significant time or effort. However, some officers see these cases as an opportunity to turn an offender into an informant who may be able to provide information that will help catch a "bigger fish." In these cases, the officer is opportunistic and, on apprehending someone for a criminal violation, immediately explores whether the person might be able to yield information pertaining to additional cases. In River City, the officers of the flex unit were not concerned about individuals possessing and using small quantities of marijuana and sometimes even small amounts of crack—perhaps one to five rocks. However, when the unit members found someone holding a small baggie of marijuana, a few joints, or a couple of rocks of crack, their first thought was that the offense provided an opportunity to gain an upper hand with someone who might be able to be pushed for information that could lead to the arrest of another, more serious, offender. When a member of the unit arrested someone for drug possession or sale and sometimes even for prostitution, the typical offer from the officer was for the individual to arrange to buy more drugs from his or her supplier and thereby facilitate the arrest of this "bigger fish" supplier. And, as evidenced numerous times, if the original arrest led to information and a second arrest of a "bigger fish," that second arrest was also done primarily to move up the food chain and try to gain access to a higher level.

Proactive Development. In at least some cases, the explicit purpose of making an arrest for possession, solicitation, or some other offense is to proactively develop an indentured informant. In other words, the officer goes out looking for persons known or expected to be involved in illicit markets, knowing that the purpose of the minor stop or charge is to flip the individual for information that will lead to a more serious stop or charge. This was often the case among the street-level narcotics officers from Central City. For example, on a slow day, narcotics investigators were repeatedly observed collaborating with officers from other units, such as K-9 or patrol, to generate new cases. A K-9 officer with a drug-sniffing dog would be enlisted to locate drug stashes in a known open-air drug market location such as a housing project. On discovering a stash, team members would direct their attention to the nearby street-level dealer, who would in turn be pressed to give up one or more suppliers on the next rung up the supply chain. Similarly, patrol officers were observed setting up vehicle checkpoints designed to uncover every order of violation, from outstanding warrants to suspended licenses to the possession of illegal weapons. To proactively generate new leads, narcotics detectives would station themselves nearby the checkpoints and swoop in when a driver was found to be in possession of drugs. Proactive patrols or probation officer-initiated "knock and talks" in known drug neighborhoods were also commonly used to identify minor violations that could then be exploited by narcotics investigators.

Choosing among Prospects. Regardless of whether an officer identifies a prospective informant through proactive or opportunistic means, he or she must make a series of determinations before negotiating an indentured informant arrangement. Once an officer has detained an individual, before he or she will pursue an indentured informant arrangement, the officer must usually feel comfortable that (1) the charges against the individual are relatively minor and therefore "not worth the hassle" of putting the offender through the system; (2) the individual is stable and street savvy; and (3) the individual has the requisite underworld connections with high-value criminal operatives (i.e., higher-level drug dealers or other serious offenders).

The officers that we spoke to maintained that they rarely pursued indentured informant arrangements with persons facing charges for violent or serious offenses. They reasoned that persons who posed an appreciable threat to society needed to be taken off the streets and thus negotiating reduced sentences in these cases was not appealing to the officers. Instead, they targeted persons being detained for minor charges or victimless crimes. Most often, they went after drug offenders for development as indentured informants. As one author notes, "I've never met so many informers that a drug field generates when compared to other forms of crime" (Grieve 1992, 58).

The next step in the screening process involves the initiating officer making a determination about the offender's character and state of mind. When first making an arrest, the officer must quickly consider the individual's mental state, general intelligence, street sense and knowledge, and ability to control his or her emotions. These factors, which are presumed to be important for an individual's ability to get information and/or contacts, keep information straight and accurate, and remain focused on the completion of a task even in the face of stressful, challenging, or dangerous situations, are all thought by most officers observed in the fieldwork in River City and Central City as critical to an informant's success. Only if the officer is convinced that the individual has the steadiness, street savviness, and social skills to successfully set up a "bigger fish" will he or she pursue working with the individual.

The final step in the screening process involves an assessment of the prospect's knowledge of criminal activity and access to the persons responsible for said activity. To make this evaluation, the officer usually queries the prospective informant about what he or she knows, who he or she knows and interacts with, and what he or she believes they can deliver to the officer. As explained by Central City interviewee Sonny: "The ones that are being arrested and working that off can actually provide a lot of good information because they know criminal activity, they participate in criminal activity, and they know the players, the people who are actually doing the crime." Federal agent Kareem describes drug users and low-level dealers as experts on the criminal world: "Just like you would go to a university for a man or woman with a PhD out of respect because they're a subject-matter expert, he or she [drug dealer or user] is a subject-matter expert in drugs, and that should be respected." Therefore, by extrapolation, an offender who may be the most levelheaded, calm, intelligent, and street-savvy individual but who is brand new in town and without any contacts outside of the people involved in their present arrest is of little use to law enforcement as an indentured informant. Without something or someone to inform on, the arrestee has no role to fill as an indentured informant and will thus be cited or jailed without delay.

The officer's three-part assessment of an indentured informant prospect usually takes place quickly and is based on limited information, but it is central to the officer's decision-making process as he or she decides whether to proceed further. Focused observation is also key in this regard, as the initiating officer can often identify cues or leads based on his or her own independent evaluation of what the perpetrator discloses. Moreover, confidence plays an important role in an officer's willingness to work with an indentured informant. If the initiating officer surmises that an accused individual is unable or unlikely to successfully execute an intelligence-gathering plan, the offender will not be offered the opportunity to work off his or her charges and will instead be promptly issued a citation or transported to jail for booking. If, however, the officer makes the initial determination that an accused person has the requisite skills and constitution to serve as an intelligence asset, the next step is for the officer to articulate an explicit deal or indenture the individual.

The Deal. At this point, the conversation becomes very specific, with the officer stating (usually multiple times) what the new indentured informant will do and deliver and what he or she will receive in exchange. One such conversation in River City went like this: "Okay, so we got this straight, right? You make three buys for me from JoJo, and they have to be legit buys. I want at least five grams on him, none of this crumbs stuff. And if you do that, then I will drop these four charges against you. You understand that?" As indicated in this quote, the deal that is worked out with a new indentured informant always contains a specific number of actions and completed tasks, often a specific target, and frequently a minimum weight or quality of drugs. In River City, the typical impromptu street-level deal was for between one and three buys from different sellers, depending on the weight that could or would be bought and whether a targeted seller was someone known to and especially wanted by the investigative unit. While very explicit expectations are stated for the number and type of transactions and/or information that are expected from an indentured informant, it is only on rare occasions that an officer will impose a deadline or time limit on the exchange. Informants who were given short turnaround times on completing actions almost always failed to realize these goals due to unforeseen circumstances. Imposing deadlines almost always led to missed deadlines. The use of deadlines with indentured informants appears to vary depending on the culture and expectations of different types of investigative units. Among those law enforcement units and officers engaged in investigations of more complex, higher-level operations (i.e., catching "bigger fish"), there exists some recognition of the need for more planning and attention to details when dealing with these bigger cases. At lower levels, especially among those patrol officers who turn indentured informants and work with them, there tends to exist a stronger expectation for things to be done immediately. This may be due, at least in part, to differences in the way productivity is gauged at different levels. Patrol officers need to show productivity through statistics on a more frequent basis than higher-level organizational units. When dealing with informants, the lack of a deadline and the absence of explicit expectation for completion of tasks can sometimes work to the detriment of officers, as some informants will try to drag out their time, perhaps hoping that the officer will either forget about them or move on to other tasks and informants. However, officers rarely forget or move on, and indentured informants are not often able to skirt their obligation to their initiating officers.

When offered the opportunity to work as an indentured informant, most offenders are immediately reluctant, and nearly all of them initially claim that they do not know of others who are criminally involved and/or that they could not set someone up for fear of being found out as a snitch and subsequently victimized. Some officers react to these protestations with apparent acceptance and matter-of-fact statements such as: "That's too bad. I was just trying to help you out. But if that's the way it is, that's the way it is." Then, as the officer moves forward with paperwork and takes steps to move the arrest process along, the detained individual is left to consider his or her situation. More often than not, reluctance and/or apprehension give way to cautiously offered "possibilities" about which people an individual "might" be able to provide access or information about.

Sometimes, an officer will give a prospective informant "one last chance" while he or she is waiting to be processed into the jail. The initiating officer will provide the individual with his or her name and cell phone number and instructions to "think about it. All I want from you is for you to give me two (or three, or four) others. Just get me those buys, and I'll take care of this here. I don't care who does them or how you get them for me. Think about it." Usually, this final offer is met with enthusiasm and the promise of a call. That call, however, rarely comes.

Sometimes, the offer to work as an indentured informant is not immediately accepted but may generate a response from an individual only after he or she has had a taste of incarceration. Here, the words of Central City investigator Miller are revealing: "It might not happen right away, and they might go to jail and think they're all tough and stuff like that. But maybe two weeks go by, and they then want to talk to you. So you do the jailhouse visit and see what they want to talk about. . . . If the guy calls you, you probably do want to take the time to go to the jail to see what he has to say."

One variation on the deal-proffering process involves two or more officers employing a "good-cop, bad-cop" strategy with the potential indentured informant. In this scenario, multiple officers work in tandem: one or more of them threatens a prospective informant with dire outcomes, and the other or others feign sympathy and support in an effort to get the individual to go along with the deal. This was a central recruitment strategy recounted by the drug informants in Mitch Miller's (2011) study, although it featured less prominently in our fieldwork. When it was used, it was most often with a reluctant suspect, often a woman, who was very emotional and distraught at the event of her arrest. River City flex unit officer George and his partner Lucky were observed using this recruitment strategy on several occasions. Both George and Lucky were white officers in their midtwenties. They were good friends, spending nearly all day, every day at work together, and frequently socializing together outside of work. George and Lucky communicated with one another very well and often could do so with only a glance or a few short words. When a woman they were arresting would cry uncontrollably and be difficult to calm down, George and Lucky would attempt to turn her through their own good-cop, bad-cop approach, in which George was the good cop and Lucky was the bad cop. Typically, Lucky would initiate the interaction, moving in on the woman with a relatively rough, uncaring, by-the-book approach. He would tell her that she was worthless, that he was disgusted at having to deal with women like her, and that he didn't care about her being upset. George would soon interrupt, telling Lucky to leave her alone and sending him away to complete some task out of earshot of the woman. George would then console the woman suspect, apologize for Lucky's rudeness, and tell her that he didn't see her as worthless. He would offer up his own assessment that she was trapped in the situation and only doing what she had to in order to get by. Nonetheless, George would claim that he could not do anything to help her because the arrest decision was ultimately up to Lucky. After a couple of minutes, with the woman typically still distraught, George would venture that he might be able to convince Lucky to cut her a break, but only if she could help the partners get a follow-up arrest or two out of the situation. At that point, either the hook was set and the potential informant was turned or she remained reluctant and subsequently ended up in jail.

Reluctance based on the fear of being identified and publicly known as a snitch is often more difficult to overcome than other types of reluctance and requires more active effort and intervention on the part of the officer. When dealing with this type of hesitation, it becomes imperative for the recruiting officer to explain how the operation will proceed and to emphasize the "very small" role that the potential informant will play. The officers were frequently heard saying things like, "No one will ever know it was you," or, "You won't even be present." When a scenario is presented that involves the potential indentured informant providing information or access without being seen, mentioned by, or in any other public way being associated with the police, the offer of informing is seen by the offender as more attractive and feasible. When a potential indentured informant can be convinced that he or she will not only benefit in their own arrest case but also avoid detection as a snitch, most perceive the proposed deal as being wholly self-benefitting and therefore something to be accepted.

At this point, it is also imperative for an officer seeking to turn an individual into an indentured informant to be able to establish a sense of rapport with the potential informant. Being able to relate to one another, on at least some level and with some degree of respect, is important. At a minimum, the prospective informant wants to feel respected and believe that the officer is sensitive to his or her needs. Moreover, individuals who feel a sense of affinity or positive regard for the officer they are working with are much more likely to enter into an indentured informant role and fulfill the role well and productively. Kareem corroborated this:

> The main thing about dealing with informants is that you have to have rapport. If you don't have any rapport with them, then first, you're not going to have good information, and second, you're not going to get all of the information that you could have got. . . . It's like you're in high school and you're dating. You're trying to tell them what you need to tell them and make them comfortable. . . . Some of them need a lot more maintenance than others. So if you let them think that you're that confidant—not necessarily their friend, because that is totally different—but they're kind of looking at you as a person I can call if I have a problem.

Once they agree to inform, most newly turned indentured informants offer to make a call and set up a deal right away. When convinced to turn on their drug provider or another criminal acquaintance, most indentured informants want to get the deal over with and satisfy the arresting officer immediately. In one instance in River City, after being arrested for selling three rocks of crack cocaine and being offered the opportunity to turn on other sellers, a woman named Joan claimed to not know of anyone she could call and instead offered to get her boyfriend to make a buy while she went to jail. Citing too many loose ends and unpredictable possibilities in such a situation, the flex unit passed on this offer. Officers almost never accept an indentured informant's offer to "do it right now" and instead explain that some planning needs to be done to be ready for such an event. Only when an officer is at the start of a work shift and has been convinced by the potential indentured informant that, for example, it is "now or never with this guy," will he or she even seriously consider immediately following through on the offer. Additionally, this reluctance to act immediately may be related to the organizational culture and workflow expectations of the investigative unit. Plans (which may have required extensive planning and resource investment) may already be place for the near future, and changing directions and addressing a newly offered opportunity could jeopardize these efforts. Also, most stand-alone investigative units seek to maintain control of their work schedule and feel very strongly that it is their imperative to impose a timeframe rather than cede control of scheduling to potential indentured informants.

On one occasion in River City, the researcher and Skye were surveilling a storefront laundromat on a busy intersection of two neighborhood streets.

While watching for suspicious activity, a tall, muscular African American man in his early twenties entered the laundromat, immediately approached a dirty, disheveled white man in his late-twenties in full view through the front window, completed a hand-to-hand transaction, and immediately exited the building. The encounter lasted less than twenty seconds. On leaving, the African American seller disappeared around the corner and was instantly out of sight. Skye and the researcher entered the laundromat to confront the scraggly white man. Skye obtained consent to search him and found several rocks of crack cocaine in one of his coat pockets. Knowing that she was dealing with a drug user who bought the illegal substance for immediate use and not wanting to spend the next several hours processing the addict into jail, Skye moved the man to the back of the Laundromat and offered him the chance to get out of an arrest: "Call your guy back and get him to come back with three more rocks." Anxious to avoid a trip to jail, where he would be forced to start to detox, the buyer jumped at this offer. Within an hour, a buy-bust plan was formulated, backup officers were in place, and the call to the dealer was made. Less than fifteen minutes later, the same young African American man returned, entered the Laundromat again, and was arrested without incident. He was subsequently offered the chance to work off his charges by informing, but he steadfastly refused.

When an arresting officer approaches a potential indentured informant with an offer to work off his or her charges in this way, it is important that this conversation and offer be made to the individual in private. Under no circumstances would an officer make such an offer either in earshot of or even while visible to members of the public. Typically, the initial indenture offer is even made away from the presence of other officers to make the opportunity seem special, unique, and truly confidential. In some instances, an officer will simply mention the possibility without any explanation or elaboration and then leave his or her name and number on a slip of paper with the potential informant. Two of the common approaches used by River City flex unit investigator George focused on him very casually providing his contact information to a potential indentured informant. At times, when making a very public arrest with numerous onlookers, George would casually mention the possibility of working off the charges to an arrestee while transporting him or her to jail and then put a piece of paper with his name and cellphone number in the offender's pocket. Alternatively, in instances when an arrested individual seemed especially reluctant to consider the possibility of informing, George would leave a piece of paper with his name and number where he was sure the potential indentured informant would later find it. In one instance, after arresting a woman named Kamla for selling four rocks of crack cocaine outside her apartment (on a deal set up by an informant), the flex unit moved inside the apartment because Kamla did not want her neighbors to see her being arrested. While in the apartment, George talked individually with Kamla and introduced the opportunity of her setting up three buys of two or three rocks from others in exchange for him not filing charges against her. Kamla claimed not to know of anyone to buy from and was subsequently taken to jail. Before leaving her apartment, however, George left a small piece of paper with his name and number on top of Kamla's purse. Less than a week later, she called and offered to work with George.

The decision of when to introduce the possibility of working off charges is in part a matter of officer preference and in part a function of the social context in which an arrest is made. The two primary opportunities for initiating such a conversation are while still at the scene of an arrest or while transporting an arrestee to jail. When an arrest is made in a way that precludes the presence of onlookers and numerous officers, having a private conversation with the individual on the scene is common. In situations when others are present and would see an officer talking with an arrested individual, it is common for the indentured informant pitch to be delayed until after leaving the scene. Regardless of exactly when and where such a conversation is held, it is important that privacy be placed at a premium, as it assures the potential indentured informant of the fact that "no one will know" and that "the only way it can go bad is for you [the informant] to screw it up."

When a potential indentured informant is deemed to be facing the right sort of charges and to be stable and connected enough to be able to provide useful information and contacts, he or she is moved into the category of "working indentured informants." It is important to note that this designation is not necessarily a permanent one. Throughout all of their time and interactions both with officers on the whole and their primary contact officer, informants are constantly being observed for signs of unreliability, instability, and intoxication. An indentured informant is considered unreliable on engaging in any one of the following common transgressions: failing to follow through with agreed-on actions, providing inaccurate information, or coming to prearranged meetings or a scheduled introduction or buy intoxicated. In such instances, if the individual is working off charges, those charges are likely to be filed, re-filed, or otherwise moved forward. In essence, the debt is called in, the deal is terminated, and the offender is handed over, without any requests for leniency, to prosecutors. Kareem described a strict accountability model to be followed when dealing with informants of this kind:

> If the plan calls for them to buy something, whether it's a gun, drugs, or whatever, and they stiff you, . . . you will have to do something. Otherwise, your business from that point is going to go downhill. If you find out they're not telling you the truth, they're gaming you, you have to address it immediately—let them know, especially the ones that are working off a charge or trying to get a reduced sentence, you have to let them know. If it's serious enough, you've got to cut them loose [dissolve the working arrangement]. . . . That's just automatic. But some things are bend-but-not-break type of things. You get them back in line and say, "Look, if this happens again, I'm not dealing with you, and I'm going to go inform the US Attorney's office that you're not cooperating and the DA's office that you're not cooperating."

Entrepreneurial Informants

Making Money. A final type of informant, far less common than the indentured informant who is working off charges, is the entrepreneurial informant, who offers to inform on others for the sole purpose of making money. Some entrepreneurs approach officers they know, typically patrol officers, and imply that they have information that they are willing to trade for money. In these instances, a patrol officer may take the opportunity to turn an informant and subsequently work a case as a way of demonstrating his or her initiative to superior officers. Or the patrol officer may choose to pass the information and contact along to a detective or investigative unit officer. This creates a bit of goodwill and also allows the patrol officer to avoid committing to tasks for which he or she may feel unprepared or for which he or she has insufficient time. Alternatively, patrol officers who pass information along to investigative units may do so as a means of demonstrating their ability to recruit informants, which is recognized as a central task of investigative units and is a critical criterion for selection to such a unit. In all of the investigative units studied in this project, the work of cultivating and handling entrepreneurial informants was relegated to only one or two officers. Other officers would routinely identify these officers as "specialists" in the recruitment and development of entrepreneurial informants and note the distinctive skills and personality required of this role. When other officers encountered an opportunity to work with an entrepreneurial informant, they would funnel these cases (formally or informally) to the officers deemed "best" at such tasks. The same was not true for indentured informants, as a wide array of officers were observed partaking in these forms of information exchanges.

We observed many cases in which individuals started off as indentured informants but then transitioned into entrepreneurial informant arrangements once they had satisfied their debt with their handling officer. In some instances, this changeover was initiated by the informant. On completing the agreed-on number of tasks, the informant might propose to provide more information and access in exchange for monetary compensation. Alternatively, when dealing with an indentured informant who was especially easy and reliable to work with, an officer might inquire if the individual would be interested in continuing to provide valued intelligence in exchange for monetary payment.

Irrespective of how the initial money for information exchange took shape, all officers in the present study voiced skepticism and at least some degree of trepidation about working with paid informants. Whereas working with an indentured informant over whom an officer holds the threat of jail and probably criminal conviction affords the officer a privileged power position in most instances, working with a paid informant substantially minimizes the power differential. Simply stated, officers report feeling less in control of the situation and therefore less enthusiastic when they have to pay for information. The level of reticence of officers was noticeably higher when the payment amounts were small. Street-level investigators such as those working in the Central City narcotics unit or River City flex unit could only offer a few dollars—typically $20 or less—in exchange for a modest drug buy or information on a stolen property operation. Most would-be entrepreneurial informants considered this incentive to be far less of a motivation than maintaining freedom. In other instances, especially in higher-level investigative units, available resources were more plentiful, and thus officers felt more at ease when paying out larger sums of money in exchange for intelligence on more high-value criminal targets. We encountered evidence to suggest that this tolerance threshold is dependent on cultural issues inside of agencies, inside of specific investigative units of agencies, and across different communities.

Regardless of resource availability, when first making a money-for-information trade with a given entrepreneurial informant, officers like to keep the monetary amount small. This is so as to not make the situation so enticing that an informant will fabricate information just to get a substantial payment. The belief is that payments of $15 to $20 are small enough so as not to lead a potential entrepreneurial informant to go out of his or her way to contrive a situation or information. With time and repeated demonstration of accuracy and reliability of information, a for-pay informant will see his or her payments increase. In our study, the River City flex unit had very limited resources for payments to informants and hence rarely paid more than $20 per transaction to an entrepreneurial informant. One informant, Tiger, proved to be very reliable and got to the point of working two to three incidents per week under the direction of George. After more than a month of always-accurate information provided in an easy and reliable manner, Tiger's pay was increased to $30, then $50, and on a couple of occasions even $100. For Tiger, a day laborer with no steady income and a nightly drinking habit, this money provided him with what he needed to get by. Over time, Tiger began to refer to himself as "one of us" (referring to the flex unit). It was evident that the heightened status and regular income made informing an attractive and easy job for Tiger. It is worth noting that, as a general rule, as payments increase, so too do the officer's expectations about the value of the intelligence payoff.

While the money that most entrepreneurial informants earn for their information is fairly small (local police agencies and officers rarely pay more than $100 per task or piece of information), there are important exceptions to this. Some agencies have established a set pay rate for entrepreneurial informants. Shawn, a narcotics investigator in a suburban police department on the outskirts of Central City, reported: "I've got a CI I pay a hundred dollars every time he gives me information. If I get an arrest, he gets a hundred bucks, and he knows that. So if he's hard up for cash and he needs a hundred bucks, he can call me up with some information; we go do an operation, and he gets a hundred bucks in his pocket." In other situations, and with other types of informants, payment may be determined at least in part by an officer bargaining for a low price. Continuing in his explanation of payment to informants, Shawn said:

> I pay them as little as possible to get what I can get. If they're willing to get me five pounds of meth for fifty bucks, I'm going to pay them fifty bucks to get five pounds of meth. Now, granted, that's about sixty thousand dollars street value of meth, but if I can pay that [$50], I'm a little stingy with them with my funds. But I also know that, sometimes, to get a big score I've got to pay [for] it. On average, our guys that are giving us low- to mid-level dealers, they get anywhere from one hundred bucks for a deal to five hundred.

The payment in some local jurisdictions is carefully scaled and laid out in official department policies or standard operating procedures (SOPs). For example, in Central City, an investigator named Orlando explained that his payments to informants were set by an official departmental scale: "It's not discretionary. And, anything over a certain amount has to be approved by the next level [i.e., a supervisor]. It's not just, 'Here's a wad of money, go pay somebody.' No, it don't work that way. . . . That's the way it worked when I was with [a different jurisdiction]. It's not a per se schedule there." The SOPs of some local jurisdictions allow for entrepreneurial informants to be paid a particular percent of the value of seized money or items. Other departments have enacted policies that deem the informant eligible to receive publicly posted rewards if the information provided leads directly to an arrest. The norm in local law enforcement agencies, however, appears to be for small, incremental payments linked to the actual seizure that results from the intelligence.

Payouts provided by federal law enforcement agencies can be much greater, especially on big cases involving high-level offenders and/or large quantities of drugs, guns, or other trafficked items. Here, again, the variation is almost always observed across, not within, agencies. This point is captured well in the following quote from Kareem, a seasoned federal investigator who has worked with several agencies: "Depending on the agency, that determines what they [the informants] get paid. There are some agencies where they get a percentage of seized monies. Our agency, it isn't like that; they're working for a certain amount. There is a maximum that we can pay them. So keeping that in mind, they're not going to get rich working with us generally."

We offer one final observation regarding citizens who seek payment for privileged information on criminal conduct—namely, that they often do not limit their marketing efforts to law enforcement authorities. Several officers that we spoke to bemoaned the fact that they sometimes felt that they were competing with members of local media outlets (most notably television news reporters) for information. Central City homicide investigators repeatedly noted that, when television reporters would arrive at a murder scene before or very soon after the police, reporters could be observed offering to pay witnesses or other knowledgeable individuals present for information to be used to shape their broadcasts. As homicide investigator Robinson noted:

The media can go against you when they put too much information out there for you. They have snitches—they pay off snitches too. That's what they do. They go to the scene there, and they'll find somebody that was actually there, that saw the body before we got there or something. They might know exactly why this person was shot. [On getting paid by the reporter, they say,] "Well [the suspect was] in the closet somewhere, and they shot [the victim] in the head twice, you know, two inches apart." Of course we're not gonna put that out on the media, but if they [the reporters] get it out there, they've bought the information pretty much. That may be some information that we could have used later. So that's gonna hurt you if they pay to put it out there.

The detectives conjectured that, if the reporters did not pay off the witness first, it is highly possible, if not probable, that such information could have been provided directly to law enforcement and used in a more effective investigative manner. Police may have had to pay for it, but detectives believed that could have secured the information if given the opportunity.

Revenge. Previous researchers (J. M. Miller 2011; Fitzgerald 2007) have noted that seasoned criminals who come forward to police with actionable intelligence are often seeking revenge on rival criminals or competitors. Generally speaking, acts of revenge are carried out for purposes of simple enjoyment or excitement or to enhance an individual's own criminal opportunities by helping to take out the competition. In our fieldwork in both River City and Central City, there were limited instances of this sort of entrepreneurial informant. Duffy, a patrol unit lieutenant with more than a decade of experience in policing, noted that, throughout his career, his experience was that informants did not have to necessarily be offered any payoff or leniency: "[In some instances, they] just tell because of competition. You know you have drug dealers telling on drug dealers. Or you have girlfriends getting pissed off with their boyfriends, and they tell on them. So, there are many reasons why someone would tell on someone."

In River City, one individual, A-Man, did offer to provide information on "all those other motherfuckers out there making it hard for me to make a living" when he was arrested for selling five rocks of crack cocaine in a deal set up by an informant. A-Man first made this offer when he was arrested on a busy city street outside a local burger restaurant early one spring afternoon. The arrest, which involved three undercover cars and two back-up patrol cars, was a notable event at the time it occurred and drew a couple dozen observers. It was in this setting that A-Man first, in a voice easily heard by many onlookers, offered to inform on others. After completing the arrest and while transporting A-Man to jail, Investigator Justin asked a few questions about whom A-Man could provide access to and with whom in the community A-Man had connections. Based on his answers, which Justin interpreted as evasive and not fully honest, Justin decided that A-Man would most likely be more troublesome than valuable as an informant and hence passed on A-Man's offer.

Some persons involved in criminal activities, however, including on occasion drug dealers, do legitimately see their competitors as "bad for business," and when they have an opportunity to inform on them, they may. In one Central City homicide case, Detective White recounted interviewing a young man about another recent homicide and learning no new information:

> I asked him if he knew anything about homicides recently. He said "Not recently, but I know about one that happened a couple of few months ago." And he went on to describe the whole entire scene. It was a homicide I responded to and I was working. I was like, "You know the dudes who did it?" He was like "Yeah." ... So I gave him my number, and I said, you know, I said, "Just give me a call." I just want to see how, you know, straightforward he was going to be. He called me like at twelve noon the next day and said, "Hey, this is the three guys' names." He gave me their names, where they lived. He was like "Man, I'm just going to be honest with you detective, they're bad for business." And I was like, okay, wow. He came down, gave me a full statement. I showed him a lineup, and he said, "Yeah, that's him, that's him, that's him." I was like, wow! You know, the whole thing. The DA was like, "You know, it's kind of unusual for a drug dealer to just come like and give you information." I was like, "They're the best people for information."'

Although this man may not have been motivated to provide information for the same reasons that motivate others, he did have a motivation, and it lead to him providing information on three murderers.

The revenge theme was also observed playing out in a more personal manner, whereby a person provides criminal intelligence to police to get back at a friend, family member, or loved one for a personal affront. Greene, a longtime violent crimes investigator in Central City, elaborated on this:

> We get good information, and in the best times [we] get it when they are angry at each other. ... If they feel like the person up in here has wronged them or something, done something wrong to them, they will, they'll go up, they'll go around and talk to us, and they'll tell us the information we need. That's the best type of information we get, when somebody's angry at someone. Most of the times, when they're angry at each other, yeah, they will tell you what is going on and where it is going to be at.

Longtime narcotics investigator Vic recounted an instance where a personal beef led to a sequence of high-quality information exchanges:

I get a phone call. I say hello, and this guy says, "Hey, I know this guy that just came out of the service [the military] named Tommy; he's my best friend. He's been mailing dope to himself from the service." We ended up taking fifteen or sixteen drug dealers down just from a phone call from a guy that was pissed off at his friend. You aren't going to believe how this one ended up. Tommy was in jail. And this guy named Mickey [the original informant], he lost his job, so he starts dealing. So Tommy gets out of jail, and Mickey calls Tommy up and says, "I need you to get rid of some drugs for me." They flipped on each other! He's waiting there in his car, and I pull up to his car, and I just said, "Mickey, you really broke my heart." He just turned around and opened the trunk, and there it [the drugs] all was. It was the same guy he ratted out that got him back.

Officers reported that upset lovers or spouses are also ripe for exploitation in this regard. Central City detective Miller spoke to this: "Well, I think a lot of the crimes are solved on people getting mad and ticked off at each other and coming back and calling the police or whatever. Domestics are great examples. Thousands of domestic cases I've handled, they've ended up telling me good stuff while I'm on that case. They tell on other things that have happened."

SUMMARY

What we see is that informants come in a variety of forms, motivations, and working styles. Motivations can be either altruistic or, more commonly, centered on attempts to either engage in self-preservation or self-advancement. It is important for investigators to understand why an individual chooses to work with law enforcement so that they can decide how best to approach and manage a relationship with the informant. Those over whom investigators hold a threat—such as prosecution or incarceration—are likely to act very differently than civic-minded or personally motivated informants.

While all informants are valuable and can provide investigators with important information for clearing offenses, they also present challenges in personal interactions, direction, and sometimes stability. It is essential for an investigator to consider these challenges when forming a plan for to go about recruiting and working with informants. These are the issues to which we turn next, and we will focus on the varying styles of interaction that are used by officers to recruit and maintain confidential informants.

FOUR

Working with Informants

UTILITY OF CONFIDENTIAL INFORMANTS

Chapter 3 maps out a host of different types of information exchange dynamics that exist between law enforcement officers seeking to solve crimes and citizens who have privileged information on criminal subculture. Making sense of the types of relationships is an important step along the way to understanding the confidential informant phenomenon. It is generally accepted that law enforcement officers need informants more than informants need the officers. Generally speaking, persons providing information to police stand to gain only modest outcomes for their role in assisting police with their investigative efforts. For example, although police sources, police buffs, and even revenge-motivated informants seek out police as a means of removing criminals from their communities, the criminal conduct in question in these cases generally does not pose an immediate and significant threat to the information provider's well-being. Similarly, while entrepreneurial informants nurture profit-oriented information exchange relations with police as a means of generating income, it is rare that this income comprises a large proportion of the individual's weekly or monthly cash intake. Indentured informants navigate a more tenuous and dependent space; after all, they are operating in a state of duress, unwillingly providing information to police in exchange for reduced charges or absolution for crimes they have committed. However, it is rare that an indentured informant is a first-time offender who has never been arrested or presumes he or she will never be arrested in the future. On the contrary, most indentured informants are entrenched members of the criminal subculture and view information exchange as an exercise in managing their criminal histories as opposed to ending them. Law enforcement officers, on the other hand, have more at stake in the information-sharing game. Given their clear outsider status in the criminal subculture, they need inside information to achieve their primary goal, namely, increasing public safety by apprehending criminals.

The value of informants to law enforcement activities is quite significant. Nearly universally, the law enforcement officers that we spoke to expressed the belief that, although informants are not the only way to solve cases, they are an integral component of the work, and without their existence, many offenses would be unsolvable. Pedro, a federal investigator who also had eight years of local law enforcement experience, put it succinctly: "I think it would be very difficult to do my job without informants at all. Can I do my job without them? Absolutely! Can I do it as effective without them? Absolutely not!" Whether they like it or not, investigators from all sorts of investigative units and types of agencies, and experienced investigators in particular, see informants as a necessity for their jobs. As Frank, a retired Central City police officer with a decade of experience working with informants both on the ground as a beat officer and as a plainclothes investigator in discretionary and vice units in addition to as a supervisor in various capacities, related:

> It's a given in police work. It's not an upside, but it's a fact, if you're going to be a cop—police officer or investigator—you have to develop relationships with people that you keep confidential. You want them to give you information, and it's a necessity.... You can't be an effective police officer, police investigator, without informants.... If you're just punching a time clock, you don't need informants. If you want to solve crimes, you've got to develop them at every opportunity.... All the good detectives had informants. The incompetent detectives didn't have the interpersonal skills or the knowledge or the motivation [to develop informants]. That's what separated the good cops from the average or the bad ones.

There is a tendency to think that confidential informants are only important to police officers seeking to solve victimless crimes, such as drug and commercial sex offenses, that are willing exchanges between two persons. In these cases, there is no complainant, and officers are left to their own devices to discover the criminal activity and assemble enough evidence against one or more of the transaction participants to justify an arrest. Given the hedonistic desires that underlie these public-order offense types, it is predictable that they occur with high frequency within the context of established relationships and marketplaces. This sets up a dynamic where vice investigators can predictably locate drug or commercial sex offenders, be they providers or consumers, with the assumption that these individuals will be privy to a host of other criminal activity within the marketplace. Referring to covert drug markets, Howard Katz (1990) identifies six different ways in which vice officers enlist the use of confidential informants: (1) to uncover insider information on the identities, activities, and product location of drug dealers; (2) to assist undercover officers in gaining entrée into a drug-dealing operation by making strategic introductions; (3) to make drug buys while being surveilled by officers; (4) to collect and relay information on drug operations taking place in secure or impervious locations; (5) to independently collect and relay information on covert drug operations to shape future case development; and (6) to serve as corroborating witnesses for the prosecution to help secure convictions. In each of these capacities, the information provider shines light on activities that would otherwise likely remain unknown or inaccessible to police. Given that complainants rarely come forward in drug and sex crimes, and given that law-abiding citizens are often not privy to the critical information sought by police, the in-the-know informant occupies a central role in vice crime investigation. It is not that the police are blind to what is going on in the vice markets but rather that they acknowledge that officers get to see only the surface activities and thus need informants to help them make their way up, down, and laterally within the covert markets. Shawn, a seasoned undercover narcotics officer in a suburb of Central City, captures this sentiment well: "We know how the bad guys work, but how do we learn how the bad guys work? Through the use of confidential informants basically training us on how the bad guys do their stuff.... So that's why we use confidential informants. They're just a resource for us to see how the bad guys are doing their stuff."

Some investigators are drawn to vice enforcement; they go out of their way to spend most or even all of their careers "chasing dope" or moving from one vice unit or taskforce to another. These officers often forgo increased pay or promotion opportunities to remain street-level investigators or carefully navigate the military-style bureaucracy to climb up the career ladder while remaining in vice-type units. It is rare to find one of these sorts of officers who does not enjoy and excel at working with confidential informants; they internalize the potential that informants represent for their success and proactively engage them and refine their usage. Orlando, a twenty-year veteran of the Central City police department, who began his career as a beat cop but was quickly promoted to commander of a multiagency taskforce due to his knack for making drug arrests, said: "I like using informants. I've always liked using informants because of the knowledge you gain. You try to keep them in certain areas, and when something happens in that area, you call that informant and say, 'Hey, do you know anything about it; have you heard anything?' The street is unbelievable. That is the main reason that you need informants, for the word on the street."

It would be naïve, however, to think that vice enforcement is the only area of law enforcement where confidential informants play an important role in the investigative process. The officers we spoke to, regardless of the type of agency they worked in (local, state, or federal) or the career trajectory they had followed, noted that informants play a critical role in the investigation of all sorts of crime. For example, Miller, an investigator who spent twenty years of his twenty-eight-year career in the same metropolitan police department as a street-level narcotics investigator, noted: "Informants do help. I mean, you're going to need them in the detective work on drugs, narcotics, home invasions, robberies, burglaries, and all those sort of things. You're going to be able to solve—I don't know what percentage—but you're going to be able to solve some on your own, but certainly those informants are going to help with the rest."

The broad nature of informant usage was captured by Orlando when he said: "Informants are needed, and I can tell you now we've solved a lot of things, shootings and different stuff, just because an informant calls and says, 'Hey, I know who did the shooting.'" This pattern was confirmed among the homicide, narcotics, prostitution, fraud, firearms, robbery, white-collar crime, and burglary investigators that comprised our sample. There is just no getting around the fact that police are not present when the vast majority of crimes occur. They do not have ready access to cooperating witnesses or obvious means through which to infiltrate criminal subcultures to piece together what happened at the time a crime took place. Kareem, a twenty-year veteran within the firearms, arson, and explosives units of a federal agency, captured this notion well:

> Generally speaking, some of the most successful agents and officers on the streets have good informants, and it's not because they are lazy [officers], it's because those people [informants] are already involved in the criminal element that you're seeking to penetrate, and that's what makes it beneficial to utilize them. So the more successful ones [agents] will have informants.... There are certain things that an informant could bring if they're already part of that culture. So that's the biggest advantage: they already know part of it

[a specific offense], or they've been part of it [the criminal subculture in general]. Or they just hang around the segment of people that you're trying to go after.

Accepting the potential utility of confidential informants and being willing to enlist them to further ongoing investigations or stimulate new investigations is only the first step. Once the officer establishes a willingness to use confidential informants, he or she must go about developing the skills to actually realize this intention. Identifying and recruiting informants comes next in the progression.

INFORMANT RECRUITMENT

All informant activities and relationships are contingent on officers identifying persons who possess relevant information, screening them for reliability, assessing their ability to efficiently amass critical evidence, and perhaps most importantly, convincing the potential informant to pass along the intelligence to investigators. Ideally, this relationship becomes an ongoing one in which the citizen with inside information repeatedly assists the officer or department in solving high-value crimes.

It is important to understand that informants come to their role and work in a variety of ways. Some, such as the police buffs or revenge-oriented types, are volunteers who initiate contact with law enforcement and offer to provide information. Others, such as the unwitting sources or indentured informants, are duped or pressured into informing. Conversely, those who are motivated by self-advancement, such as the entrepreneurial informants, have varying degrees of dedication, enthusiasm, and as discussed below, reliability and credibility.

In some instances, the "recruitment" of an informant occurs through an accidental meeting or because the officer was simply in the right place at the right time. On rare occasions (e.g., those involving select civic-minded or previously employed entrepreneur-oriented informants), a citizen will contact the police and indiscriminately offer information to anyone interested and willing to talk. In such an instance, the officer who answers the telephone, is flagged down on the street, or simply happens to be present in a precinct station when the person walks in may recruit the informant with little to no effort. That said, these individuals are often ignorant of the bureaucratic processes that go along with offering up inside information on criminal activity and thus require coaching by the agent taking in the intelligence. Altruistic "regular folk" who offer information may be responded to with relatively low levels of skepticism, although it is still necessary for the officer to uncover the motivation of the individual and the accuracy of the information that he or she provides.

Most entrepreneurial informants who come forward with information seeking to exchange it for monetary compensation are well versed in the bureaucratic expectations that go along with such a transaction. These are individuals who have usually worked with one or more agencies in the past, and this makes for a more efficient negotiation. The exchange of information for a monetary reward can be streamlined and beneficial for all involved, although officers often approach such deals with caution and skepticism. The initial information gained from this type of informant, and all interactions that follow, may go smoothly, but the informant-for-hire will likely be viewed skeptically and used as a departure point for other investigative activities designed to determine the veracity of the intelligence.

The indentured informant arrangement (highlighted in chapter 3) is the most common type of informant. Unlike the volunteer or entrepreneurial informants, indentured informants must be explicitly convinced to cooperate with the authorities. In common law enforcement parlance, this is known as "turning" an informant. Learning to turn an individual into an informant is a skill that individual officers must largely learn on their own or from observing and perhaps assisting their colleagues. There is no formal written resource or training on how to turn an informant, and police departments, training academies, and even academics have long viewed this important process as something that simply happens, although the mechanics of *how* it happens have been neglected. This is an unfortunate circumstance, as nearly everyone we encountered in law enforcement recounted that they had to either "figure it out on your own" or be mentored by a senior investigator in order to have any idea of how to effectively and efficiently manage the use of informants. Manny, a twenty-year-plus veteran of federal law enforcement, clearly expressed the desire for some guidance in this respect:

> Working informants? I don't know that that is taught. I don't recall ever being taught that. I recall getting [instruction on] interviewing, where they teach you how to interview somebody and get the most out of that interview so you can tell if the guy is full of crap or not, you know? And [we were taught] how to expound upon that interview and take the interview to where it needs to be to get the information you want. But as far as going out and building informants, yeah, I don't know that that's taught.

In many instances, it appears that attempts to provide training materials to local agencies and officers have stimulated little more than general discussions and cautionary tales about relationships gone wrong and cases being sacrificed due to poor recruitment and inadequate supervision of new informants. While organizations such as the FBI, the International Chiefs of Police, the Police Executive Research Forum, the National Institute of Justice, and the Bureau of Justice Assistance make manuals and seminars on informant usage available to staff, use of these materials is self-initiated and intermittent. As early as 1990, Howard Katz, writing for the National Institute of Justice, warned that "the use of informants is controversial, repugnant to the general public, and always under attack by civil libertarians. The contemptuous attitudes that will be generated by the mere use of the term 'police informer,' require that officers must always be judicious and ethical in developing and using informants" (1990, 11–12). However, despite the fact that his report was titled *Developing and Using Underworld Police Informants*, Katz failed to provide instruction on how to develop individuals as informants. Many of the points conveyed in reports such as this amount to common sense and lack the level of background and precision needed by officers who are new to the informant game. For example, Katz suggests that prostitutes may be effectively used as informants, as they are often in contact with and knowledgeable about local criminal activities and networks, but he provides no further information about how to work with them.

The officers that we observed and interviewed in our fieldwork consistently maintained that there is no set way to identify, screen, and convert an informant, as every individual—both informers and officers—brings a unique approach, personality, strategy, and set of skills to the relationship. As Alonzo, a fourteen-year veteran of a metropolitan homicide unit, related:

> It's no cookie cutter in terms of relationships [between] the street and police. . . . I just think like the only way to get anything done is speaking truth to power; there is no real curriculum to how this thing gets done. There's not a set policy in most [local] departments; this is just what we do with informants. To me, they're just people, folks. And in my situation, working the street the whole time since the mid-eighties, I have never met a stranger. So my informant might be the aunt of the victim, and maybe the mother doesn't know their relationship. You know what I mean?

In this quote and elsewhere during the interview, Alonzo conveyed that he was self-taught in his use of informants and came to build his techniques around what he perceived to be the strengths of his personality and tips he received from more experienced officers. That said, the extant literature—typically those works geared toward law enforcement practitioners—does provide some very general insights on finding individuals with knowledge of criminal activities who may have some type of motivation for working with law enforcement. For example, John Madinger (1999), a twenty-five-year veteran law enforcement officer at the local and federal levels, breaks informant recruitment down into four distinct stages: background, foundation, construction, and closing. These stages are detailed and elaborated below.

Background Stage

During the background stage, the investigator seeks to gather as much intelligence as possible on a prospective informant to determine their intellectual capacity, motivations, and overall strengths and weaknesses as a potential information source. Kareem, a federal law enforcement officer, touched on this: "From the start, you've got to dialog with them to find out what they can do because you don't want to send a guy who knows nothing about drugs into a drug deal. . . . You have to figure out what their niche is and fulfill that particular niche, not move them around and say, 'Hey, I've got an informant; he's a one size fits all.' You have to utilize them based on what their skill set is rather than trying to force a square peg into a round hole."

Personal information about informants, including where they are from, with whom they associate, to whom they are related, where they hang out, what they like and dislike, their substance-use patterns, and numerous other facts, are seen by many investigators as being critical to knowing how and why an informant comes by his or her criminal intelligence and how and why he or she may be willing to come forth and share this information with law enforcement. Gathering this personal information can amount to an investigation in its own right. Pedro explained that it is imperative to put in the time and effort on the front end to determine "who" an informant is before tapping him or her for information about the wrongdoing of others:

> When you sign up a CI, you don't just go out on the street and say, "Hey, I want to sign you up as a CI." I know more about that CI than he does or she does [about him- or herself]. I've gone through all of the checks, everything from background to fingerprints to criminal history to the vehicles they drive, the places they lay their heads, different babies' mommas. I know

everything about that informant before he is signed up to be used. . . . You have to tip your hand slightly to an informant to know what's going on.

Some of this sort of background investigation is straightforward, especially if an officer is pondering turning an individual pursuant to an arrest. In that case, the substance of the arrest provides important insight about the perspective informant's potential area of expertise and access. As Miller explained: "For instance, if I arrest you selling drugs, I know that's what you do. I just want you to keep doing what you're doing but do it for me. I just need to be able to know if you can go in and do the same thing and keep doing it for me, and I keep doing my research on you. I pretty much know what you're capable of."

Madinger (1999) notes that, at a minimum, the background stage should always include running a criminal history report on a prospective informant. This is a rather quick step and is usually practical even in those cases in which an officer is thinking about turning an arrestee into an indentured informant immediately after an arrest. It is generally believed that the details of a criminal history report will let an officer know whether the offender is a career criminal and will also provide some insight into the types of crimes and criminal subcultures with which the arrestee has prior experience. In the best-case scenario, the potential informant will have a lengthy criminal record; this is one indication that the individual is significantly integrated into the criminal subculture and will have firsthand access to criminal intelligence and connections to facilitate subsequent actions.

While a criminal background and the potential to facilitate subsequent criminal transactions is a more or less de facto requirement for becoming an informant, these traits are also indications that an individual may not be fully reliable, responsible, and honest. This is a conundrum for law enforcement officers, who are simultaneously drawn to and repelled by certain individuals due to these individuals' criminal involvement and connections. As such, investigators who wish (or need) to use confidential informants in their investigations need to trust and believe in their informants while at the same time viewing them and the information they provide with skepticism.

Shawn explained that he actually trusts only "maybe one half of one half of what they [potential informants] say" and always does a thorough background check on them:

I'll look at their criminal history. Anytime I pull in a confidential informant, I run their criminal history. I'm looking for obstruction of officer charges at the same time as some pretty big felonies. I'm not even going to put myself in that liability [if the person has impeded the police in the past]. Obviously, most of them are going to have criminal histories because they're going to be peddling dope or guns or whatever. But if it's that, they're not really, really bad; then I'll look at working with them. If their history is really bad, it ain't happening; I won't work with them.

Beyond the basics of observation and running criminal history reports, savvy investigators describe that gleaning background information involves asking probing and direct questions based on the information at hand. This is illustrated in the following comments made by Kareem:

That's the whole nature of building intelligence; when you talk, you ask them a non-obvious question like, "What other types of drugs do you know about?" Or, "If you're in the drug game, are you involved in gangs and guns?" If I find a gun in the car, it's important to say, "The gun didn't just appear; you bought it from somewhere," because if you're a felon, I know you couldn't have bought it legally. So, I'll ask, "You know someone that's supplying guns?" So you have to ask those questions; it's like peeling back the layers of an onion. So now that I see what you're in, I'll run your criminal history. Maybe I see you're involved in aggravated assault with a group of people, and now I may ask you, "Hey, if I wanted to go ahead and do a home invasion, who would I call to do something like that? Who's doing those types of things?" Now there's another area to work. I want to squeeze that particular lemon until I get all of the juice that I can at that particular time of contact. That's what makes a good agent, asking the non-obvious questions. So every stop has the potential to produce an informant because they all recognize, "Hey, my freedom is in jeopardy, so I need to let them know what else I know to limit the freedom of my jeopardy."

Where time is not of the essence, seasoned investigators noted that they will often take the opportunity to gather more detailed and reliable information on a prospective or active informant. Frank noted that this is time consuming but value-added work:

You never want a situation where the informant is out there doing things, and you're not monitoring what they're doing. So sometimes you might have an informant on the informant. That way, you'll know if he's still selling drugs or whatever. . . . Then I have to start watching my guy to see what's going on. And of course, that's how you find out your informant is on target. . . . It's not going to happen the first five minutes of the conversation; it may take an hour-long conversation. If you're willing to dig, dig, dig, you may be able to get something out of it.

Officers note that it is prudent to think of the background stage as never ending, as a smart investigator is always seeking to add to his or her understanding of the skill set, motivations, and personality traits of the confidential informants with whom he or she is working. For example, Kareem noted:

> You've got to constantly be doing your background information. So you might have someone else watching that person [the informant] or at least someone that you can ask, whether it's another officer on the beat or whoever, "Hey, have you seen this guy [your informant] on the street lately?" "Yeah, he was hanging out on the corner with so and so," or, "I picked your guy up the other day; he was with these other guys." Well, it's important to know if those other guys are dope heads, and he hasn't come back and given you the information. So it's about vigilance, constant vigilance. . . . Three-hundred-and-sixty-degree vigilance makes for a good agent and informant. . . . The guys that are able to have that balance, a good rapport, the 360-degree vigilance, they are the ones that actually know how to directly lead and not have the informant direct them.

In the end, the background stage is all about the investigator gathering as much information as possible about a potential informant's access to criminal networks, motivations, lifestyle, criminal-offending patterns, and reliability. Collectively, this information will inform how the officer proceeds in terms of the types of information-gathering efforts that are commissioned of the informant.

Foundation Stage

Once the background stage is complete, Madinger (1999) notes that the investigator is wise to transition his or her efforts into the foundation stage. At this point, the officer is advised to embark on deliberate and purposeful rapport building to gain the individual's buy-in and trust. Listening and demonstrating respect and empathy for the potential informant are key factors in this regard. Kareem maintains that it is important to approach the potential informant as a "subject matter expert" you respect: "You've got to be willing to learn from them because you're becoming a criminal, in theory; you know, when you're undercover, you're playing pretend criminal, and you know this guy [the informant] is a real criminal, so you've got to be willing to listen to little things that they know because they know better than you do."

Officers noted that mutual respect and empathy are cornerstones of the foundation- and rapport-building exercise. Without some ability to respect one another (and there may be challenges for both parties to achieving this), communications will be stymied and information will either not be communicated completely or accurately or not be communicated at all. This is captured well in Kareem's follow-up statement:

> You have to understand that, even though you're dealing with a guy or a girl who could be a potential criminal, they're a person first. So the more humble you are, the easier it will be for you to get that rapport cycle going, and the easier it will be for you to listen to them on things they know about. You may know the law, but they know the street. So there are things that they can teach you. You know that you can learn from them. And so the more eager you are to acknowledge that, the better off you're going to be. Like I said, if you're very humble but able to step on the gas when you need to, the informant is not going to take advantage of you. To me, that makes for a good relationship of handling an informant.

Respect and recognition of one another's humanity are important in establishing a relationship with an informant, just as they are in any relationship. While law enforcement officers may not fully respect community members (see chapter 5) and potential informants are recognized as criminally involved and not the types of people officers are likely to be friends with, there is a primary need for respectful interactions. Alonzo explained: "I want a real relationship because these people, they're comebackers. . . . It's just being real with people. This police thing is not all high and mighty, you know, 'I'm better than you.'"

While respect is about recognizing the value and intrinsic contributions of individuals, a positive sense of rapport also needs to be developed between an investigator and his confidential informants. For many people, rapport is about how one presents oneself to others and how that presented self is perceived, processed, evaluated, and responded to. The way one presents oneself in particular contexts or interactions provides others with intelligence about one's statuses and attitudes. Rapport is about more than just this, though. Rapport is based on a shared set of statuses, activities, or other characteristics. In order to locate and exploit the similarities that can lead to rapport, an investigator needs to know about the individual with whom he or she is dealing. Therefore, knowing details about a potential informant's lifestyle, values, activities, likes and dislikes, and so on are important when building rapport. Kareem spoke to this in the following quote:

So one of the things I would do on a first meeting with an informant is I would always dress closer to the way my informant dresses, so even if I have a suit on and I knew I was going to meet an informant, I would change because I want the informant to say, which has happened, "If I asked you to go buy some dope from somebody or introduce to somebody could you do that?" That's the highest compliment because if they're saying they could actually take you [to a deal], at least to him you're believable. If you're believable to him, he could sell you to [other criminals]. So that's the part of building rapport.

Once the investigator has built rapport with the potential informant and feels comfortable that he or she is a viable information asset, the next step is formulating the deal. This is done in the construction stage.

Construction Stage

Madinger (1999) notes that the construction stage is where the nuts and bolts of the informant-agent agreement get hammered out. Once the officer has internalized the needs and motives of the potential informant, he or she must present a proposed solution to partially or fully meet those needs. This includes convincing the person that the terms of the deal will be honored; describing confidentiality, safety, and retaliation concerns; and explaining potential outcomes associated with testifying and case development. Kareem described this process:

> So it's all about building rapport, and it's not just based on building charges, you know, because some of them [potential informants] are willing to go to jail and do their time anyway. So after you build that rapport with them and say, "Okay, here's what we need to do," then they're going to give you a nod. With an informant, they want to know what you can do for them. So if you go in and all you're talking about is what they're going to do for you and how they're going to do it—X, Y, and Z—but you don't even express concern for what their charges are, whether they go to prison, or what they will be doing with their life, they will shut down. It will be the expected rapport, it will be policeman/bad guy, but you'll have some rapport. So it's about connecting with them in some kind of way. . . . So the whole thing is a sizing-up thing. So when you're sizing them up, they're sizing you up the same way. They want to know, "If I go in as a CI, and you're working undercover, are you going to get me killed?" How you talk to them matters. If they [officers] give them [informants] the sense that the relationship is worker and employee . . . they can see, they can sense that. They can see that this is a relationship where you don't really care if they go in this house and get their brains blown out. . . .

That's no good. . . . Once you build that rapport you can kind of tell if they're telling the truth a little bit better. Those things are not necessarily written down; that's why not everybody in different agencies has informants, because some guys just can't do it.

The construction stage also involves establishing the parameters and guidelines for the relationship between the handling investigator, the informant, and the larger investigative process. The investigator needs to establish his dominant position in the interpersonal relationship and reiterate the expectations for the informant as well as establish how tasks, communications, and all activities for the informant will be handled. Shawn explained this:

You don't take any shit off of the guy. You know, he works for us. You don't work for him. You know, is he starting to call the shots, and he wants us to do it this way, and this way, and this way? You gotta tell him, "You work for me, I don't work for you. You're going to do it my way, or it ain't going to happen." Now, in our line of work, you've got to be able to manage that, because obviously he knows the way the deal happens, and if we go in there and start changing that up, it's going to throw red flags or whatever.

The officers that we spoke to made it clear that there is no room for a "nice-guy" approach during the construction stage of the informant recruitment process. This is the point when a clear demarcation of power in the relationship is firmly established. The construction stage ends with the officer setting the proverbial hook into the potential informant. Once the potential confidential informant has been identified, approached, and offered an opportunity and has subsequently agreed on a transaction, the recruit is all but established. All that remains is for the hooked individual to be reeled in and put to work.

Closing Stage

Madinger (1999) identifies the closing stage as the fourth and final step in the informant recruitment process. At this stage, the investigator reviews the details of the proposed deal and gets a commitment from the informant to follow through on his or her end of the deal in exchange for the officer doing what he or she has committed to.

While this stage of the process sometimes goes by quickly and without fanfare, it is critical to the police-citizen information exchange. An individual who has been arrested and is talking with an officer while in handcuffs, in the backseat of a patrol car, or in some other setting that is literally controlled by a law enforcement officer is not a person who is free to negotiate on an equal plane. Rather, the closing moment in this type of interaction is a final statement and reminder to the newly indentured informant about their tasks and responsibilities. As in the frontier days, when individuals engaged in a symbolic blood oath, or on the modern-day playground, when two school kids lock fingers for a "pinky swear," it is at this moment that both parties understand that the deal has been consummated.

In other instances, and especially with informants who are not indentured informants, closing can be a more prolonged and more even-handed negotiation. For example, a civic-minded source may assert that he or she is not willing or able to accomplish a requested task on the officer's proposed timeline, or a paid informant may not be willing to secure three buys in a given day but will agree to do two. In these circumstances, when an officer does not maintain a position of power over the prospective information provider, he or she must be more patient and savvy in closing the deal. Regardless of its brevity or interactional flow, the closing stage is important because it crystalizes the "fine print," so to speak, of the verbal contract between the officer and the informant. Informants may not pay attention to or even notice this "fine print," but once an agreement is reached, this is the part of the negotiation that will be held over the informant and will serve as the criteria against which they will be evaluated by their law enforcement contacts.

For many law enforcement units—such as vice, narcotics, or street crimes units—the ability to identify, turn, and work with informants is considered a key skill and a central task of day-to-day work. In the police units in which we conducted our fieldwork, an officer's potential ability to recruit informants was one of the major qualities considered when selecting new officers to be added to the units. The criteria for assessing this central skill are rather nebulous and fluid, and when supervisors and current unit members were queried about how they judged candidates' presumed skills in this area, responses were inevitably some form of: "It's a gut feeling"; "It's something you need to judge by the type of person they are"; or, "There is no set criteria; it's a feeling you get about a person—you just sort of know." A candidate's personality, interaction skills, and most concretely, way of interacting with colleagues, the public, offenders, and suspects are the data that are drawn on in making such as assessment. In order to be able to recruit and develop an informant, an officer needs to be personable, adaptable to diverse others, and generally able to talk a good game and be persuasive. However, all of this is irrelevant if an officer cannot locate individuals who see value and reason in working with the police. In short, without a motivated person to be recruited and turned, there can and will be no police-citizen information exchange.

WHAT MAKES A GOOD INFORMANT?

While the above discussion has focused on how law enforcement investigators identify and fish for potential confidential informants among the people they arrest or otherwise come into contact with in the community, we have yet to address what type of person investigators identify as a "good informant." As is the case with any job or position of action or responsibility, there are some qualities that are considered more desirable and others that are considered less desirable, as well as characteristics that are interpreted as indicators of a likely good informant.

In conversations with both current and former informant-managing law enforcement investigators, we discussed the idea of a "good informants" in the abstract (i.e., focusing on qualities and characteristics) as well as concretely (i.e., requesting officers to recall and describe their "best" confidential informants). Interestingly, and rather unexpectedly, most investigators had difficulty recalling whether any of their informants were "better" or more valuable than others. On reflection, most investigators that we interviewed struggled to identify any one informant as the "best," responding with some variation of: "Well, it depends on what you mean by 'good.'" Instead, the officers often explained that the situational contexts in which informants were utilized guided what type of informant, information, and interactions would be valuable or helpful. Despite the frustrations such a conclusion may elicit, the answer to what makes a good informant was a resounding, "It depends."

When pushed to identify what qualities or characteristics they believed were most desirable, the officers identified a few issues. First, several investigators stated that it was most important to them that an informant have solid personal connections. Without connections to the criminal community as well as to the community in general, an individual is very unlikely to have (or be able to readily gain) information that would be otherwise inaccessible to the police. In the simplest terms, Pedro said that, when he looks at individuals as potential recruits for a confidential informant role, he is looking for "somebody who can give you what you need. . . . If they can give you what you want them to give you, then they're a good informant." In other words, a good informant is someone who can fulfill the pressing intelligence needs of officers. From this vantage point, it is the outcome that is important, not anything about the individual.

Knowing who is or is not likely to be able to provide the desired outcome of the role is an issue that can be seen as related to a couple of social statuses, but it is also something that officers believe needs to develop over time and with experience. But, overriding all other individual qualities or characteristics, a potential informant, according to Miller, has "got to be somebody that's active, somebody that looks the part, somebody that can talk and mingle with those kinds of people." An informant must be able to fit into the world that he or she moves in and from which he or she garners information. If it were not for such a social requirement, officers could themselves simply go into the community, introduce themselves to targets of their investigations, and ask question themselves. But, largely due to officers "not being from around here" and presenting statuses incongruent with the environment where an investigation is occurring, informants are necessary.

Another simple way to express this idea was voiced by Shawn, who succinctly stated: "I want somebody who obviously knows the bad guys; you know, they're in 'the life.'" An individual who does not "know the bad guys" is not going to be very likely to get intelligence on the bad guys; hence, that individual fails to fulfill one of the fundamental qualities of a good informant—being able to provide needed information.

When officers did talk about particular individuals they recalled as especially good informants, the theme of being properly connected and in touch with the criminal aspect of the community was recurrent. As officers recounted particularly colorful, eccentric, or very highly motivated informants, they always rounded out their descriptions with an explanation of the "payoff" or benefit that was realized as a result of the work of the particular informant. It took Miller a few minutes to be able to identify his best informant. He eventually named two informants he had worked with, both of whom had the following laundry list of qualities:

> They know how to intermingle. They were a little cleaner than just a bum on the street, of course. They could get into the higher tiers; they could get into the clubs, the strip clubs, the bars, and they could intermingle with the higher-end people. . . . They drive a halfway-decent car. . . . They've got to be able to talk; they've got to learn their jargon, learn what they're talking about because, you know, on the street, things are happening. It's a whole other

language.... So all of these things play a part in it—the personality—and none of [the] guys like working with dirty, dirty informants.

Kareem highlighted the fact that outcomes, as opposed to personal characteristics, are what officers use when defining good informants:

What makes them [informants Kareem has worked with] really good was their street IQ. Their street IQ was off the charts, and generally speaking, he [one of Kareem's best informants] was almost one hundred percent on for what he said being actually accurate.... So it was his reliability, his street IQ, and the fact that he was self-motivated to the point where I would have to say, "You need to slow down; we can't move that fast." So, a little bit high maintenance, but he was worth it.... That's why I said these guys are subject matter experts, but we have a tendency to look at—because of the different mistakes they've made in their life—that they're unintelligent. They're highly intelligent. Sometimes, they know the state and federal laws better than some officers do and some attorneys, because it's important to them. They know, to them, information is currency just as much as drugs and the other things they're doing, so they know "If I get a nugget of information, I'm not going to use that until I'm able to get value for value".... So the ones that you don't have to coach, the ones that know it to the point where I was finished with them. So I fought because he was already sentenced. My case was done. He was able to know, "Hey, this is valuable. This is information that is valuable to me, and so I can utilize that information."

When asked to describe his best informant, Kareem, who claimed to have worked with dozens of informants throughout his career, focused heavily on what the informant was able to produce or provide to him as an investigator (i.e., the outcome) rather than what the person brought to the table in terms of personality or social background. The only quality that Kareem mentioned, besides being able to provide information he needed, was social intelligence, what he called "street IQ."

Sex/Gender

In general, age, race, occupation, relationship status, employment, socioeconomic status, and other statuses were not commonly seen as being related to whether an individual could be an information-producing confidential informant. Such issues were, depending on the situational context, not considered to be highly relevant to ability. One personal trait, however, was frequently identified as being valuable and important in a majority of contexts:

gender. Women were commonly explained to be superior to men in fulfilling the role of informant, a conclusion that simultaneously reinforces women's rights and delivers a slap in the face to hegemonic masculinity and its influence on law enforcement activities, values, and beliefs. Simply stated, women are perceived as being more likely to have a motivation to inform on (some particular types of) others, to be more willing to trade information for their own self-preservation and benefit, and to be more easily manipulated by skilled investigators than men are.

Officers surmised that women provide different avenues of entrée into criminally involved worlds and, by the nature of how they are seen by others (typically in a subordinate role and not as a threat of any form), may have access to settings, conversations, and hence information that would not be so available to men. The sentiment was that women, because of their generally more social, open, and accepting nature, may be more likely to be amenable to conversing (and subsequently working with) investigators as well. Alonzo was fairly adamant in conveying his position that women are much more valuable and likely to be accessible than men:

> The best way to learn a neighborhood is to get to know the women, because the women know everything. . . . Women are more apt to talk to me. I don't know why—I mean I can surmise why—but most of the time, I talk a little shit, and I'll get their attention. My intro has always been women. With men, it's hard to get through to them; they're always checking you out, like, "What does this motherfucker want? All he wants to do is lock me up." With men, you get the name recognition later, after we've had our experience. . . . Cats look at me before I start talking, and they see the little glasses, the fucking necktie, the cheap bullshit suit, and they're like, "Oh, that's a fucking nerd." You know what I mean? That's until they know me. I mean, they may [only] know my last name or something like that. So you know, they [men] have to cut through that and see where you've been. They want to hear something come out your mouth because . . . they want to make sure.

Similarly, Sonny proclaimed a strong preference for working with female informants over males, stating that they are more likely to be able to gather useful information: "I'd say females are better informants, depending on what type of crime you are investigating. . . . Especially the females that are attractive and young; they usually tend to call the attention of the perpetrators or suspects, and they would actually become good sources of information. People like to brag on what they do, so females are good for that [getting information from men]."

Taking this a step further, Sonny said that his ideal informants were not just women in general and not just women who might be privy to private conversations and actions of individuals actually being investigated, but rather "female bartenders. If they are attractive, they get to know who the players are, and usually, once those guys have a couple of drinks, they start to talk about it [crimes they've committed] or start to show off with money and things and stuff like that. Or [they] brag about what they've been doing."

A second type of woman that is seen as especially valuable is the low-level, often street-walking, prostitute. These women are often well integrated into the community—seen and known as a member of the community—yet are also able to spend intimate time with men who are criminally involved. Many men will bare all, including secrets (disclosed both intentionally and accidentally), to prostitutes. Contrary to common belief, one of the most desired and most frequent interactions between a prostitute and her customers is conversation (Tewksbury and Gagne 2002). As such, prostitutes are often rich sources of information about at least some men and their activities in the neighborhoods where the prostitutes work.

In River City, Tammy was a regular informant of Justin's. Tammy lived off of her income from prostitution and worked a fairly wide geographic area. At least a couple of times a week, she would be seen working street corners and parking lots of convenience stores and coming and going with men both to alleys for sexual liaisons and to houses for drug sales and use. Tammy was friendly, approachable, and loved to tell stories. Therefore, Justin found her to be a great informant, especially considering that, more often than not, she contacted him after learning about some event or transaction that she thought Justin might be interested in.

In addition to these types of women, who have access to information via their jobs or because they simply spend time around men, investigators also identified ex-girlfriends and ex-wives as especially good and valuable informants. These women are valuable repositories of criminal intelligence not because they could go out and actively collect information but because they already have the information at their disposal due to prolonged intimate and/or emotional relationships with criminally involved partners. Furthermore, they may be motivated (highly in some cases) to get back at or get some sort of revenge on an ex about whom they hold information. Pedro explained this circumstance well: "I bet I've solved more cases by pissed off ex-girlfriends or wives than anything else. Because when things are hunky-dory, they know nothing. And as soon as the guy or girl has gone to the next best thing, they're left out in the cold. They're pissed off, and they now have a motivation. And some of those types of informants don't necessarily have a criminal or checkered past." Manny also spoke about this type of informant: "There's an old saying [among law enforcement officers] that there's nothing better than the scorn of an ex-girlfriend. If you can get a girlfriend or a wife to flip, I mean they're gold, because the bad guy is always going to come back to that girlfriend or that wife. He's always going to be in touch with her and with [his] mama too."

Although women, especially those who, due to their jobs or physical attractiveness, may have different (and some would argue better) access than men to both other members of the community and information in the community, there are law enforcement officers who have negative opinions about female informants. Some skeptical investigators perceive women as more needy, more unpredictable, more emotional, and more of a hassle to manage than male informants. Just as sexism and hegemonic constructions of masculinity shape the views of those officers who feel that women make especially good informants, so too do these same sets of beliefs determine how other investigators perceive and define women as being less desirable informants. Shawn was quick to express his personal disdain for working with female informants because of both what he perceived as constitutional differences between men and women and the fact that he felt restricted in how he interacted with them:

> I personally don't work with female informants. . . . I don't want to put up with all of the emotions and all of the changes and all of that kind of stuff. I let the females [officers] do that; they can relate to them a little bit. Guys you can manhandle a little bit better. You can threaten them more. Females, I think they're going to shy away from that, you know; they don't like to be bullied. . . . Guys? I can call a guy's bluff in a heartbeat and throw down some paper, throw my arms up in the air and call him on his bull crap, and they'll come clean.

Similarly, Ranger, who has worked for multiple local law enforcement agencies in the greater Central City metropolitan area, said that, although he has worked successfully with female informants, he prefers to work with male informants. He attributed this to characteristics and qualities he ascribes to women in general as well as to his own lack of comfort when it comes to working with women:

> I don't want this to sound the wrong way, but women are just—especially informants and cops—they're just catty bitches. And that's okay. . . . Women

don't work well together. Men don't really work well together either, but they work a hell of a lot better than women work together. The best CIs, the best relationships have always been the male-female, male cop–female informant, female cop and male informant. They always work way better.

SUMMARY

What should be clear at this point is that working with informants is both potentially very useful for law enforcement and potentially risky and frustrating. The use of confidential informants, of all varieties, is critical to gathering intelligence and providing information about and access to offenders—especially drug traffickers. Without informants, law enforcement investigators would be hard pressed to learn the intricacies not only of who is involved in criminal activities but also how, when, where, and with whom. Whether informants provide information in exchange for leniency on charges or for monetary payment, as an act of revenge, or simply because they believe that doing so is morally right, the information accessed by law enforcement speeds up and provides greater validity and reliability to investigations and also reduces resource expenditures.

Working with an informant, however, typically necessitates its own investigation—into the informant. While the information provided by an informant can be indispensable, it is critical for law enforcement to ensure that this information is accurate. This means that it is necessary to know about an informant's background, his or her general trustworthiness, and especially the likelihood that he or she has access to offenders so as to be able to provide police with useful, accurate information.

Not all informants are alike, which means that the way a law enforcement officer works with individual informants is going to vary. Critical factors shaping the nature of the relationship and work are intelligence, gender, and reputation. Each of these factors influences how an officer handles an informant, through all of the stages of recruitment and initiation of work. Some informants can be pushed hard, while others need to be handled somewhat gently, slowly, and supportively. How informants are actually used and managed is just as, if not more, important than how and from where they are recruited. These are the issues we turn to next.

FIVE

The Game

THE IMPACT OF COMMUNITY CONTEXT
ON INFORMANT USE

Given the ever-widening and persistent war on drugs, metropolitan police officers find that law enforcement efforts are becoming increasingly intertwined with narcotics enforcement. Departments are progressively being segmented into specialty units that focus their efforts on select types of criminal offending. Although many of these specializations (e.g., commercial robbery, sex crimes, and financial crimes) have no direct link to drug markets, most specialty units find themselves routinely bumping up against drug offenders as they investigate and resolve the crimes that fall under their purview (e.g., homicide, property crimes, burglary, and auto theft). Furthermore, nearly every metropolitan police department now has one or more specialty units dedicated exclusively to narcotics enforcement. These units were the focus of our fieldwork in River City and much of our fieldwork in Central City. Law enforcement officers whose work focuses on street-level drug policing face situations, individuals, and organizational issues that challenge their beliefs about both the criminal justice system and human nature. While drugs are commonly pointed to as a scourge of society and targeted as the issue that extends and ripples into nearly all other social ills in a community, it is the actual people involved in drug use, trafficking, and policing who are the contact points for issues that both frustrate and solidify the values held by police focused on drug offenses.

PLAYERS IN THE MODERN URBAN LANDSCAPE

The commitment that officers show to their work and their communities arises out of a desire to protect the "good folks" and their communities from being harmed by the "bad folks." In the eyes of narcotics officers, the world is highly stratified, with very clear demarcations between "good folks" and "bad folks." "Good folks" are the law-abiding citizens of communities who invest in their homes, their communities, and their children and neighbors. Good folks come from all economic levels. They support the police and are believed to recognize that the police, while force-wielding authority figures, are both members of the community and a special class of citizen who is both responsible for and dedicated to maintaining order, structure, and peace. Good folks are those who do not regularly use drugs, who supervise their children, who speak and interact with others (including the police) with respect, and who care about their neighborhoods sufficiently to work with both one another and law enforcement to maintain and improve the community. It is the good folks that the narcotics officers included in this study see themselves as working for and for whom the officers care the most. Good folks, according to Sergeant Perez, "deserve better than to have to live around these scum [drug offenders]." Sergeant Perez's words and views diffused to the other members of the River City flex unit and became a commonly expressed sentiment. Although they did not use the same terms or references, all of the flex unit members clearly distinguished the "good folks" from the "bad folks" that they targeted in their activities. However, while catching the "bad guys" was seen as the important task that guided all of the unit members' activities, the real goal was serving the community and working to protect (or regain) the positive aspects of community. Here, the reflections of Goldman, a midcareer female investigator, are instructive in understanding how she perceived her role in the community:

> I work every day, and I have a lot of heart and dedication in my job—that's why I come to work every day. I try to make my job fun and—not necessarily entertaining to me—but motivational to me to want to do something, to want to help somebody. When I decided I wanted to become a police officer, that was my motivation. I like being a person that people call for help, but unfortunately in the dope game, I don't know how to help them because they don't want to help themselves. The only thing I know how to do is lock them up.

The goal of protecting the community for the good folks was frequently frustrated and frustrating due to a perception that supervisors and departmental administrations were not committed to it. While acknowledging that these higher-ups paid lip service to this goal, officers felt that there was a lack of tools or resources available to aid them in doing anything to truly help those most in need of help. Thus, while the administration's expressly espoused goal was to protect the community, the organizational commitment to that goal was seen as inadequate, and the organization was subsequently considered to be responsible in part for limited or failed attempts at community maintenance. Those who bring down the quality of life for the good folks in the community are clearly devalued by law enforcement officers on the street.

In addition to the good folks, the community is also comprised of some other classes of civilians, including "troublemakers," crackheads and addicts, hos, "head cases," and thugs. Each of these classifications of persons presents very distinct behaviors and interactional schemes with the police, and each comes with its own somewhat unique set of challenges. Members of these groups also have varying degrees of possibility and promise for functioning as informants.

"Troublemakers" are law-abiding citizens who actively oppose what they call "police oppression" and who, as officers put it, "stand up and yell all the time about how cops are bad." Community activists who generally obey the law but speak out against police practices and policies were described by the street-level investigators in our study as "dangerous, you really can't trust them," and "stupid people who don't understand what we [the police] do and are only interested in getting in the media." Troublemakers are handled carefully when encountered, but officers discuss them privately in strong, emotional, and extremely negative terms. For example, Lucky said one day: "Just let me catch one of those Citizens Against Police Brutality people doing something wrong—man would I have fun with that. You know they're really just a bunch of thieves and crackheads anyway, or at least they've got kids who are thugs. I'd love to pull one of them over and get to write them up. Hell, I might get lucky and have them try to resist!" We observed that citizens who did not support the police, and especially those who voiced opposition to the police, were despised and ridiculed by officers. However, although officers may tell grand stories about what they would do if and when they had a chance to interact with such an activist, such occasions in fact bring out a very careful and methodical approach from the officers. Troublemakers can do just that—make trouble—for an officer, and no one wants to "get into a jackpot [bad situation] if you don't have to." In this regard, troublemakers are seen as dangerous and at times present more of a threat to an officer's career than do criminal offenders.

One Friday during the time of his fieldwork in River City, the researcher was riding with George when they pulled into an alley and George saw two

African American teenagers talking, quickly shake hands, and then separate and walk in different directions. Thinking that they had just stumbled on a drug deal, George continued down the alley, pulled up behind one of the teens, stopped him, and asked what he was doing. "Nothin'; just getting a phone card from a guy I know," the boy answered. "A phone card, eh? You sure it wasn't a rock you were getting?" George countered. "No, man; it's a phone card," said the teen, and he started to put his hand in the pocket of his jeans. George stopped him, patted him down, and found only a phone card in the teen's front jeans pocket. "Okay, you seem to be telling the truth, go on." With that, the interaction was over. The researcher recorded the incident in his field notes, and he and George got back in the car and continued with the day. However, that evening, while at home, the researcher received a telephone call from a lieutenant in the River City Police Department Internal Affairs Unit. It seemed that, on returning home, the teen had reported the incident to his mother, who called the unit to complain that George had harassed her son, aggressively interrogated him, and choked him in an effort to search his mouth for hidden drugs. The researcher was asked about the incident, reported what he had seen happen, and was thanked by the lieutenant. When he returned to the district office on Monday, he was greeted enthusiastically by George: "Doc! Man, am I ever glad you were with me last week! Can you believe what that no-good do-gooder bitch said about me last week?! I owe you, Doc; if you hadn't been there, I'd be a pile of shit right now!" Although in no way known to be a criminal in any form, the "no good do-gooder" was immediately labeled as an enemy of the police and categorized as a troublemaker.

Crackheads also present narcotics unit officers with challenges. They are considered problematic because they are often highly unpredictable and frequently desperate for their next hit of crack. For officers, this means that these individuals can be easily manipulated and managed and will frequently agree to do anything an officer requests of them so long as they believe they can and will be able to secure more drugs in the near future. However, officers are hesitant to work with crackheads because their follow-through is tenuous and unpredictable at best. Although crack addicts know who's who in the street-level drug market and may agree to immediately go to a dealer and make a buy or introduce an officer to a dealer, they are also known to be easily distracted and to change their behavior without warning. On more than one occasion, we witnessed crackheads agree to make a drug buy or to go to a nearby location to see if a particular target was present only to have them go to a different location, make a drug buy but use the drugs, or wander off and forget about the task they had been repeatedly briefed on and dropped off to complete. Crackheads sometimes ripped off the police for drug-buy money. While officers were very reluctant to front money to crackheads for making buys, they sometimes had no alternative means of attempting to get buys made. As informants, crackheads, and anyone else perceived to be seriously addicted to drugs, are considered to be unreliable and very difficult assets to manage. Crackheads need constant supervision and repeated instructions on how to complete tasks. Even then, narcotics officers recognize that the chances of addicts successfully completing tasks are often slim.

With open-air drug markets come commercial sex markets built to satisfy the sexual desires of drug users and others that may frequent these socially disorganized environments. "Hos," the prostitutes that staff these sex markets, are usually thought by officers to be relatively predictable and typically very compliant once they are informed of an officer's identity. This is not to say that some prostitutes will not attempt to run or fight with an officer when being arrested for solicitation, but that is the exception rather than the rule. The commonly recognized potential problem that prostitutes introduce is that many are renowned for accusing officers of sexual improprieties. Officers believe that a prostitute will do this as a way to try to get her (or, on rare occasions, his) arrest dismissed. Accusations of sexual assault, abuse, or solicitation against an officer are usually accompanied by threats of lawsuits, although these almost never occur. In River City, every one of the flex unit officers has either been personally accused or have close friends in other units who have been "put in a jackpot" by a ho. Because of their recognition of this, all of the male officers take special care to never be alone with a prostitute. At least one other officer, ideally a female officer, is always present when a flex officer is with a prostitute. In this way, a case of the prostitute's word against the officer's is often (although not always) avoided. The problem, however, is one of resource allocation: to tie up the time of multiple officers for a simple prostitution citation or arrest is inefficient. Furthermore, when an arrested prostitute is approached about the possibility of working as an informant, the presence of a second officer can be problematic (as discussed in chapter 4). In such cases, all discussions with prostitutes that may need to be in private are done out of earshot but close enough to allow visual contact at all times.

Hos are frequently considered to be good potential informants. Such women (and the occasional male prostitute) are members of the street community, recognized by other members of the street community, often interested in making money in any way possible, and wishing to avoid jail. Prostitutes are accustomed to the world of barter and exchange, so when they are presented with an opportunity to barter information for leniency or freedom, they are likely to see value in such an opportunity. Prostitutes who are newer to street life and street work may also be more fearful of arrest, prosecution, and jail. As such, just as with a marginally involved, low-level, first-time drug dealer, the new prostitute may be especially interested in avoiding criminal justice processing and hence be ripe for the picking as a potential informant.

One of the unfortunate but well-known facts about American criminal justice is that jails have become one of, if not the primary, source of mental health services for millions of Americans. In order for a mentally ill person to get to jail as a service recipient, however, he or she first needs to be in contact with the police. Mentally ill street people, or "head cases," are among the most undesirable persons with whom officers must interact. These individuals are typically unpredictable, usually believed to be prone to (unprovoked) violence, and untrustworthy in any reports of information. As such, drug unit officers (and, for that matter, all police officers with whom we interacted) prefer to avoid contact with head cases and, when possible, will pass off any interactions with mentally ill contacts to patrol officers. The mentally ill are never relied on as informants, and all information that they offer to officers is viewed skeptically at best and most often as delusion and fantasy.

"Thugs" are members of the street community who live criminally involved, usually drug-involved lifestyles that emphasize resistance to authority (especially the police). They are widely known to seek out instant gratification and use strength to dominate weakness (Anderson 1999; J. Katz 1988; Wright and Decker 1996). Thugs, also sometimes known as "perps," "corner boys," or "dope boys," are the often highly visible members of street communities that aspire to live a "fast life" of drinking, drugging, wealth, women, fancy cars, expensive clothes and jewelry, and other accoutrements of material success. This is not to say that thugs necessarily have all of these indicators of "success," but these are the things that many thugs desire and strive to attain. Thugs see themselves as leaders in their impoverished urban communities—even if these "communities" are only a block of a street or a set or two of buildings in a public housing project. Because of this, thugs expect deference and signs of respect from others in their community. Such expectations are where interactions with drug unit police become problematic. Thugs rarely interpret their interactions with the police, especially drug unit police, as respectful and deferential. Consequently, thugs react to the police with oppositional manners, and this merely intensifies the negative perceptions the police have of them. Police generally do not trust thugs, as thugs are known to want to demonstrate to any onlookers their masculinity and superior social status, which includes being smarter than, stronger than, and out of reach of the police and the law. Because of their expectations of signs of respect and admiration from others, thugs do not typically warm to drug unit officers' overtures regarding the potential of being an informant. In order to be successful in turning a thug into an informant, police find it most beneficial to approach the thug with a strategy that acknowledges and respects his or her "special status" in the community—although doing this while also trying to get a thug to inform on "his people" can be a delicate balancing act.

OFFICERS' BELIEFS THAT THEY UNDERSTAND CITIZENS BUT NOT OFFENDERS

The officers we studied not only exhibited the strong belief that they were striving to make their communities safer but also generally believed that they could understand and relate to the "good folks" in the community. However, understanding those individuals that they targeted in their work—the "bad guys"—was something that no veteran metropolitan officer felt was achievable. While officers whose work focused on policing drugs, drug dealers, and drug users did claim to be able to decipher and predict the routines and habits of such persons, they almost always considered it to be beyond their comprehension to understand *why* these individuals did what they did.

While stopping short of suggesting that they could understand all of the motivations, values, and actions of the drug dealers, prostitutes, homeless persons, robbers, burglars, and assorted other public nuisances with whom they interacted daily, the officers in this study shared the belief that, "because we see it all and we interact with them all the time, we know what they're thinking and what they're going to do most of the time." The officers applied this same view to law-abiding "good folks" and even to other officers in the departments where they worked. As was frequently expressed, the officers in the River City flex unit and the Central City narcotics units knew what it meant to be a "good" community member, and they had all started as uniformed beat officers, so they had experience in the role of beat cop as well. Exposure to and interaction with good community members translated into deeper understandings and stronger affiliations between officers and community members. However, the exposure and interactions of even those officers with years of experience focused on drugs, prostitution, and other forms of vice only yielded recognition and the ability to predict behaviors, not a deeper understanding of the reasons for such behaviors.

Officers consistently espoused the belief that they could empathize with the motivations of drug dealers, distributors, and users. Officers commonly acknowledged that the users of illicit drugs and at least some of the dealers are people who are structurally disadvantaged, without pro-social support systems, and are "trapped in the hood" lifestyle. Therefore, the officers believed that at least some dealers and users are not morally culpable for their lifestyles. But even so, it was inconceivable to most officers why dealers and users made the decision to live life in such ways. Flex unit officers recognized that structural disadvantages and institutionalized forms of racism, sexism, and class structure exist, but they saw these limitations as obstacles that can, should, and would be overcome by individuals if only they would make a conscious decision to do so. So, although officers believe that they understand the reasons drug dealers, distributors, and users engage in drug-related behavior, there is also an acknowledged lack of understanding for why this is the chosen behavior of these individuals. Structural disadvantages are perceived as issues that create a poor starting point, but not as issues that necessarily need to have a lasting impact on those who wish to overcome their circumstances. With this as a starting point, we will examine the ways that metropolitan law enforcement officers who are engaged in the active and ongoing battles of the war on drugs perceive, define, and create as suitable targets for aggressive policing those who engage in illicit exchanges, such as drug dealers and prostitutes.

DRUGS, DEALERS, AND HOS: SCOURGES ON THE URBAN LANDSCAPE

Drug dealers, drug distributors, and prostitutes are the classes of people focused on by flex unit, narcotics unit, and other street-level specialty unit officers. In the eyes of these investigators, such persons are the worst of the worst in the community, the primary reason for community problems, and "the core of what's wrong with this country." It is not a revelation that law enforcement officers hold negative views of offenders, especially drug-involved offenders. But understanding the ways that such offenders are negatively defined by officers allows for a deeper understanding of how and why officers interact with such persons, including when enlisting or recruiting them as informants, in the ways they do. Whether officers are dealing with offenders to be policed or potential informants to be assessed, screened, and developed, what the officers believe about such individuals as moral, ethical, and thinking people establishes the basis and framework for the ways in which information exchanges are structured and conducted. Major Button of the River City police referred to dealers as despised entities that were nearly impossible to rid the city of. During one meeting about Jay, a repeat offender working as an informant who had not been heard from in a couple of weeks, Major Button told George: "Oh, c'mon. Jay's not dead. He's like a cockroach; he'll turn up again."

Drug dealers were commonly referred to as "sellers of death" and described as "the reason this community is as fucked up as it is." Drugs are widely perceived to be destructive to individuals, families, and community networks. Those who provide drugs are thought to be exclusively self-interested and willing to do anything and everything to maximize their profits without giving any thought to any consequences for others. In a colorful yet clear manner, Justin described the drug dealers of River City as "scumbag shit-heads who don't care about anything except themselves and will do whatever they can to help themselves and not give a shit about anyone else." This strong sense of self-interest is also perceived as being a reason that such individuals are dangers not only to the community but also to the police themselves. It is also believed that this disregard for authority is likely to be accompanied by a willingness to resort to violence and to use "any means possible" in resisting policing efforts. As such, drug dealers are not only despised but also viewed as universally dangerous and constant threats regardless of the time, place, or circumstances.

However, despite being despised and a target of daily activities, drug dealers are also recognized by essentially all experienced law enforcement officers as universal and nearly impossible to stop collectively. While day-to-day efforts lead to the (temporary) removal of street-level dealers, it is expected that there will always be a replacement dealer ready and available, and few dealers are removed from the streets permanently or for prolonged periods of time. At the individual level, dealers are, as Major Button put it, like cockroaches and will inevitably return. On the collective level, drugs and the people who deal them are seen as inescapable. As Vic put it: "I don't want to say that I'm a liberal, but the war on drugs is war that can never be won. There's just too much money in it."

Law enforcement officers also consistently and vocally believe that drug dealers are simply not to be trusted. This makes for difficulties when officers are considering using arrested dealers as informants. In order for an informant-investigator relationship to be productive, there must be some degree of mutual trust established between the two parties. Ironically, however, drug dealers and investigators have no trust in one another, and both can and will easily and quickly point to former interactions and relationships with members of the other group that were negative and use this as evidence of why trust should not be granted. For officers, the lack of trust and absence of respect for drug dealers means that, from the outset, many drug dealers are seen as inappropriate for development as informers. The only dealers that are commonly believed to be suitable as informers are those at the bottom of the drug-market hierarchy. Dealers with the least experience with the criminal justice system and its processes and those least integrated to the network of drug activities are most likely to be seen as potential informers. Although these low-level dealers are still seen as a menace to the community, solely self-interested, and incapable of empathizing with the victims of the drug trade, these qualities may help an individual be turned into an informer. Once an individual has been arrested, self-interest and disregard for others can be exploited as motivators for working with the police. In such cases, the dealer-turned-informer is not perceived to be the least bit interested in any long-term consequences that may arise from his or her informing activities and is only assumed to be concerned with gaining freedom and being removed from the criminal justice process. In these ways, then, the negative qualities law enforcement officers associate with drug dealers can actually be exploited to turn these individuals into informers.

Prostitutes, the second most common type of offender that is encountered by street-level vice officers and exploited as informants, are also viewed in strongly negative terms. Officers see prostitutes as immoral women who are unwilling to engage in real work. Moreover, many officers presume that prostitutes have (usually multiple) sexually transmitted diseases, such as HIV, and commonly deem them to be uncaring about the fact that they spread these diseases to others. As will be discussed in more depth in chapter 6, the belief that prostitutes are "dirty" directly influences how officers interact with them. When arresting a prostitute, officers minimize physical contact, seemingly expecting the presumed STDs of the prostitute to be transmitted through nonsexual contact. George and Lucky went so far as to carry disinfecting wipes in their vehicles and habitually used these products to clean handcuffs after removing them from prostitutes. After they had announced themselves as police to a soliciting prostitute, both George and Lucky would don latex gloves prior to touching the prostitute. Taking it a step further, Sergeant Perez, who was well known for his skill in getting prostitutes to solicit him, typically liked to get prostitutes to get into his car so that, when he announced himself as police, they would be less likely to attempt to run. Because of the frequency of having prostitutes in his car, the sergeant carried a container of disinfecting wipes with him, and after having a prostitute in the car, he would meticulously wipe down any and all surfaces that may have been touched by the prostitute, including the seats, door handles, and dashboard.

Yet prostitutes were also seen as both a common and useful part of the urban landscape, and some officers even saw them as simple fodder for fun, diversions, and games. Officers are sometimes reputed as engaging prostitutes for sexual services. Other times, even when working with a prostitute as an informant, officers may go too far in their interactions with the prostitute. Vic reflected on officers he had known in the past: "Female informants, they got in a lot of trouble with that. They [the officers] sometimes thought it would be good to go out drinking with them [female informants], and usually it wasn't." Alternatively, Richardson recalled active attempts by prostitutes and sometimes by other female offenders to work off their charges in another way: "One of the traps that police fall into, particularly [when dealing with] women who are trying to work off a case, is they'll [these women] create some scenario where they'll entice the officer to have sex.... And they know if they can ever get you [to] compromise yourself with drugs, alcohol, or women, then no longer are you working them, now they're working you, and so the temptations are there." Ranger related another instance in which a known prostitute was (unknowingly) used by an undercover unit to initiate a new unit member:

> The guys that are working the prostitutes, they're wired, and they have a code word for when to move in and bust her. And I was working with those guys one night, and here's this guy, this officer I'll never forget, Darren, as pure as the driven snow.... Anyway, the law back then was that, in order

to—entrapment was big, so you had to be very careful. But when you pulled out the money and you were agreed with the money, well, that wasn't enough back then; she had to actually do something. Whether it's touching you, start undressing me, start undressing you, whatever that had to happen. So she starts unbuttoning his jeans, and he's giving the code word, and everybody is just giggling, and he's like, "Don't you suck my dick! I told you not to suck my dick!" And he finally jumps out of this pickup and yells, "I'm a cop, lady!" So apparently she got her mouth around his dick, and he was pissed! Man, he was pissed. But you know what though? That's your initiation right there.

Very clearly, the officers interviewed and observed in this study saw prostitutes as inferior beings—valuable for information and entertainment but not respectable or worthy recipients of their day-to-day work.

While officers appear to assume that all prostitutes have HIV, when this assumption is confirmed (typically by a prostitute's self-disclosure), officers become hyper-vigilant and avoid all forms of contact they can. During the arrest of a prostitute who agreed to anal sex with all four of the flex unit officers for $50, the young woman cried and begged not to be taken to jail, telling the officers: "I have AIDS, and they'll not give me my drugs there." Although George, Justin, and Lucky had been careful about what they touched in the woman's small apartment prior to this disclosure, on hearing this news, George immediately returned the unit vehicle, brought in latex gloves for all of the team, and proceeded to gingerly and slowly open drawers and look under furniture in a search for narcotics. Prior to being taken to jail, the prostitute was allowed to smoke a cigarette. When she was handcuffed prior to transport, she tried to hand her unfinished cigarette to Lucky. Even though he regularly smoked at least a half of a pack of cigarettes a day, he responded with a loud: "Don't give me that! I'm not touching that!" In the property room later that same day, when logging in a baggie of marijuana seized at the prostitute's apartment, George told the clerk: "You don't want to touch this without getting some gloves first. It may have AIDS on it."

The fears of HIV and assumptions about all prostitutes having HIV is in direct contrast to the training that all officers receive regarding HIV and its transmission and the personal lives of the unit members. Justin, George, and Lucky were all well known for refusing to use condoms in their own sexual encounters. While Justin was married and claimed to be monogamous, both Lucky and George dated widely and frequently and enjoyed entertaining the rest of the unit and selected patrol officers with tales of their sexual escapades. Reflecting the values and attitudes of carefree teenagers, they said they never used condoms, claiming, "I don't care what they say, you can tell when a chick is dirty." When encountering a woman who had sex with men for money, the assumption was that of course she was "dirty" and required special precautions for interactions.

FRUSTRATIONS WITH REPEAT OFFENDERS IN "THE GAME"

When asked about the biggest frustrations with their jobs, officers focused on policing the drug trade cited the fact that they repeatedly encountered the same offenders over and over, often spotting individuals back on the streets again shortly after having been arrested. Officers spent most of their days riding around searching out street dealers, prostitutes, informants, and other targets. As they did so, they would frequently point out individuals they knew and had arrested in the past: "Over there, that tall guy, that's Smith; we busted him just last week. Looks like the courts did their job yet again!" or, "Hey, slow down. Isn't that the guy we busted with four rocks on Tuesday? What's he doing back on the street already?" Such comments were common, and while officers clearly expressed frustration over the situation, they also saw it as "just the way it is."

Officers who spend more than a few years on the streets not only see the same individuals over and over, and often arrest these individuals repeatedly, but also (sadly) come to recognize and know offenders' children and other extended relations. Realizing not only that their efforts fail to bring about change in the behaviors of particular offenders but also that, despite their efforts, a second generation of dealers has emerged can be especially disheartening and discouraging for some officers. While touring in a well-known high-crime, high-drug-activity neighborhood, Sandy said that, in her few years on the streets, she has come to realize that "it's been generation after generation. You know, mama, grandma, great-grandma living like that, they just seem not to know any better or want any better for themselves."

In cities all over the country, especially in high-crime, socially disorganized, and poverty- and drug-infested communities, officers get to know offenders, offenders get to know the officers working in the neighborhoods, and the two groups see each other—both formally and informally—quite frequently. In some ways, this is to be expected. Officers and offenders are both located in a small, geographically restricted world, where the success of each group is contingent on being in high-visibility locations. Officers need to be visible and accessible to the general community so as to be seen as "doing something." Officers also need to be seen by drug dealers as a means of deterrence. Drug dealers need to be open and available to customers, so being visible to officers and the general community is a potential cost of business that needs to be managed.

While there are clearly benefits to drug dealers seeing law enforcement officers in their neighborhoods and being aware of the presence and threat posed by law enforcement, there is also a downside to this. When officers, whether as individuals or as organizational units, operate on a predictable schedule, drug dealers (and presumably other types of offenders as well) can fairly easily adapt and arrange their own schedules around those of the police. Cruz, a seasoned narcotics unit investigator, explained: "I think they all learn. You know. What time of day they can do what they can do, you know? They be like, 'He a slug; he ain't going to stop. He can see us doing stuff, and he won't stop.' They know. Like with us, they know our schedule and they learn fast. Cause they want to keep up their criminal activities so they going to know the best time to do it without getting caught." Sandy also reflected on this:

> They know the routine, the routines of the officers. They know who is and who's not going to the police. They know who are rookies and who's not. They know how to play on your emotions. And they study your every move. When you think they are not paying attention, they're paying attention. They know our procedures better than we know. They know nine times out of ten how many cars are going to show up, how many at one time on certain calls. . . . They know, they know. They have all that figured out. They know what times the most aggressive officers work, and they won't sell during that time. They will drive by the precinct and see your car, if you're there or not. They're very organized.

The relationship between officers and drug dealers is a two-way street, and it is managed by both parties. This means that dealers will engage with officers, but only when the dealers know that they will not be arrested. Officers, both patrol officers and drug unit investigators, typically know who many of the drug dealers are in their neighborhoods. Moreover, they recognize that the drug dealers all know who the officers are, when they are present in their neighborhoods, and, for the most part, how to interact with particular officers while avoiding "hassles" or legal processing.

These relationships work, to some degree, to the benefit of both parties. Sincerity may be absent, but there is acknowledgement and a form of respect between the two parties. As expressed by Woods, a Central City violent crimes investigator: "As far as relationships, it kind of depends on the officer, . . . but everybody knows what role the other person is playing; I mean, there is no ambiguity there or anything." Officer Young put it a bit differently, explaining how he talks to known dealers on the street: "You know, you don't get mad. And they don't get mad at me for doing my job. And I'm like this, 'Don't take it personal. Let's not make it personal. I'm doing my job. My job is to catch you, and your job is to not get caught. You got caught today.' And then they calm down. . . . That's my job."

The relationship between officers and street-wise, often criminally involved individuals is recognized for what it is by players on both sides of "the game." For officers, the game is not only well known but also typically seen as unwinnable and expensive and a cause of frustrations. Johnson continued his explanation of the strategic yet unwinnable ongoing interactions with dealers: "I wouldn't say it's anything as sophisticated as a chess match, but it's kind of like that in that it is perpetual. There is no beginning or end to it. . . . It's a game. Everybody knows what role they play, and everybody plays it to an extent."

In order to continue with any significant degree of motivation and enthusiasm, officers report that they need to view their jobs and the actions of those that they are policing in the "right perspective." This means not taking one's failures (or successes) personally, knowing that it is possible to interact with offenders in respectful, safe, and mutually respectful ways, and trying to look at the big picture rather than seeing the specifics of a particular interaction or dealer as indicative of one's overall efforts and value. Richardson, a homicide investigator, summarized his way of thinking about his job as follows: "Some days I win, some days he [a drug dealer] wins. . . . These guys are professionals in their own way, the dope dealers I'm speaking of, and they respect that also. It is a mutual respect. . . . What is that old saying, 'There is honor among thieves'? Yeah, if you catch a guy fair and square, it has been my experience, for the most part, that they respect that."

However, even though a few officer-dealer relationships suggest a modicum of mutual respect and cordialness, the fact remains that officers quickly become frustrated by their experiences of repeatedly encountering the same offenders in the street-level dope market. For many officers, time brings with it resignation, and they settle into a view that the game they play with drug dealers should be approached as merely the way they go about doing the requirements of their job, realizing that those with whom they are competing are also "simply doing their job." Acknowledgement of this approach can be clearly seen in the words of Central City's investigator Greene:

> I tell them. I say, "Man, you know, I'm not mad, I'm not angry, I don't give damn . . . cause that's your job." And it might not be. . . . But this is their profession. Yeah. I catch you now, you go to jail. If I don't, he sells. The old saying in the NCAA tournament goes, "The winner talks, and the loser walks." That's the way it is on the street. It's like the winner talks, the loser walks. So when he loses, he's going to jail. If he wins, he walks and talks about it; he brags about it. It's like knowing when you get rid of him, then somebody else is just going to take his place. . . . My mother always told me, or my grandmother always told me, "There's more than one way to skin a cat." It's like playing chess. I may have three moves. I might not use this move today. I might use a new one. I may use that move later on in the week. . . . I'm a firm believer that, certain days, it's that guy's turn to go to jail that day. Some days you don't get it. Like, today I got a cat. I know he had it, he was going. He had drugs on him. . . . I didn't have enough probable cause to just come to him and do a full scale search or even do a pat down. Didn't have probable cause. So, you know, that day, today, wasn't his day to go to jail. But tomorrow, in the same situation, tomorrow I may have more probable cause."

Sandy, who recognized that his approach had changed over time, largely due to frustrations and a sense of being unable to effect true change, expressed even more resignation than Greene to the state of his relationship with drug dealers:

> I tell them it's not personal. After I arrest you, if I see you tomorrow, I'll be like "Hey, what's up?" Because I used to take it home with me, and I felt like the system was letting me down, and it wasn't designed for the police, it was just designed to generate money for the city. That's the way I felt. I was like, stop taking it personally, it's just the thrill of the hunt, just to see if they really are smarter than we are, just to figure out how they're doing it, and just be amazed at some of the stuff they come up with. It's just amazing. So that's the way I look at it now.

Sometimes, it may not be the exact same offenders that are encountered repeatedly but rather more-or-less interchangeable individuals that work in the same places doing the same exact tasks (e.g., selling or distributing drugs, organizing sellers, etc.) that were done by recently removed offenders. Investigator White from Central City spoke to this: "The problem is, usually, when you shut down a house, within a week or two, the house is right back up. Yeah, it's just somebody else comes in and takes over." So, while not necessarily dealing with individual repeat offenders, the constant repetition of cases with more or less interchangeable facts, situations, and players is a major source of frustration for narcotics unit officers. In addition to the other structural and procedural issues that frustrate officers, simply dealing with the same types of scenarios day in and day out becomes disheartening and frustrating.

While officers commonly use the analogy of "the game" to describe their work, this does not necessarily mean that their work is seen as being without benefit to the community. In some instances, especially for officers who are skilled at carrying out interrogations that are not readily recognized as interrogations, valuable information can be obtained. Here, the words of Tyrone, a sergeant in a narcotics investigation unit, are instructive:

> It's adversarial; it's a game of chess. They make a move, you make a move. Sometimes, we make a move first, then they make a move. That's all it is. It's a game to them. . . . And they see it that way. . . . It's nothing personal, and they don't really see it that way either. You know, most of them, when we arrest them, they'll tell us what's going on; they'll snitch a lot. They'll snitch on each other.

The game can have payoffs for both officers and offenders. Officers can make some impact on the proliferation of drugs, and dealers can help themselves, especially if they are able to trade information for leniency or other benefits. Policing is a trade-off. The winnings may not always be substantial, but there are benefits to be gained for both sets of players.

PERCEPTIONS OF AND FROM THE COMMUNITY AND OTHER OFFICERS

Interestingly, although the officers in the River City flex unit and various tactical units in Central City held strongly to their belief that the reasons drug dealers and prostitutes choose to live the lives they do were incomprehensible, they simultaneously held the strong belief that others in the community, or even officers in other departmental units, were not able to understand their perspectives, experiences, and approaches. We observed that officers in drug and homicide units often felt isolated, misunderstood, and very frequently simply disliked by society. Sometimes, community members simply want absolutely nothing to do with police officers. This was illustrated in the following story about an offender that had been shot, told by Sergeant Johnson of the Central City homicide unit:

> He asked me could I contact his family. Let them know where he was, that type thing. I said okay. He gave me the number, and I called. I said, "Hey, how are you doing? This is Sergeant Johnson from [the Central City Police Department]." Click. Okay, try again. "Hi, this is Sergeant Johnson from [Central City Police Department]." Click. Then I called back a third time, because—I don't have to do this now because he's not dead and he's over eighteen—but because I just feel for people. I tried again, and of course it went into voicemail. I left a message: "I was calling to let you know that your brother has been shot. If you would like to know more information, answer the phone." Ten minutes later, I get a call back: "Oh, I'm sorry, my phone was going out." You just have to break down that barrier, because a lot of people just don't like the police, don't care what kind of police you are.

The challenges of working in a street crimes unit, homicide unit, or a tactical taskforce focused on drug interdiction are believed by those in such units to be special and somewhat unique to their work. Throughout the time that we spent with police units in River City and Central City, officers would point out interactions or tasks that they would do and try to explain: "These are things the community doesn't see that we do. People don't understand what it is we have to do deal with on this job." As we encountered new situations, officers would ask us if we were starting to see things "differently." After tense, violent, or argumentative interactions with arrestees, onlookers, or other members of the community who were not law enforcement officers, it was common for an involved officer to ask us some form of the question, "Now do you see what we mean?" As researchers, we were granted unfettered access to officers' day-to-day activities and interactions with citizens of all kinds. It became readily apparent that the officers had no problem exposing us to the stresses of the job and the underside of the community that contributed to the attitudes and views of the officers.

This perceived lack of understanding did not only apply to the general public; many of the investigators we observed felt similarly misunderstood by patrol officers and supervisors. We found that narcotics and homicide investigators believed that what they see and do is different from what they know patrol officers see and do (because they were all patrol officers at one time).

So drug unit officers believe that they know and understand patrol officers but that patrol officers do not know or understand the stresses, expectations, and social worlds of narcotics or homicide investigators. This view can negatively impact crime-control outcomes. Although the sharing of information, especially from patrol officers to narcotics investigators, is important, it is not uncommon for patrol officers to express frustration with investigators who do not reciprocate, do not act on the information in a timely manner, or are perceived as "not really doing anything other than riding around and looking for people to jump out on." This is reflective of the well-recognized hierarchical pecking order of specialty units (Manning 1980; Marx 1988), in which the "special" work of such units is not fully understood and is at least sometimes viewed with jealousy by people in lesser units or assignments. Detective Cappelli, a six-year veteran of the Central City homicide unit, offered the following assessment of patrol officers:

> They're like kids. . . . They take orders. . . . Usually, they'll listen, and they look up to you because they know this is where they want to be one day. . . . But on day watch is where they put all the old crusty veterans who never done anything, and they're the ones who are gonna be the smart asses and all that stuff. You know them. That's when they'll come to me. Like he'll come to me and say I'm having a problem. "Hey, God damn it. Get off the fucking scene Jimmy. What the hell are you doing? You know better than that." You know, we'll all jump his ass.

The investigators that were observed throughout all departments expressed a similar sentiment when it came to police supervisors both inside and outside their units. In most metropolitan police departments, supervisors often gain command over units specializing in types of police work for which they have no prior experience. In other words, the sergeants and lieutenants that oversee homicide or narcotics units often come from patrol backgrounds and have never held the rank of investigator or worked within a criminal investigations unit, let alone gotten their hands dirty doing homicide or narcotics work. This garners them resentment and a lack of legitimacy among seasoned homicide and narcotics investigators, who see themselves as "walking the walk" while supervisors only "talk the talk." It was not uncommon for the investigators we observed to assess their supervisors as being out of touch or ignorant of the rigors of the work of the unit. For example, Detective Duffy, a sixteen-year veteran of the Central City homicide unit, offered the following comments about the unit's supervisors:

I have more time on the department than most of the majors I have served under. Just because they wear a different color shirt doesn't make them smarter than me or, you know, more experienced or . . . I mean, [our current unit major] was never a homicide detective. None of the sergeants were ever homicide detectives, with the exception of Sergeant Martinez. So what are they gonna tell me about homicide investigation that, you know, I can't tell them?

A similar sentiment was expressed by Detective Richardson, a ten-year veteran of the same homicide unit:

As a lead homicide detective, you're the man. By God, you have the authority of the chief of police. If, all of a sudden, you look up and there's a captain over here or a major or even a homicide commander walking through my crime scene, kicking my shell casings by accident. So I cuss him like a dog. I told [one homicide unit commander] to get his ass off my homicide scene. [And my friends later said,] "What the hell are you doing? Are you an idiot? You're our commander; you should know better."

The lack of respect for other types of supervisors is generally even greater. This is captured well in a follow-up story told by Detective Richardson:

I had a guy that was a patrol zone major at a crime scene where two officers had gotten shot. And there's this major on the phone with [the chief of police] walking right through our shell casings and stuff. And I said, "Hey, you, get the fuck off my scene! Get out of here!" Cause you, you have to protect the crime scene. He goes, "You don't talk to me like that. I'm on the phone with the chief." I said, "I would tell his fucking ass to get out of here too. Get out of here. You're kicking my shell casings." And it embarrassed him, and I don't give a damn. God damn you, if you're stupid enough to walk in here and do that stupid shit, you deserve what you get. . . . I don't work for him. I don't. Just because you got a white shirt, I don't work for you. I work for these two officers who just got shot and their wives and their children, you know? Everybody forgets what the hell they're doing around here and who they really work for. We work for the public. . . . That's my crime scene, and see, people forget who they work for, and when you become an upper-echelon supervisor, you forget who you really are sometimes. You know, you think your rank is this, [but] your rank is not more important than me solving that homicide. You know, and that's where you have problems. They know me. When they see me on the scene, they say, "He'll cuss me out." And it's out of respect. It's out of fear. Because they don't want to get embarrassed, and that's why I have the reputation as a jerk or a butthole or whatever. . . . But then again, that's why I'm successful at what I do. I cannot stand incompetence. I can't stand somebody to come in here and mess up my scene. Because nobody's gonna care as much about this homicide as me. They're gonna go home, they're gonna go back to their office, they're gonna go eat their lunch. I'm there until the end.

.

SUMMARY

What we see in this chapter is that narcotics unit police investigators have a very highly structured, bifurcated view of the work they do and the people who inhabit the world in which they work. The world is seen in largely "us versus them" terms, and the police usually see themselves and their colleagues as aligned with the "good folks" of a community. The "good folks" are the hard-working, upstanding, not-criminally-involved, civic-minded, and involved individuals "who are just trying to raise their kids, live their lives, and not be bothered by anyone." It is this segment of the community that narcotics police feel an affiliation with, an affinity toward, and a responsibility for. The police like to envision themselves fighting against the "bad guys" in an effort to preserve a particular form and structure of community life for the "good folks."

The "bad guys" are seen as universally bad, and in almost all instances, they are not considered to be contributors of anything positive to the community. Whether in an effort to attribute some human qualities to these "bad guys" or as a result of education and/or experience, the police regularly interact with bad guys in the community whom they feel they can at least superficially understand. Individual community members who pursue illegal activities to support themselves (and perhaps their families or others) are recognized as sharing a core value with the police, but the means by which that value is pursued is seen as unacceptable and not understandable.

Here, an interesting paradox is introduced in the views, values, and knowledge of such law enforcement officers. Officers often acknowledge the structural, economic, and political forces that create and maintain poverty and an urban underclass. However, while (supposedly) recognizing that there are valid and tangible reasons for people to be underprivileged and pushed to a life of crime, these same law enforcement officers also believe that individuals can overcome such structural impediments "if they only try." This sentiment is reminiscent of what was commonly believed about domestic violence victims thirty or more years ago (and is still present to some degree): "Why don't they just leave?" Today, we have a much better and more frequently acknowledged understanding of structural impediments that make it hard for domestic violence victims to leave their abusers. However, our observations showed that, at least among narcotics police, there is not an understanding of why people living under disadvantaged circumstances don't just get out of their neighborhoods or situations.

Although they may be useful as confidential informants, civilians known as "thugs" and "hos" are universally looked upon with repugnance and complete distrust by law enforcement officers. Such individuals are perceived as scourges on the community and thought to bring violence, fear, disease, and threats to families. They are also acknowledged as potentially powerful because they have the ability to "strike back" at officers and investigative units through allegations of improprieties and abuse. Such persons are believed to be interpersonally dangerous in interactions and are also recognized as potentially likely to try to "get back" at officers in any way possible.

This potentiality, coupled with the fact that, even when caught, such offenders are likely to spend little or no time incarcerated, leads to high levels of frustration among law enforcement officers. In playing "the game," narcotics police find that their efforts are often for naught or, at best, yield minimal negative consequence for targeted offenders. Officers become exasperated when they see individuals they have targeted, spent significant time investigating, arrested, and followed through to court end up back on the streets carrying on with the same behaviors as previously, and all within a short period of time (days, weeks, or months). Therefore, seeing their actions (and those of others) as plays in a giant game is a way for law enforcement officers to make sense of their time, efforts, and expenditures and to minimize personal frustrations and the accompanying consequences.

Throughout this process, narcotics law enforcement investigators come to feel isolated from everyone around them, including their peers, supervisors, community members, families, and essentially anyone who would or could represent the "good folks" of the community. The war on drugs is focused on the "bad guys," but the war takes its combatants away from support systems and similar others. Thus, in the end, those who are fighting our war on drugs are not enthusiastic about the war, do not necessarily believe that they are winning the war, and in fact may argue that the war is a lost cause.

SIX

Maintaining Relationships
with Informants

Once an informant has been identified, recruited, and turned, he or she will
be put to work by his or her primary/managing law enforcement agent. At
this point, the informant will be asked to provide information about
unsolved or unknown crimes, set up and make drug buys while under surveillance, introduce officers to criminal-world contacts, or engage in other
types of "work" requested and directed by the managing officer. It is well
documented (Alvarez 1993; Billingsley 2009; Natapoff 2004) that the execution of said work is time consuming, resource draining, and carries with it a
host of potential downfalls.

As we have argued throughout this book, informants serve an integral role
in the police-citizen information exchange. In particular, they provide law
enforcement officers and agencies with a number of important services and
resources. In some instances, informants play an interactive role, working
side-by-side and hand-in-hand with undercover officers to provide officers
with an entrée into illicit scenarios or with initial participation opportunities
in illegal activities and transactions. At other times, informants have a more
social role, providing introductions and facilitating undercover officers'
establishment of an identity and place within a criminal subculture or group.
Also, as we found in our fieldwork experiences, a common form of work
informants engage in involves the one-way provision of information about
the behaviors of criminal actors, including about who is doing what where,
when, with whom, and how. In still other instances, the informant will be
asked to take on an active engagement role wherein he or she is asked to
arrange and complete a drug transaction, which is either observed by law
enforcement from afar or documented through the exchange of marked cash
and captured through a hidden audio or video recording device worn by the

informant. Directly observing an informant conducting a criminal transaction provides the officer with a means to collect evidence for use at a later time (most likely for an arrest, although in some cases to try to turn a new informant). When an informant uses marked money to make a drug buy out of the direct eye contact of officers, officers subsequently approach, search, and arrest the seller with the marked money. The takedown of the seller in these cases is usually completed immediately or very shortly after the informant makes the buy. The longest elapsed time between such a buy and officers moving in on the seller that was witnessed in our fieldwork was just under two hours; however, in most instances, such a takedown comes within minutes of the informant completing the buy and notifying his or her managing officer that the buy is complete.

With this understanding of the common roles played by confidential informants within the police-citizen information exchange, we begin this chapter by exploring the organizational requirements imposed by law enforcement agencies on how officers document and officially manage their informants. We then move into a discussion of the actual working activities of the informant-officer team, highlighting the various styles of interactions that officers have with informants and some of the means by which managing officers can and do work to maximize the benefits derived from an informant while simultaneously guarding against potential pitfalls.

ORGANIZATIONAL REQUIREMENTS FOR STRUCTURING AN INFORMANT-OFFICER RELATIONSHIP

Common across all law enforcement agencies is a requirement that any and all confidential informants must be officially documented, or "registered," with the agency (Fitzgerald 2007; International Association of Chiefs of Police 1990; U.S. Department of Justice 2005). Core components of the registration process include documentation of the confidential informant's basic identifying and criminal history information, the code name or number assigned to the informant, and signed materials explicitly establishing any remuneration or considerations to be realized by the informant in return for his or her voluntary cooperation. Typical too is the inclusion of a waiver of liability that confidential informants are required to sign prior to embarking on their information-exchange activities. Additionally, in many agencies, all confidential informant registrations must be reviewed and approved by the registering officers' supervisor (or a designated superior officer). Mark, a three-year veteran of a federal agency, succinctly described the approval process of his agency as it relates to the use of entrepreneurial informants:

> There will be an initial approval to get those funds. . . . We send a jacket [case file] to our coordinator, who handles the money to get preapproval to pay the source so we know exactly how much money we can offer that person. So we send in that information [the items detailed above], give them an outline of the case, and say, "Hey, we want preapproval for a fifteen hundred dollar payment." We have to do a quick fingerprint with our portable [fingerprinting device], get some biographical information, and submit all that to a supervisor, and that goes all into a locked safe.

Some investigators welcome this procedure and see it as a means of protecting themselves. Orlando cautioned: "You're just asking for trouble if you don't document an informant and something happens. Otherwise, some kind of accusations come out, like you're stealing money or you're paying this informant too much money. There has to be a paper trail when you deal with informant. That's just bottom line. I mean, you're setting yourself up for disaster if you don't have a paper trail."

While official requirements for registration and approval and any other paperwork are acknowledged and known by all officers, some of these requirements appear to be disliked and not infrequently ignored, only partially completed, or in some other fashion less than fully and accurately fulfilled. Officers consistently considered the paperwork requirements of registration and approval by a superior officer to be bureaucratic, time-consuming distractions from "real police work" with little or no meaning or value for the officer on the street. As some officers also argue, introducing the "formality" of registration and paperwork can be unsettling to newly recruited informants, who see it as a means by which their identities could be leaked to others, resulting in their being labeled snitches on the streets. Simply stated, many officers believe that some informants, especially those who are serving in a one-way provision of information role and are not intrinsically beholden to the information exchange (i.e., they are not paid entrepreneur informants), will be reluctant to be registered and will therefore not follow through with their role and activities if forced to do so. In these instances, the managing officer will usually chose to treat the individual as an undocumented "source of information"—as opposed to a "registered confidential informant"—to gain access to the intelligence the individual has at his or her disposal. It is important to note that these terms are official designations assigned by the agency, not by the officers on the ground. In the bureaucratic sense, the term "informant" is reserved for those persons who provide criminal intelligence and have been subject to the formal registration process. Per the formal standard operating procedures (SOPs) of the individual law enforcement agency in question, these individuals have been formally vetted and can serve as repeat providers of intelligence in the police-citizen information exchange. Alternatively, most law enforcement organizations reserve the term "source of information" for persons who serve as one-time intelligence providers and have not been subject to the formal registration process. Kareem explained it a bit differently: "The way our system is set up is that, if we plan to use them [an informant] repeatedly, we have to document them. We can use them as a one-time source, but if we plan to use them repeatedly, we have to go through and have them properly documented." Shawn, a seasoned narcotics officer in Central City further summarized this situations:

> You have CIs, official documented CIs, and then you have sources of informa-
> tion. A source of information can be totally random and anonymous. You
> don't even have to record their name. . . . So yeah, they're not technically a CI,
> but they're a source of information. You see, some of the sources don't want to
> become CIs. They don't want to be photographed, fingerprinted, and all of
> this kind of stuff and be an actual file in the office with all of their information
> [documented]. But we know their phone number, we know who they are, and
> every now and then, you get a phone call [from them], "Hey, you might want
> to look at this apartment complex." Then, of course, that gives us enough
> information to start an investigation. On the flip side, they don't get paid.

The officers in this study consistently noted that a positive and productive relationship with an informant is predicated on the two parties developing a functional interactional dynamic and at least some degree of mutual trust. They frequently noted that the formality of the bureaucratically imposed "sign up" process inherently threatens this rapport and nurturing of trust, especially when it comes immediately at the heels of an arrest. Officers feared that asking an individual to come to the office and complete paperwork prior to that person getting to know the officer and deciding whether the role is one they are ready and willing to fulfill would discourage most (if not all) potential informants from following through and working with law enforcement.

As a result of the officers' disdain for paperwork and possibly also due to their commitment to "get the job done" and not lose a likely informant because of his or her reluctance to be registered, many informants are never formally registered. In a way, this means that undocumented informants are key components of many criminal investigations, even though they have never been (officially) vetted by the agency. In effect, officers take advantage of the fact that the SOP allows for the use of "sources of information" and manage to circumvent the rules. Ranger confirmed this: "I'd be surprised if 20 percent of CIs are on the books." Our fieldwork exposed us to many instances where informants were not registered because they simply refused to "go official" yet still voiced a willingness to work with the handling officer. In these situations, the officer was left to decide between strictly abiding by departmental policies, treating the person as an unregistered and unpaid "source of information," or simply refusing to embark on an information exchange with the individual (and most probably losing access to information about one or more investigations). Treating the person as a "source of information" was consistently seen as appealing to officers, as it allowed them to circumvent the paperwork requirement, go forth with the information gathering, and thus advance the investigation. Not surprisingly, officers reported that, in most cases, they find a way to extract the relevant information from persons who are unwilling to become registered informants and to utilize them as key components of investigations. Furthermore, it was not uncommon for a single individual to be treated as a "source of information" on multiple occasions, something that is technically not allowed under the stated policies of most agencies. Not surprisingly, under these circumstances, managing officers are not likely to disclose the details of these cases to supervising officers or anyone outside of a small, trusted circle of partners and other unit members. Oftentimes, the existence of undocumented informants was not even included in investigation files, as officers were able to "get the information in" without attaching it to a particular source.

It is simply a fact that some individuals have access to critical criminal intelligence but are highly reluctant—or even simply refuse—to allow for an official record of their work to be documented. This reluctance may be especially common and strong in the case of informants being recruited to work off charges. When these individuals are initially arrested and provided the opportunity to turn on others, the situation is fluid and fast-moving, and officers are likely to be provided with information about events and individuals that needs to be acted on in a very short period of time. Under these circumstances, little time exists for the officers to develop rapport and trust with potential informants, and thus these individuals may not want to be registered. Even though officers have the upper hand in these situations and the authority to refuse to work with potential informants unless they do agree to be registered, in a practical sense at least some information or opportunity is going to be lost if officers decide to stop, take an informant to a precinct, complete numerous forms, submit the forms to a supervisor, wait for them to be reviewed and approved, and then return to the streets with the informant. In many instances, officers believed that all possibility of acting on provided information would likely be forfeited by strictly following department policies and procedures. The question then becomes an ethical one for officers: is it worse to not follow procedure and work with an undocumented CI or to lose information that could solve a case?

We observed that individual officers respond to the reluctance of informants to be registered and to the immediacy of information's value in different ways. Just as Shawn pointed out above, some officers were happy to work with individuals as "sources of information" rather than "confidential informants." Other officers denied even being tempted by that possibility. For example, several officers argued that it is imperative, for the protection of the officers, the integrity of the cases, and the legal well-being of the informants, to have all paperwork completed and all confidential informants registered with the department. Perhaps not surprisingly, officers working in state or federal level agencies almost uniformly claimed to follow this this by-the-book approach, while city-level officers were more apt to admit to playing it free and loose with the rules. For example, Stan, a member of the River City flex unit, suggested that it could be more efficient and effective to make it a practice to *not* register informants. Noting that some informants are reluctant to "go official" and that the time and formality of doing the registration paperwork can significantly delay (or even lead to the loss of) an investigation, he surmised that not registering informants was a common practice in his street-level narcotics unit:

> You know, for our purposes, we generally avoid it [registering informants] unless it's going to be a paid source. Then we have some procedures that we have to go through. But for the most part, it's kind of, especially if somebody is a little nervous, . . . like if we're in my car, or we're in a room by ourselves, my partner and a source, or maybe it's just me and a source, I would say, "Look, I'm not taking notes. I'm not taking this down. Anything you tell me stays between us." So my documentation there too is minimal. The one exception is if they're paid, and that's a whole set of procedures we have to go through, and that stuff gets sealed.

We concede that Stan's experience, along with those noted intermittently among officers from the metropolitan police departments in Central City, may constitute rare events in the landscape of law enforcement in general. Nonetheless, these instances make an important point that documentation and registration of informants is not universally seen as important or necessary.

There are serious repercussions for officers who are found to be repeatedly working with an unregistered informant. Doing so is almost always a violation of departmental policy and may subject an officer to disciplinary actions. However, the officers interviewed in this study could recall only rare instances when officers faced formal disciplinary actions for their conduct associated with the use of informants. They more commonly recalled informal intervention on the part of supervising officers. Members of the River City flex unit described one occasion when the precinct commander learned that unit members had gone several months without bothering to fill out the requisite paperwork or register any of their informants. Realizing that he was therefore potentially subject to exposure and the wrath of superior officers in headquarters, Major Button notified Sergeant Perez that no flex unit officers would be allowed to leave the precinct until all of the unit members had fully completed paperwork on all informants used by the unit during the previous six-month period. Not surprisingly, when the unit members were informed of this, they were not pleased. Nonetheless, they spent the entire day in the office completing forms. The only time anyone left was to go meet an informant to get his or her signature on registration paperwork. Two days later, George spent nearly four hours correcting the registration information that he had done after Major Button had returned most of it because it was "all fucked up."

Our fieldwork interviews suggested that, when informants are registered and paperwork is done within federal and local law enforcement agencies, it is frequently done some period of time after an informant starts to work with an officer and that it is not infrequently done by someone other than the informant's managing officer. For example, in the River City flex unit, several officers—Justin, Lucky, and Sergeant Perez—were well known to be very poor with paperwork and to often not have the necessary information for completing paperwork (of all varieties, not just for registering and documenting the activities of informants). Because of this, they often passed off their paperwork to George or Skye. As part of his duties, Sergeant Perez is required to complete numerous forms and documentations of the unit's activities. However, it was noted that he strongly disliked "being tied to a desk and having to do this stuff that really isn't important anyway." As a result, his desk was usually strewn with piles of forms and requests for information from superiors that simply piled up for days or weeks at a time. One day in late summer, Sergeant Perez was sitting in his office, leaning back and simply staring at the piles of paperwork, when he commented in an exasperated fashion:

> I know I'm going to have to start staying up in this office and stay on top of these things. I dread it because I know that will drive me stark ravin' crazy, but that's how it's gonna have to be. I've been spending too much of my time rollin' on the streets. I realized this the other day when I was in court and I realized I never see any other COs [commanding officers] there. I'm there all the time, but I very rarely see any other COs there. So I guess, like it or not, I'm gonna have to start doing things different here.

This attitude lasted a couple of hours. Later that day, the sergeant was back on the streets looking for prostitutes and drug dealers. The piles of paperwork were smaller, but not by very much.

In some regards, delegating the task of completing paperwork to those who are more detail oriented and better organized is a productive trade-off. It means that, when paperwork is completed, it is done more accurately and to a higher quality, and those who pass off their paperwork are freed to spend their time on tasks (such as working with informants) at which they excel. Additionally, we observed that, when one officer was doing paperwork for another, it was not uncommon for the officer doing the paperwork to ask the other officer questions both about specific information needed on forms and about more general topics, for example: "Justin, this guy Sam, does he ever hang out over on Oak Street?" or, "This girl Betty, do you think she might know my guy Bill?" In this way, information was shared, investigations officers were directing could be facilitated, and new lines of investigations could be opened. Although there are some benefits that may be realized through the process of completing paperwork and by officers interacting as they do such tasks, the fact remains that the officers nearly universally did not consider such activities to be "real police work," even when they acknowledged the potential benefits.

RELATIONSHIPS AND INTERACTIONS WITH INFORMANTS

Beyond formal documentation, the actual ways in which officers work with and interact with the confidential informants that they manage vary significantly and sometimes substantially. Some officers viewed and interacted with informants as people with their own interests, emotions, skills, needs, and personalities. For example, Kareem noted: "There are some [informants] out there who are experts. So the one thing you do is you always respect their expertise. They have knowledge, and you need to respect that you're dealing with a skilled person." Others appeared to view and interact with informants in more impersonal ways, seemingly perceiving them as a tool of the job and as one-dimensional beings. Vic epitomized this type: "I'd treated them [informants] like they were dogs because they knew if they didn't work with me that they're going to prison." While both approaches can be productive and yield valuable information that facilitates investigations, different types of informants are likely to respond better to one of the two styles. In general, it appeared that officers developed their own styles when it came to working with informants. An officer's style largely reflected his or her personality, daily interactional style with all persons, and values and attitudes regarding diversity and persons with lifestyles other than his or her own. As Frank, a retired officer from Central City, noted, "some detectives work out of fear, some work out of mutual respect, and some just intimidated people."

The style of working with informants varies on three dimensions. First, officers interact with their informants on a personal level to different degrees, ranging from getting to know their informants as people, including perhaps meeting their children and/or partners and knowing about their daily activities outside of their informing role, to knowing little if anything about their informants beyond their names, addresses, and phone numbers. Second, the relationships that officers develop with informants come with varying degrees of authenticity, genuineness, and mutual respect. And third, how strict officers are with their informants about completing tasks and following through on agreed-on information varies.

Personal Relationships with Informants

Officers contended that it was rare to develop a true relationship built around genuine trust and feelings with an informant. Most officers felt that this was by design and reflective of what they would deem a best practice for such relationships. Nearly all of the officers encountered in our fieldwork and interviews viewed using confidential informants first and foremost as a "necessary evil" (see Mericle 1994, 63) of their work and thus believed that informants should be kept at arm's length. However, this is not to say that all

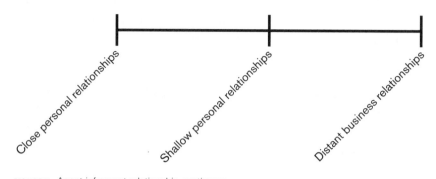

FIGURE 3. Agent-informant relationship continuum.

officers who worked with informants saw them in a completely impersonal way. Officers conceded that it was possible for some officers to develop some form of personal relationship with select informants. As two individuals spend time together, regardless of the fact that they operate on different sides of the law, it is not uncommon for some points of similarity or shared interests or experiences to be uncovered, such as a similar upbringing or a mutual interest in sports, cars, or fitness. In other instances, a personal relationship will be grounded in a relatable life event, such as the death of a family member, the loss of a job, or a pregnancy. Instances where the officer empathizes with the informant's situation can make for a closer relationship moving forward. As with the development of any social relationship, feeling empathy or identifying common interests and experiences provides officers with an opportunity to see the informant as "real" and truly a person. Our fieldwork and interviews suggested that it is useful to conceive of these types of personal relationships on a continuum (see figure 3), ranging from the rare instances when officers develop close personal relationships resembling friendships with their informants to relationships in which officers adopt a cold and callous approach and make it clear that the relationship is hierarchical and strictly about the exchange of criminal intelligence. Most officer-informant relationships are best described as falling somewhere in the middle ground of the continuum, with officers fostering a shallow personal relationship with their informants to garner trust and commitment.

As an exemplar of an officer who gets to know informants as true individuals and persons (far left end of the continuum in figure 3), Justin shows that there are both personal and professional advantages that can be realized from nurturing a close personal relationship with an informant. Of all of the River City investigative officers, Justin had the largest established cadre of informants, most of whom were indentured informants working off charges he held over their heads. Despite the fact that he was well known for his poor paperwork and lack of detail in many reports, Justin maintained a well-organized, detailed set of information on all of his informants, whether they were indentured informants or entrepreneurial informants. Justin noted this information primarily on three-by-five-inch notecards that he kept in a metal box in the trunk of his car. He recorded all of the basic contact information about informants, including their names, aliases, addresses, phone numbers, contacts, and common places to find them. He supplemented this with personal notes on informants, such as their drugs of choice, their personal likes and dislikes (including food, drink, sports teams, etc.), information about with whom they did and did not get along, their family members, and anything else that helped him to know his informants "as real people, because even though they may live out here on the streets and do things different than you and I, they are really people. They deserve to be treated like they are."

Many of Justin's informants were women, often drug abusers who, at least on occasion, engaged in prostitution. While not particularly handsome, Justin came across as a genuinely kind and caring man. As such, the vast majority of Justin's female informants thought the world of him. When they saw Justin, the women's faces would brighten, and unless they were being chastised for not doing something they were supposed to do, they wore big smiles and acted almost like middle school girls around a boy they had a crush on. Justin treated his informants, especially the women, very well. He remembered their birthdays and usually even sent a card. He often gave his informants money, even when they were not working for him. He bought food for them, both fast food meals here and there and, on occasion, a bag or two of groceries. He would shuttle informants to doctor's appointments or a child's school. And it was not uncommon for Justin to see one of his informants out on the streets and stop to casually chat, often not ever broaching the subject of any illegal activities or a need for any information.

As a very outgoing, caring, and empathetic person in all aspects of his life, Justin aimed to develop "personal" relationships with his informants fairly quickly. Moreover, he came to hold genuine, positive personal feelings for many of the confidential informants with whom he maintained longstanding information-exchange relationships. In fact, he had what very nearly approached "friendships" with many of his long-term informants and made it a point to maintain regular contact with them. Whenever Justin would be conducting street-level surveillance on a case, he would spend at least part of the time making calls to his informants, checking up on them, and putting in the time to nurture his relationship with them. Conversations typically centered on the informants' personal or family relationships, financial situations, how they were doing in school, or, if they were employed, how they were faring at their job. Even when his informants were off the streets (incarcerated, in a residential treatment program, etc.), Justin was willing to put in extra effort to maintain contact. For example, during the fieldwork period, Justin was observed both receiving and writing several letters to Shelly while she was in drug treatment. In the case of an informant named Tammy, an overweight, pale-skinned prostitute in her early twenties, Justin was seen calling her parole officer on several occasions, attempting to smooth over some minor situation she encountered with her supervision. One day, after hanging up from a call with Tammy's parole officer, Justin explained: "I just hope he will give her a break. She really is trying, and I just want him to know that." It was clear he was motivated by genuine feelings, not just a desire to keep their working relationship intact.

At times, Justin's generosity and big heart led him to get hurt by his informants. While he outwardly staunchly denied it, he clearly felt hurt when Shelly disappeared a few weeks after coming out of an in-patient drug treatment facility and was ultimately found in a crack house. Similarly, when Tammy violated her parole one too many times and was sent back to prison, Justin's demeanor and mood clearly darkened for a couple of days. However, true to his personality, he did not give up on Shelly or Tammy, and he continued to maintain contact with them in spite of their transgressions. These women's failures were seen as the women failing themselves and failing their primary supporter, Justin. Although no one in the unit would say it in front of him, behind his back Justin was known as, in Skye's words, "a softy. He's really just a big damn teddy bear."

Justin was not the only officer we encountered who approached his informants in a parental and supportive way. Skye knew her informants' interests and actively sought out opportunities and support services for them. Both Justin and Skye spoke in authoritative yet supportive ways to their informants, treating them with respect and care yet clearly taking the role of the caregiver and responsible adult.

The idea of knowing one's confidential informants on a personal level can also be important for knowing how to best motivate and reward them. Ranger, who spent ten years on the street doing both patrol and undercover work in one of the nation's ten largest cities, recalled that, when working with informants, he often remunerated informants in other ways than with money or leniency on charges:

> A lot of times, it would be like, "Help my family out." You know, so, "My mom is about to get her check, but her benefits are about to get cut. What can you do for us?" Or the state got involved with their [an informant's] kids, and you go to bat for them when it was feasible.... So it was sometimes the "what can you do for my family" kind of thing. Or, "My brother's in prison, and he comes up before the parole board in a year. What can you do to try to grease the skids on that?" So those kinds of things were quite common.

Central City investigator Alonzo describes his personal, as opposed to financially driven, approach to informant motivation in the following story that begins with him reflecting on how he turned two entrepreneurial informants (drug dealers seeking to stamp out their competition) into long-term police sources:

> We [initially] established a relationship because they [the informants] wanted to get him [a competitor drug dealer] out of the area. He was taking a third of the market share and was vying to take even more than that. To this day, we're still cool when I see them [the informants] in the street. It didn't really go on paper with what they told me; they more or less produced the witnesses for me. You know, the homeless or the indigenous people of the area, they set the cases up for me. That benefits them; I'm not giving them anything for that or Crime Stoppers money. The kind of guys that I'm working with, that's not what they're looking for. It's a trust thing.... To me, that's a good informant. I don't want the kind you give money to.... I don't ever want anybody to tell where they did it for money. With narcotics [investigators], I never understood why we give them all of that fucking money, especially a percentage from the seizure on the eventual warrant we would serve. I would say, "I don't like giving them money because they're going to start kicking balls on the fairway and give us some bullshit to deal with." So I made up my mind when I came to homicide—what, going on fourteen years now—I said, I just want my gig to be different. I said, the stories I hear in the streets in terms of me never doing people wrong and just getting the information and so on, that's the informant to me. People in the street know me.

For others, the idea of relating to informants or becoming friends with them was seen as too strong of a way to view an informant relationship. Julius, a seasoned federal investigator currently in a supervisory position, had a different view of taking a friendly approach with informants. He described the ways that the "friendship" part of an investigator-informant relationship could be both beneficial and tolerable for both parties:

I think there is some personality there. Informants are the same way we are; they don't trust the police, so you have to be able to build that trust relationship. And, you know, as weird as it sounds, because you know you're dealing with someone that you don't want to go to dinner with or be your buddy, but there has to be a level of, you know, maybe just say being cordial. But there has to be some trust too, not really a friendship, but it's got to feel that way. So we can talk about anything, and what you say is going to stay with me—other people aren't going to know about it. I'm going to protect your identity, and you know, they've got to feel that they're speaking to you. I think that's probably more important than you being able to take the information and do something with it—it's getting to the information to begin with.

Previous scholars (Pogrebin and Poole 1993) have argued that officers will sometimes develop very positive emotional feelings for some informants. In some instances, officers may see personal similarities with an informant and may develop a quasi-friendship with particular informants. These sorts of relationships would be positioned somewhere in the middle of the continuum depicted in figure 3, under the heading "Shallow personal relationships." For instance, on several occasions, Central City investigator Miller was observed asking informants about the health of their relatives or how their employment efforts were going. Miller was a very talkative guy by nature and found it easy to make small talk with people, even if he shared little with them in terms of personal background or life experiences. Manny, a seasoned federal investigator, acknowledged that, although at the core he viewed informants as tools, he also recognized that the cultivation of a personal relationship with informants, especially one that would provide a regular and reliable flow of information, necessitated caring and attentive interactions. Manny did not hesitate to pull ten bucks from his wallet for an informant, so long as they were providing information in return.

Others, such as Orlando and Kareem, argued that it was necessary to have at least some form of meaningful personal connection between an informant and a handling officer in order for the relationship to be a productive one. This could be as small as helping an informant out with mundane or very small aspects of life, such as providing bus fare or listening to personal stories or problems. In this middle-ground approach, officers asserted that it was important to invest time and effort in getting to know (potential) informants, and not simply so as to find their vulnerabilities for exploitation. Kareem summarized this strategy:

So you have to spend that time getting to know them as a person before you really ask them for their business. Otherwise, it's just going to be a business relationship with not much rapport. . . . So it's about connecting with them in some kind of way. You know, finding out where they're from and all that kind of stuff. You know, showing them that you have some concern, because deep down everybody wants at least that. I always do that beforehand. They want to know that someone actually cares about whether they do well or do bad. . . . [A good officer is one who] understands that, even though you're dealing with a guy or a girl who could be a potential criminal, they're a person first. So the more humble you are, the easier it will be for you to get to that rapport cycle, and the easier it will be for you to listen to them on things they know about.

Similarly, Orlando cautioned against getting into anything close to a personal relationship with an informant but also advocated that all law enforcement officers need to "treat them [informants] as humans." Respectful and professional, or as others have referred to it, "business-like," interactions are what are perceived as most beneficial. Orlando elaborated on this:

An officer that talks down to them, looks down on them, and treats them like shit—an informant is not going to respond to that, and that's where you get yourself where they don't want to talk to you to get valuable information. . . . They're looking at this officer like, "I don't want to do shit for him, but I know I don't want to go to jail for five years." So it's like two evils: "I'm going to do this because I don't want to go to jail, but this son of a bitch ain't getting nothing out of me after I get through doing this."

The common wisdom among these officers was that it is simply dangerous to get too close to an informant. To do so may compromise the power differential in the relationship and may lead an officer to take shortcuts, fail to verify information obtained from an informant, or in some other way not do all that he or she knows is right, proper, and necessary in such situations. As Miller reflected, "you start to build a little too much trust in them and trust them too much, and that can be dangerous. And then, a lot of times, that's going to come back and bite you." Many officers considered it to be dangerous and inappropriate to let informants know about an investigator's life or interests or to give informants information about a case.

Most officers, however, said that they actively worked to maintain a personal distance from their informants and strongly maintained that it was important both personally and professionally to do so. These individuals would be positioned on the right side of the continuum shown in figure 3 above, as they pursued impersonal business relationships with the informants with whom they engaged in the police-citizen information exchange. Shawn explained this as follows:

> You're not just going to eat lunch with them every day and have no purpose or meaning for the lunch other than the fact that you've built a relationship with this guy and you want to go have lunch with him. If you're going to lunch to talk about some cases, go for it. But you have some liabilities there if you start to befriend them and becoming really good friends and pals or whatever with these guys because, remember, they're bad guys, they're criminals. They're going to exploit you the best they can, and they might be trying to befriend you and, the next thing you know, they're turning on you, making false complaints. Then your job is in jeopardy. So you have to draw the line somewhere and say "Okay, you're going to build a relationship with them, but is this going too far, and is there going to be a liability?" The way I tell my guys is, okay, to look at them as a professional property. I mean, you use them in a professional manner, and they're a tool to do your job.

Looking at informants as a resource, as a form of property, or as tools rather than necessarily as people is common and was at the core of much of the advice that experienced officers offered about informants. Pedro explained his view of informants:

> You never build that friendship, and they are never your friend. It is always a business relationship, right? You're never going to call me on my personal phone, and you're never going to show up at my house. I mean, it's very business-like throughout the whole way. Anytime you see police officers or agents in in trouble with CIs, they've crossed that line somewhere there.... You know you're not standing around talking shit; I'm not asking about his three-year-old kid. That's in the beginning stages. When you start to sign up a CI, you want to get to know that person as much as you can and ask them questions, because there are motivation things. I know if a guy's got a sick two-year-old that he's struggling to find the money for treatment, I know that's his motive. I can exploit that if I have to. But, again, there is no friendship, it's a professional relationship.

Lucky, George, and Mickey were extreme examples of officers at the far right of the continuum in figure 3 (i.e., those who prefer cold business relationships). They knew essentially nothing about their informants beyond their names, criminal histories, and how to contact them. For example, Mickey's relationship with Betty consisted of nothing unrelated to Betty's required drug purchases or the charges Mickey held over her head. Mickey's lack of knowledge about Betty and his discomfort being around her was evidenced one day when she was called to the precinct to meet with Mickey (and the rest of the unit) to go over plans for a drug buy he wanted her to make the next day. When Betty arrived at the office, several unit members were not yet at the office, and Betty, Mickey, George, and the researcher were sitting in the unit's office, chatting and waiting for the others to arrive. After less than five minutes, Mickey had run out of small talk with Betty and was talking about restaurants and movies with George, basically ignoring Betty. After about fifteen minutes, Betty asked Mickey if she could smoke, and Mickey asked the researcher to take her outside, telling them to "just hang out until Sarge and the others arrive." With nothing to talk about with Betty, Mickey was clearly uncomfortable in interacting with her. Whereas most officers made efforts to spend at least some time with their informants individually, Mickey did not. He explained: "I don't have anything in common with them; I don't know them. I don't know what to talk about with her."

Among the River City officers, George, Mickey, and Lucky all thought that Justin was "out of his mind" because of the way that he interacted with his informants. Asked about these concerns among his coworkers, Justin responded with statements such as, "They don't realize that these are just people," and, "If you treat people nice, you get a lot more from them." And, in fact, there were tangible professional payoffs for Justin. While not a common occurrence, on more than one occasion Justin got a call from or was flagged down on the street by one of his informants for a "just thought you might like to know" type of conversation. Some of these unsolicited tips led to successful investigations, while others were not considered worthy of pursuing, but in all instances, Justin expressed appreciation and either paid the informant on the spot or made a point of providing them with groceries, beer, or some other "present" shortly thereafter. Central City officer Alonzo, who also went out of his way to nurture close and lasting relationships with select informants, described having these sorts of unprovoked information exchanges as well. Below, Alonzo describes his long-term and fruitful relationship with a street prostitute:

> I had a prostitute, her name's Madison. She's helped me with about five murders. I have had a ten-year relationship with her. She's helped me with five murders; I solved three through her. Her resume is impeccable. . . . I was driving one day and she came up to the car. Turns out, the guy that did the killing the night before was on the porch across the street. And she jumped in the car. I used to give her like a dollar—that's all she wants. Like, I'll give her a

dollar because I know she's going to go up here and buy a soda until she turns a trick; I understand what's up with her. She pointed him [the shooter] out to me. So I said, "Damn!" So I told the lead detective at some point [to] get in touch with her, . . . "Here are the hours she works, the corner she works at night." He fucked it up . . . . I was like, "Dude, she's been sucking dick on the same corner for about fifteen years. I mean, what effort did you put into this shit?" So I go back out and get her, and she comes in and she testifies in court.

Authenticity and Strength of Relationships

Many officers could not be readily placed at a single location on the agent-informant relationship continuum depicted in figure 3. Instead, these officers could more aptly be described as relationship chameleons, as they varied their approach depending on the situation. For example, retired Central City narcotics detective Vic said that his method of interacting with informants varied depending on how and why the individuals came to be informants: "The guy that wants to make money, I use kid gloves with [him] because he can walk away anytime. If I had cases on you, I treated you like shit. You know, I would lie to them, I'd treat them like they were dogs because they knew that if they didn't work with me that they were going to prison." Vic held the power in the police-citizen information exchange, and he used that power without feeling any need to privilege the feelings or humanity of the informant. But he also recognized that a hard-line, aggressive approach would be counterproductive when dealing with informants over whom he did not hold the threat of prosecution and incarceration: "You gotta be more friendly and supportive of the ones that don't need your ass."

The salient point is that, anytime an officer interacts with an informant, regardless of his or her overarching orientation to officer-informant relationships, the interaction may or may not reflect the officer's true feelings about the informant or how the officer actually perceives the informant as a person, a resource, or someone meriting his or her time and attention. All officer-informant relationships can be either authentic or artificial, especially those that include nurturing and parental-like guidance and supervision on the part of the officer. As discussed above, Justin's relationship with his female informants was usually very nurturing, and they were authentic relationships in which Justin functioned as a pseudoparental figure. Interestingly, Justin was either the same age or several years younger than the female informants he worked with. The fact that Justin checked in on these women, gave them advice about and encouraged them to pursue pro-social and legitimate sector activities, and was simply there for them as a sounding board and emergency support system established him as the parental figure and the female informants as the children in their relationships. It was not just Justin's actions that reinforced these roles. The deferential and sometimes embarrassed ways that Tammy and Shelly would talk with Justin, particularly the thank you notes and polite updates on their activities that these women would send to Justin, were reminiscent of an adolescent or young adult child interacting with a parent.

River City investigator Skye also developed authentic nurturing relationships with some of her informants. Skye's approach to an authentic, nurturing relationship, however, was a bit different from Justin's approach. Skye provided emotional support to some of her informants, but she shied away from providing financial support to them or from intervening in their legal cases in any way other than what she initially negotiated. Several of Skye's informants were witnessed asking for her assistance with other officers or parole officers. In a few instances, she contacted one of her fellow officers to request a "favor," but only when she personally knew the officer involved and the incident was small (i.e., a citation for drinking in public or a loitering ticket). One of Skye's informants, Skeeter, an African American man approximately fifteen or twenty years older than Skye, seemed to enjoy conversing with her. When contacting him, she would acknowledge his desire for "normal" social interaction and spend five to ten minutes talking with him about his family, his activities, and general small talk topics. After speaking with Skeeter, Skye would always be quick to remind any others who were around that he was not to be taken lightly: "You have to remember who he is, though; he can be a bad motherfucker. That doesn't mean that you can't treat him with respect. It just makes things work easier. But on one level, I think he's a good person."

Other times, the supportive and nurturing relationships that officers tried to present to their informants were clearly artificial in a way that was fairly obviously to observers. The question of how these relationships were perceived by the informants is one that cannot be answered here, but observed interactions suggested that the informants did not necessarily realize that their relationships with their officers were completely artificial. In River City, both George and Mickey developed long-term working informant relationships that had a transparent artificial nature to them. George luckily fell into his relationship with Tiger, who developed into one of the most productive informants seen by anyone in the district in a long time. Tiger was an alcoholic who worked menial construction and miscellaneous labor jobs. He had previously worked as an informant for an officer in another district of the city, and in his relationship with George, he quickly proved himself reliable and valuable. Mickey developed Betty, an attractive single woman in her midtwenties, into an informant following her arrest for possession of crack, which she claimed to be transporting for her boyfriend. Tiger lived in a rundown apartment and had little money or material possessions. Betty lived in a nicer apartment, was a university student, worked a part-time job, and although her apartment did not have an abundance of furniture or other furnishings, she did have drawers full of lingerie and numerous sex toys in her apartment. It was rumored on the streets that she worked as an escort, although Mickey was never able to definitively confirm this. Interactions between George and Tiger and between Mickey and Betty were cordial and superficially friendly but did not go beyond discussions of work issues or immediate activities. As noted above, Mickey knew very little about Betty's life, and George also knew little about Tiger beyond his address and common hangouts (Tiger did not have a phone). The lack of interest and inquisitiveness of Mickey and George became apparent when they were witnessed learning simple and basic facts about their informants (such as where Tiger was working or what Betty was studying in school) from other flex unit members who would engage Betty and Tiger in casual conversations.

When Tiger was in the district offices to work on setting up a deal for George, it was common practice for George to excuse himself from Tiger's presence during downtimes (such as while waiting for a call back from a target) and ask others, including the author, "Can you stay with Tiger for a little bit?" Mickey spent more time in Betty's presence but tended not to interact with her or talk with her very much. If Betty initiated conversation, Mickey would allow her to talk, but he displayed to others that he did not listen when she talked (except for when the conversation was about work). While Betty was talking, Mikey turned his back to her, engaged in some form of paperwork, or did something on his computer. When she paused, he would frequently ask her a question without realizing she had just been talking about what he asked.

Both George and Mickey complained at length about Tiger, Betty, and their other informants. George would complain that Tiger was dirty and not very smart or that he talked too much (Tiger did fill time with his own conversation). Mickey seemed to enjoy making sexual comments about Betty and querying others about what they thought her sexual life was like. He also complained that Betty did not seem sufficiently interested in working with him; she was, however, working with him in an indentured role. Both Tiger and Betty continued to work with George and Mickey, and they never gave any indication that they realized they were viewed in a negative way. In fact, Tiger and Betty spoke of George and Mickey in positive ways, suggesting they liked their officers.

At other times, situations arose where one of the River City flex unit members did not want to or was not willing to work with a particular CI. Informants are valued and viewed as important to an officer, but only so long as they are providing the officer with fruitful intelligence on open investigations and/or generating leads on new cases. If an officer perceives an informant to be holding back information, telling "only part of the story," or conducting him- or herself in some other way that indicates a lack of reliability or trustworthiness, he or she is likely to be dropped from the officer's stable of informants. A variety of things will lead an officer to define either a current or prospective informant as unreliable and not worthy of use. The most common reasons that the officers in this study cited for defining an informant as unusable included failing to keep appointments for personal meetings or phone calls, showing up drunk or high, or getting involved in serious felonious activities. All of these factors were perceived as putting the officer into situations where the potential costs outweighed the potential benefits of working with the informant. When an informant was perceived to likely cost more than they were likely to benefit the officer (in terms of productivity, potentially blown deals, and/or taking too much time and energy to be managed), he or she was dropped as a paid or voluntary informant or simply processed into the system instead of being offered the chance to work off charges.

Like any relationship, the one between an officer and an informant is a two-way street. Just as officers can develop positive or negative feelings about informants, informants can develop positive or negative feelings about officers. Some informants exhibited very strong attractions to and bonds with particular officers and would simply refuse to work with or even be in the presence of other officers. Other informants developed very strong negative feelings about particular officers and, in extreme cases, simply refused to work with certain officers. Our fieldwork suggests that female informants often exhibited strong negative feeling toward female officers. The reason behind this pattern of female-to-female aversion and conflict was not consistently apparent, although at least some instances suggest that jealousy may have been the guiding force in such situations. Shelly, one of the informants with whom River City officer Justin had an authentic nurturing relationship, refused to work on any task or situation that involved Skye. Shelly made no pretense of her distain for Skye, and she did not hesitate to tell this to anyone willing to listen, including Skye herself: "I'm not working with that one; no way. That dyke gets on my nerves, and I won't do it." Referring to Skye, Shelly told Justin: "You know I'd do just about anything for you, but not that one. No way. I just can't, and I won't work with her." This situation would put Justin in a bit of a difficult position, as he and Skye were typically partners and almost all of their significant work was done as a team. Justin and Skye talked about the situation, and although Skye was offended by the treatment directed at her by Shelly, she acknowledged the importance of the deals that Shelly was setting up for Justin and graciously stepped back and took a minimal role (i.e., serving as back up and staying away from the physical areas where Shelly was) during work involving Shelly. Justin suggested that Shelly's attachment to him led her to see Skye as a threat to their relationship, despite the fact that Skye was open about being a lesbian. Shelly always made a point to mention her dislike of Skye: "Because she's a dyke, and I just don't like those types." Yet her actions suggested she was jealous and therefore did not trust Skye. The unit officers handled these situations professionally, although Shelly's strong stance did make interactions tense at times. However, the unit recognized the value of a good informant, and this guided the resolution to the situation.

An officer's informants, like his or her firearm, cellphone, and other standard-issue pieces of equipment, are respected as private and not to be intruded on. Interestingly, our fieldwork revealed that the value and private nature of informants superseded that of other equipment and possessions, including vehicles, handcuffs, flashlights, and even food some officers kept in their desks and vehicles. Driving another officer's vehicle (which doubled as his or her take-home vehicle) was common practice, whereas talking to another officer's informant without the managing officer involved was a major norm violation. Cars, handcuffs, and food could be easily replaced, but a good informant directly contributed to an officer's reputation and career progression (see chapter 7) and thus was not seen as being so easily replaced. Therefore, it not only was deemed impolite but simply was not tolerated to "mess with someone else's CI."

Regardless of the type of personal relationship that officers either do or do not develop with their various informants, they universally view their informants as both a tool to help them conduct their business and a valued piece of personal property. This was most definitely the approach of the officers in the agencies in which we conducted fieldwork. Each informant was viewed as a primary possession of one officer, and interactions with and use of the informant was restricted to that officer. The idea of intruding on another officer's or another agency's informant was reacted to strongly. Manny described this: "Poaching somebody else's informants, that's bad juju right there. If they're with your agency, and they're sitting right next to you, that's one thing. Yeah, but if you've got somebody that is documented for another agency, you kind of leave them alone. . . . It's territorial, unless you're given permission by that other person."

The unwritten but strictly adhered to rule about working with informants is that the officer who develops an informant is the only one who works with that informant. It is wholly that officer's choice as to if and how he or she deviates from this agreed-on doctrine. The fieldwork underlying this project put us in direct contact with dozens of officer-informant information exchanges (ranging from newly developed relationships to longstanding ones), and in all instances, the informant communicated either primarily or exclusively with only one officer. While other unit members occasionally interacted and talked briefly with some informants—especially when an informant came to the district office to meet with his or her contact officer or when the unit was working with an informant to plan a buy or other activity—these conversations and discussions took a backseat to any discussions or comments from the contact officer.

In River City, it was not unusual for an informant to simply show up at the district office to report that he or she had information about a transaction scheduled to transpire soon (usually that same day). If the informant's handling officer was not working, temporarily assigned elsewhere, or simply not available, the unit would thank the informant but tell them: "You know, we'd love to do that today, but without so-and-so here, we can't." On several occasions when Mickey was either testifying in court or on vacation, Betty came to the precinct and told the other unit members who came to greet her about a deal she knew of scheduled for that day. On at least two occasions, the upcoming transaction she reported was supposed to involve a significant quantity of drugs and money, yet without Mickey, the other unit officers immediately rejected the idea of working the cases.

A few investigators indicated that they were open to granting fellow officers restricted access to the privileged resources provided by their CIs.

However, they made it clear that they expected to control the situation and be centrally involved. In short, the investigators operationalized a one-way street where they decided if the prospect of information sharing was on the table and, if so, under what terms. Only the officer who worked with an informant contacted that informant. If the informant initiated contact with the unit, other officers only spoke with him or her to greet and direct him or her to the primary officer. Tiger was an informant who often simply showed up at the station. This was Tiger's only real way of communicating, as he did not have a telephone. It was not uncommon to see George give Tiger quarters and instruct him to hold on to them to use for calling George from a pay telephone. When Tiger walked into the station, he was recognized by the front desk clerk, who would immediately page George to come to the front desk and receive Tiger. If George was not in the station, another unit member would go up and talk with Tiger. On days when George was working but on the streets at the time Tiger showed up at the station, the greeting officer would quickly surmise if George needed to be paged (and usually he was). If George was off work, in training, in court, or for another reason not available, Tiger was told so by the greeting officer and sent away with instructions of when to check back. Even when the unit was working on a case with Tiger, such as setting up a buy or surveillance on a dealer Tiger was seeking to set up, George was the only person to talk with him in any detail. Sergeant Perez sometimes asked Tiger a question or two while planning an event, and one of the others occasionally asked for clarification of something Tiger said, but direct and longer verbal exchanges did not occur.

In River City, the exclusivity of informant relationships was most clearly demonstrated with Justin. In part because he had been in the River City flex unit the longest, and undoubtedly in part because of his outgoing, supportive, and easygoing personality, Justin had the largest collection of informants of the unit officers. Justin's relationship with his informants was also very different from that of the other officers. As discussed above, Justin had a very authentic, caring, and nurturing relationship with at least some of his informants and regularly maintained and initiated contact with them. When he would call or stop to pick up one of his informants, it was not necessarily to get investigative information. He often called or stopped to see his informants to check on how they were doing and to see if they needed anything. As a result, Justin's informants, especially the women, were very protective of him. When we met these typically poor women who smoked crack and either turned tricks or dealt in stolen property while staying with various friends (or strangers), they would make a point of telling us things like: "I really love Justin. He's not like those other cops. He's a good guy; he takes care of me." The personal relationship that many CIs perceive having with their handling officer is critical to their trust in the police, and the exclusivity of the relationship establishes the necessity of only the handling officer interacting with the CI. A cornerstone of the limited CI-sharing arrangement was the expectation that an informant's primary officer be present during the information exchanges and that a violation of any terms on the part of the fellow officer would result in permanent termination of CI-assisted collaboration. There was a clear "you burn me only once" mentality in this regard.

As a general rule, the officers we observed treated all but the most unreliable informants as special and valued entities. Mickey developed Betty as an informant after finding crack in her purse when she was pulled over as part of a traffic stop. From the very first time he talked to Betty outside of her car in the parking lot of the gas station where she was stopped to the point that he started setting up deals with her, Mickey handled all conversations and contacts with Betty. Mickey was the only officer who knew Betty's cellphone number and the one responsible for decisions about what to do with the information she provided. Betty, and all the information that she produced, was considered Mickey's property. Much like a piece of livestock or a pet, the officer who obtained an informant was the one who garnered all of the value and payoff from the informant.

Officers treated good informants similarly to a beloved piece of property that one takes precautions to protect and insure. Officers would watch over their informants to provide protection as well as to make sure they knew what the informants were doing, where they typically spent their time, with whom they associated, and what problems they encountered. While we observed instances when officers would loan out one of their informants for a specific case or consent to an informant meeting with a fellow unit member if they were unavailable during a timely information exchange, the vast majority of officers described informants as their "property."

It is important to appreciate that informants are almost always involved in social circles that are (at best) marginally legal and often populated with nontrusting persons who are primarily or exclusively interested in only their own well-being. Informants, then, are no different from most other individuals whose lives center on the streets; they face potential dangers consistently and contend with the unknown on a regular basis. As such, they tend to exhibit a strong allegiance to particular officers, who are often the only people on the force they trust. For example, Miller explained that, although he might encourage an informant to talk with a fellow officer in his absence, this would be highly unlikely to actually occur:

> You've got to remember that the informants are going to go with the people they know and trust—that's the one they're going to call. If I tell my informant I'm on vacation or something [and] to call you, they're not going to call you. They'll say, "Well, I'll wait until you get back, and we can talk." They're not going to call you. They don't know you. They don't trust you. Remember, it could be a life or death situation for them.

One responsibility for an officer who works with an informant is to protect the informant. Almost all informants are *confidential* informants, meaning that they should not be known as an informant to anyone outside of the immediate chain of command of the officer or unit with which they work. If an informant becomes known in the community as a snitch, he or she, along with his or her family, loved ones, property, and anything else with which he or she may be associated, could be in danger. Almost all of the officers encountered in this project endorsed the veracity of the saying, "Snitches get stitches." This is a widely believed fact not only among law enforcement officers but also among informants.

Because of the potential dangers faced by confidential informants, it is important for officers to strive to maintain the confidentiality of the identity of informants and to protect them from becoming known or suspected of being informants. Snitches are disdained, and community members are often very vocal about their animosity regarding snitches. Therefore, there is a well-recognized stigma associated with informing. Current events, urban myths, and in some communities, well-worn stories of retaliation against snitches emphasize the message that community members should not snitch. As a result, it is important for investigators managing informants to be aware of the dangers that may accompany the disclosure of an individual's status as a snitch. Central City investigator Miller stated that he was always aware of the need to insulate his informants, especially from being openly and formally labeled as informants: "You're always trying to figure out how to keep them [informants] out of court. That's always got to be in the back of your mind from the start, 'Okay, how are we going to keep him out of it?'"

However, as with most things, this is not the universal view or perspective of investigators. Some law enforcement officials see informants as disposable tools that are (theoretically) all but interchangeable. With such a view, the value of an individual informant is obviously reduced, and the accompanying responsibility reported by some officers to protect both the identity of the informants and those informants' safety is reduced or eliminated. Among the officers we observed and interviewed—although some officers expressed a more callous view of informants—the prevailing attitude was that officers could, should, and would go out of their way to protect their informants. Even if officers who kept their informants safe did not do so for the moral reason of protecting someone who was helping them out, they realized that doing so was a way to avoid more problems while also deriving the benefits of gathering information. Federal agent Mark, while discussing how other officers interacted with informants, lamented that, unfortunately, some law enforcement officers did not see a need to protect their informants and did not realize the multiple benefits of maintaining their informants and keeping them safe in the community:

> Other guys that are just hounding around and texting [informants] and are just not letting the source work. And, at the same time, they are really putting the source's safety at risk. Those are the ones of us not doing a very good job. To me, I don't want to get anybody killed. I've heard guys talk like they don't give a shit. But to me, I'm not going to be that guy. I don't care how skanky or what kind of dirt bag [the informant is], I'm not going to be the one to get them killed. I'm not going to have that on my head.

It is important to recall that most informants are individuals who were initially drawn into their roles as informants by being identified as criminals. Persons who are not sufficiently intertwined in criminal circles and contexts do not have capital within the police-citizen information exchange. Those individuals are processed through the judicial system and most likely sentenced (although lightly) for their offenses. However, individuals who possess knowledge of and/or access to larger criminal enterprises are welcomed into the police-citizen information exchange and offered the opportunity to avoid judicial processing by working as informants.

Strictness of Imposing Expectations on Informants

Most informants, and all who are developed as a result of being indentured, are explicitly expected to produce information, initiate underworld introductions, or complete other tasks (such as drug buys) for their managing officers. Not all informants maintain their interest in working with the police, and despite entering into an explicit agreement with an officer to "do X, Y, and Z in exchange for A and B," some informants drag their feet or try to back out of their agreements.

Informants apply a similar consistency and diligence to completing their negotiated terms of work as children apply to tasks assigned to them. Some informants will work fairly consistently and diligently so as to complete their commitment and be able to move on as quickly as possible, whereas others procrastinate and require officers to repeatedly remind them of their agreements. Some indentured informants simply never seem to get around to doing what they have agreed to do, and in the end, their handling officers either file formal charges against them or work with a prosecutor to get a case against them reinstated and moving through the courts. Officers seem to give individuals who agree to work as informants pretty broad leeway, however. Some indentured informants remain "active" while they "look for an opportunity" to produce actionable intelligence information for months or, in some cases, over a year. Not surprisingly, since among River City flex unit members he had by far the largest stable of active informants, Justin reported having several informants who had never worked for him but with whom he kept in contact so as to remind them that they still owed him. Regardless of the number of active indentured informants they had, all of the investigators we interviewed claimed that they maintained a running mental or written log of the how many deals each of their informants owed them in order to work off their charges.

While Justin and the researcher were driving around River City one day trying to track down an individual reported by some tips to be dealing crack, Justin pointed out a public housing community building: "See that building there, second one from the corner? That's where Willie lives." The researcher replied: "Willie? Who's he? I don't remember any Willie." Justin explained: "Ah, I got him—let's see—must be just over a year ago now. I got him over in the Sussex projects with about twenty rocks. He owes me three deals on that one. I should call him; he hasn't done anything for me yet." With that, Justin picked up his cellphone, looked up Willie's number in his set of 3-by-5-inch cards where he kept his informants' contact information, and talked to Willie for about five minutes. Justin reminded him that he was still on the hook for three deals and that Justin could still file charges against him and prosecute him. Willie claimed that he did not have any information and could not set up any deals. Still, Justin reminded him repeatedly (but politely) that he still was in debt to Justin. After hanging up the phone, he had a look of skepticism on his face: "He says he doesn't have anything now. I don't believe him; he's connected. He's gonna do me those deals though. We might stop back there later." However, as the day progressed, new tasks emerged, and Justin did not go back to Willie's apartment. In fact, over the remaining months of fieldwork conducted with the unit, Willie's name was never heard again.

Other officers were much less lenient with informants. They were explicit about their expectations and followed up with newly recruited informants soon after an initial deal was struck. George was perhaps the most diligent member of the River City flex unit when it came to following up with indentured informants. He would repeatedly call them, search for them in the community, and on finding them, more or less threaten them by saying that he would move forward with filing charges against them if they did not come through with valuable information quickly.

In most instances in which indentured informants who had agreed to provide information or make buys from other sellers did not follow through with their promises to call or come to the precinct offices, the officers who made the original arrests would go forward and file official charges against the individuals. However, the officer would not usually do so until between one and three months had passed without some sort of serious follow through on the part of the informant. In one case, George moved forward with charges after a low-level drug seller failed to follow through on his initial promise to come forward with information. Although George claimed he was disappointed and did not want to do this, he said: "Fuck 'em. They had their chance. I've given them all kinds of time, and they just decided they'd rather go to court and go to jail. I can't help them. They had their chance." Even when a newly recruited indentured informant completed some, but not all, of their agreed-on tasks, officers sometimes moved forward and filed for a direct indictment. In these cases, officers reported feeling "used" and "burned," and they exhibited no reservations about moving forward with the indictments, believing that these individuals had "asked for it."

During a normal day with little going on in River City, Justin received a call on his cellphone from Rodney, a man he had arrested several months prior on minor charges. When he arrested Rodney, Justin had made initial overtures to him about the possibility of working off his charges, but Rodney was not interested because his charges were quite minor. Therefore, Justin was surprised to hear from Rodney but nonetheless agreed to meet him. Together, Justin, George, Lucky, and the researcher met with Rodney in the parking lot of a fast food restaurant. Rodney greeted Justin enthusiastically and tried to hug him, and it was immediately clear to anyone watching that he was drunk. Rodney explained that he had a court appearance scheduled for the next morning on a drug possession charge: "I just can't go in there again," he said. "So how's about I make a buy for you tonight?" Justin refused due to the fact that that Rodney was drunk. Rodney initially denied being drunk but, after several minutes, admitted it: "I've had a couple of drinks because I'm so worried about court tomorrow." Justin stood fast on his refusal to work with Rodney that night but told him: "Give me a call next week; we can probably do something then." Rodney was not happy and was still calling after Justin as we drove away. Not surprising to Justin or anyone else, Rodney never did call back.

The above instances reinforce that detectives follow both formal and informal rules when engaging potential informants. Formal rules apply to the legal and departmental policies that govern these relationships. Informal rules, on the other hand, apply to how the investigator chooses to guide those interactions in such a way that maximizes the quality and quantity of actionable information that comes from them and helps produce the most consistent and manageable dynamic between the players involved in the equation.

HONESTY, CRIME, AND THE PROTECTION OF CONFIDENTIAL INFORMANTS

One of the most important aspects of a successful officer-informant relationship is that the officer be honest with the informant about the potential outcomes of the information exchange. While it might seem tempting for an officer to promise an informant anything they desire and then disappoint them when such promises cannot be kept, this approach is likely to lead to that informer never trusting the officer again and, at least in some instances, contribute to a reputation on the street that the officer is untrustworthy. Others writing to provide advice to officers working with informants are adamant about the importance of dealing with informants in an honest manner (Alvarez 1993). While an officer could certainly make promises to an informant, get the information needed to solve his or her case, and then tell the informant, "Too bad; what I promised you is not going to come through," this approach would work for only a very short period of time. Different informants often belong to the same or overlapping social circles, and rumors about any officer's reputation for dishonesty are sure to spread quickly. While a good reputation can also be established through word of mouth, negative information always seems to spread more rapidly and be more convincing.

Treating others in a respectful and decent manner is the golden rule that parents strive to instill in their children and one of the basic building blocks for the establishment of any productive and smoothly functioning relationship, and it is also deemed critical that officers treat their informants in this way (see Motto and June 2000). This holds true regardless of what an individual officer may think or feel about a particular informant. Very promising informants can easily be lost because of something they overhear on the street or in the precinct house or the way they interpret something an officer says or does in their presence. As Carmine Motto and Dale June state, "officers should handle informants with respect and refrain from using . . . derogatory descriptions" (2000, 54). Informants are people, with feelings and a sense of pride, and they are often suspicious of police officers to begin with. If and when they feel that they are being denigrated or made fun of, distrust arises, and they are likely to seek some way to retaliate to maintain their sense of dignity and pride. This may mean refusing to cooperate any further with the police, providing false or misleading information, or in extreme situations, even providing information that could lead officers into seriously dangerous situations.

While it is important to appear respectful, honest, and interested in the informant, most investigators tend to see such persons as flawed, inferior, and at best, of questionable moral character. Investigators sometimes refer to informants as "snitches," "bitches," or "scumbags" behind their backs. Investigators also commonly believe that they are using informants and that the position of the informant is likely an uncomfortable one. However, officers are primarily concerned with demanding that tasks be done, information be collected, and contacts be made with others. More than once, investigators pragmatically expressed some version of the following: "It's a tough spot they're in, but they got *themselves* in it, so it's not my problem."

Although, on the surface, it may appear that the power in the officer-citizen information exchange is tilted in favor of the officers, in reality, informants possess the information, contacts, and social capital that officers need to access in order to be successful. Even in instances in which indentured informants who are working off charges choose to stop cooperating, they still control the relationship. Even when the consequence of pulling out of a deal is being "sent into the system," the informant holds the greater power in the relationship. Being arrested and booked into jail is not the end of the world and, many times, not even necessarily a very significant event for many individuals who work as informants. Few of these individuals are newcomers to the constraints of the criminal justice system. While going to jail may be undesirable for these persons, it may be less undesirable than other options, including feeling that they are being disrespected and "used" by law enforcement officers.

In order for informants to be truly valuable and be able to move within their day-to-day social world seeing and knowing of criminal activities, they sometimes need to either engage in some degree of illegal activities themselves or take advantage of opportunities to engage in illegal opportunities. For some informants, working with the police means that they know they are protected as they engage in small-scale drug, theft, prostitution, or other illegal activities because they cannot be arrested, as this would remove them from the streets and from access to the information and knowledge their managing officers want and need from them.

In other instances, at least according to some officers, it may be important to work with an offender—whether as an informant or not—in ways other than arresting them in order to facilitate gaining information about other (presumably larger and more important) criminal activities. Although speaking about offenders in general, Woods, a former patrol officer who, at the time of our fieldwork, was working as a violent crimes investigator in Central City, said that he often prefers to work with people to resolve their disputes or problems because there are a number of ways this approach can benefit him in the future, only one of which is learning of information about criminal activities:

> If I can cut them a break, they might trust me to give me some information next time or, you know, help me out if I am ever getting my ass whooped or something, they might actually be apt to pull somebody off me or whatever. But if they are just getting sent to jail left or right, they don't feel like we are even listening to them when we take them to jail. They are not as apt to trust us and they're not going to feel like they can work with us. Talking to the low-level users might give us information on the dope boys and stuff. If we are constantly locking those people up, not cutting them breaks, they're not going to talk to us. They are going to say, "Alright, you go ahead and lock me up for my possession. I'll be out in a couple of days, and I'll be on my way." They don't feel any need to work with us either if we keep locking them up.

There were obvious instances of some officers we encountered in our fieldwork ignoring or overlooking their informants' criminal activities. Even

though some officers explicitly and specifically knew that particular informants were engaging in particular illegal activities, they did not deem these
offenses as being significant enough to offset the value of the information the
informants provided. One of Justin's primary informants, Tammy, was frequently seen by River City officers on the streets prostituting herself. In such
instances, both the flex unit officers and, for the most part, the patrol officers
(who knew that Tammy was Justin's informant due to Tammy having told
them so) would simply either ignore her or tell her to move to a less visible
location. When Justin saw Tammy out working, he would make a point of
either driving by where she was standing or slowly walking, or parking near
her location in a conspicuous place where he knew she would see him. This
almost always led Tammy to either move to a different (and less obvious)
location or head home. When other flex unit officers saw Tammy, they would
pass along to Justin when and where they saw her, "just so Justin knows
where to find her if he's looking for her." Even though Tammy was seen getting into cars pulling up to her, riding with men up and down alleys, and
getting out of cars in alleys, she was never subject to arrest or citation. Tammy
was a very good entrepreneurial informant and was eager to work for Justin
whenever she could. In fact, not only was Tammy almost always available and
eager to work for Justin (usually by making drug buys) but she also would call
him at least once a week: "[I wanted to] see if you've got anything for me. You
know, anything I can do to help out." In short, Tammy was a well-known
prostitute, but she was largely permitted to work whenever and wherever she
wanted so long as she continued to provide information and was willing to
make drug purchases when requested.

This is not to suggest, however, that the River City flex unit officers truly
trusted or held their informants in high regard. As others (Levine 2009;
Pogrebin and Poole 1993) have previously reported, informants should not be
trusted, and although some officers developed friendly, personal, and authentic relationships with their informants, the fact that the informants were
"different" from the officers and were really just whores/thieves/thugs at the
core remained central in officers' minds. Occasionally, informants promised
information and then did not come through with it, or they claimed to have
been shorted by drug dealers or had some other explanation for why they
came back from a drug buy with no drugs and no money. Brenda, a gaunt,
bleach-blond, middle-aged woman with only about two-thirds of her teeth
remaining, was one of Justin's indentured informants. One day, after being
sent to a particular address to buy crack but coming back nearly fifteen

minutes after the time she was expected to, Brenda explained: "Justin, you know how it is on the street. I was goin' up there, and I run into that guy I told you about who's been hassling me for the money I owe him. I didn't know what to do. I don't trust him, and he's been getting' pretty demanding. So I had to give it to him. I didn't want to, I really didn't, but I had to. So if you'll give me some more money, I'll go back and I'll get the buy this time—I will. You know you can trust me." Justin simply told Brenda: "Nah, I understand. These things happen sometimes. I know that. We're done for today, Brenda. Go home." Losing the buy money was a cost of doing the job. Justin had to answer to Sergeant Perez for the loss of the money, but there were not any significant repercussions. It was an accepted fact that informants ripped off everyone in the unit at one time or another. It was simply treated as a cost of doing business with them.

There was a widespread sentiment among the officers in this study that informants should always be treated as potential threats to unit security. In short, it was assumed that anything they saw or overhead about police operations could be leaked to other offenders and that this could seriously compromise the success of law enforcement activities. Motto and June advise:

> You have to be very careful about telling an informant about any case. Whether you trust him or not, you should not give him information unless it is important that he know this information to successfully work the case. He should be informed only on a need to know basis and only when the time is appropriate. To give him any additional information serves no purpose other than to make him knowledgeable and put him in a position to bargain, perhaps with the other side (2000, 164).

Furthermore, it was commonly assumed that any information given to an informant could and would find a way to come back and "bite" the agent. It was not that informants should not have access to any information, but that giving information on a "need to know" basis was a best practice.

The major thing that an informant needs to be protected from is becoming known in the community as an informant. The primary responsibility for this, of course, falls on the informant. But the managing officer and the entire law enforcement agency with which the informant is working also take part of this responsibility. Confidentiality regarding informants' identities (as well as their roles, relationships, and other information) is the responsibility of all law enforcement officials but most of all of the informant's managing officer.

The vast majority of informants realize that, in the community, being labeled a snitch is highly stigmatizing and can very likely lead to violence, threats, and at the very least, ostracism. To be known as a police informer is to lose any trust others in the community may have in one and to lose many, if not most of, one's social contacts. It is especially likely that an individual who is known or even suspected to be an informer will lose access to illegal goods and services (including drugs) and social circles and events (including persons engaged in criminal activity). A number of potential negative consequences for the individual can arise from being labeled as an informer. Perhaps most importantly and most obviously, informants can be subject to physical danger. While discussing the experiences of "regular" community members, Duffy noted: "If they [Central City drug dealers] feel that you are snitching or talking to the police too much, you will be intimidated. You're gonna have people walk past you and say things because you have the individuals that are on the streets who will tell, and they will be out in public and tell. And then you find later on that something has happened to them. So yeah, there are a lot of threats out there. That's just how the community is." Note how the assumption is that of course this is how drug dealers operate, and of course individuals known or suspected to be "talking to the police *too much*" (emphasis added) will be harassed or attacked.

In many communities, residents' fears of retaliation for being labeled as a snitch are considered very real by both law enforcement officers and community members. Invariably, communities are replete with stories of dire consequences faced by informants who were subject to retaliation for their betrayals of the street code. As a result, many community members prefer, not surprisingly, to avoid any actions or activities that might be perceived by others (whether drug dealers themselves or anyone who might pass such information on to drug dealers) as "talking to the police too much." This reluctance, based in valid fear, was explained by Central City's Investigator White:

No one ever wants to get involved. . . . They want to be uncooperative; they just don't want to get involved. . . . 'Cause they figure that, if it is somebody fighting, that person might have a knife or a gun. And one thing about stuff happening here—it never stays a secret for long. They know who ratted them out within a day or two, and then they worry about it. It's easier, and I think they look at it as safer just to not get involved. . . . They're just trying to look out for number one. I mean, if they help us, what are they going to get from us? A pat on the back, a "thanks a lot," maybe a get out of jail free card in the future. If they rat someone out or are perceived to have done so, they might get shot or stabbed, or their house might get broken into, or you know, whatever, their car gets vandalized. . . . If they do a little cost-benefit analysis, they make the right decision for them.

Similarly, another Central City officer, Investigator Greene, related a story about drug dealers actively working to obfuscate opportunities for community residents to communicate with the police and provide information about drug dealers' activities. As this seven-year veteran female investigator recounted, at one time, she and others would attend church in the neighborhood so as to provide a cover and opportunity for "good" residents to have access to the police:

> But even the people in church who wanted to use the church for that reason just won't talk. "You won't even know that we're there. We'll come in dressed out, won't even look like police." They're like, "No," 'cause the drug dealers have already come there on a Sunday during a service and threatened them. So now they're afraid. . . . They don't even want to give the impression that they're helping the police.

The police also have a vested interest in protecting active informants, as well as invested and involved community members, from exposure. This is not necessarily an easy task, and according to many officers, protection is not necessarily something that can be guaranteed. Community members live in their local communities, and they see, interact with, and are in the presence of drug dealers in their communities every single day. As such, they are vulnerable. Officers know this, but they are limited in how and how much they can protect individuals. As Central City homicide detective Duffy noted:

> What kind of protection do we have for them? I mean, you know, we are not able to live with them twenty-four seven. I mean, we are a twenty-four seven operation, but we cannot be at your doorstep twenty-four seven, and we can't be in one area twenty-four seven. And they [drug dealers] know how many police we have coming to work every day. They know that, and they know about witness protection, but do they know anybody that ever went into witness protection? No. When they go to court to testify, do they feel safe? No. And they will tell you that.

When an officer's informant is exposed, it means losing the individual as a productive informer. When an informant is targeted for revenge by others in the community, it means that crime has occurred, which contributes to the negative organizational issues associated with increased crime and necessitates the investigation of an additional case. But perhaps the most harmful and longest-lasting consequence of an informant being exposed is that future attempts by that officer to turn other community members into informants may be more difficult. After all, if an officer failed to protect the identity of one informant, why should others expect to have a different outcome?

There are several means by which managing officers can enhance the protection of their informants, and we witnessed them all numerous times during our fieldwork. At their core, all of these methods center on avoiding any situation that might allow community members to associate the informant with any police officer. So as a foundational, cardinal rule, officers generally tried to avoid any and all direct contact with or acknowledgement of an informant in public. While it was true that some officers, especially those who had personal relationships with informants (e.g., Justin and Alonzo), did see and interact with these informants outside of the confines of the police department, these contacts were carried out only after the officers ensured that there were no or very few others present to witness the interaction. For example, Justin would often communicate his desire to meet with his informants by driving by them on the street and making sure they saw it was him. Most officers avoided directly calling their informants, as they never knew where the informant would be when the call came in, in whose company they would be in, or if there were any other circumstances that could make for an uncomfortable situation that the informant would need to explain. Instead of calling, officers would frequently search out their informants and make themselves visible to them, signaling to the informants the need to initiate contact with their officers.

While the officers observed in our fieldwork recognized the importance of not making contact in public and thus universally avoiding doing so, some informants needed to be reminded of this rule and why it is important. This was most clearly seen during times when informants were actively working with officers in the community. When an informant was scheduled to meet someone, make a buy, or do some other task, officers drove the informant to a spot at least several blocks from the general vicinity of the planned activity and instructed him or her to walk to the destination site. Some informants considered this a hardship and frequently complained. River City informant Shelly, for example, disliked that Justin would drop her off in an alley or behind a small shopping center five or more blocks from where she was going when she was scheduled to make a drug buy, although she said she understood why he did this. Shelly complained about the "long distance" of the walk, both to get to where she was supposed to go and to then turn around and come back. She begged Justin to drop her off just down the street from the dealers she was going to see, swearing: "No one will see me; no one will even notice. They'll just think you're a john dropping me off." But Justin would not agree, explaining to her, as he did nearly every time she worked for him, that, while he knew the walk was a burden for her, it was for her safety. To convince her of the importance of taking such a precaution, he asked her if it was really that much he was asking for from her, considering how much she cared about him.

In some cases, an informant would still be on the scene when officers followed up on a drug buy to arrest a seller. In these instances, the informant was treated just like every other person present. He or she was rounded up, detained, searched, and "arrested" along with everyone else. Alternatively, a plan might have been laid prior to the event that, when the police arrived, the informant was to run, and rather than chasing him or her, the police would put out a call over the radio describing the informant and asking for assistance in finding and stopping him or her. This would be a fake radio call, typically accomplished by the officer either not pressing the button on their radio or making the call over an unused and unmonitored channel. More often than not, however, if the informant was still on the scene, he or she would be processed just like all others present. Typically, the informant would either be issued a fake citation and then released or be cuffed and put in one of the unit's cars for transport to jail and then dropped off at or near his or her home. However, if the real offenders are being arrested and transported to jail, the managing officer cannot claim to be taking the informant there as well, as the actually arrested offender will see that the informant was never processed into jail and thereby likely become suspicious. The point, regardless of how it is actually carried out, is to instill in the minds of any and all onlookers that there is distance and no relationship between the informant and anyone from the police.

GETTING A FREE PASS ON FUTURE CRIMES

A common assumption among those who are not law enforcement officials is that individuals who work as confidential informants are provided a free pass on some, if not all, crimes that they commit while working with the police. Being able to offend unimpeded would be a great motivation and attraction for many criminals. If all a person needed to do to continue with his or her own illegal activities was to inform on other offenders, the trade-off would be very attractive. However, this is largely not the case. When informants do get the benefit of officers—either their handlers or others—looking the other way about informants' criminal activities, it tends to be for very minor offenses, and this occurs only if an officer can easily justify a greater good coming from his or her lack of intervention.

When queried about whether they allowed informants to offend with impunity, nearly all of the officers we interviewed and observed steadfastly insisted that they did not allow informants to continue with any serious criminal activity and that they would certainly intervene and arrest their own informants if they engaged in such activity. For some officers in some agencies, both policy and practice dictate that any known incident of criminal activity by a confidential informant will result in the informant being dropped and any and all benefits that the informant was accruing being canceled. In response to a question about whether he ever lets informants continue with any illegal activities, Central City narcotics investigator Shawn steadfastly insisted:

> If I find out one of my guys [informants] is buying or selling on the side or anything else on the side, he's gone, and they know that from the get-go. Don't let me find out. I know they're going to do it. I mean, they're perps. I know they're going to do it. But don't do it in my city. Don't let me find out about it. . . . Because he [an informant] knows from the get-go that if you commit any crimes and get caught, you're done. Cut off.

One of the most commonly encountered zero tolerance rules espoused by investigators who work with informants is the prohibition on criminal activity. This is not to say that all investigators believe that their entrepreneurial informants have reformed their ways or have suspended all illegal activities for the time period during which they work with the police. Shawn acknowledged this and was reconciled to the fact that many of his informants probably did continue with at least some criminal activity. Similarly, Kareem said that he insists that his entrepreneurial informants do not participate in any illegal activity beyond what he knows about and what is part of their investigation activities. He emphasizes to his informants that, if they do commit any crimes that he or anyone else becomes aware of, they will not get a free pass and will in fact be prosecuted. This could mean the loss of a case or evidence in an investigation, but Kareem said that enforcing the law is the highest priority: "They [informants] don't always stop the criminal behavior, and you can have an informant get locked up. You can even have an informant get killed because they're still involved in the streets, or they could just be a drug user and that could cause, you know, various issues because, if they're on some type of supervised release, that could mean that they have to go back to jail."

The belief that any informant essentially has immunity from arrest and prosecution is something that many officers are aware of and that some officers find detrimental to the public's view of law enforcement. Officers recognize that the "immunity for information" trade-off is a common myth, and most officers adamantly deny that such practices exist. Orlando explained: "No, that don't happen as much as people think it does. I think that an officer on the street might take heed of someone saying, 'Hey, I'm an informant.' But most good informants are not going to tell the officer that they're an informant. . . . It makes it hard when they start committing crimes, but I've not had any nuns as an informant either. But the fact is, unfortunately, you have to work with what you get." This attitude and approach are fairly common, especially among more experienced officers. Frank, who retired after thirty years in law enforcement, including five years as a member of the Central City vice unit, explained that he does not believe it is wise to intervene in a situation if an informant gets arrested or in trouble with another officer:

> I had a standard rule, and I would tell all of my cop friends in uniform divisions this: "If anyone tells you that they're my informant and that you shouldn't be locking them up because they are [Frank's] informant, lock them up. Because, unless it's me calling you and telling you that they're my informant, I probably haven't heard from them in a while." One of the pitfalls is trying to do things on the informal level, specifically dropping a charge without going through preclusion or losing evidence so that nothing happens. That's the old, old, old days, and they don't work nowadays.

However, other officers do admit to "helping out" when informants get into legal trouble or to trying to run interference on "small things" their informants may get involved in. Pedro explained that, while he does not make a practice of intervening if and when an informant is arrested or in trouble with any law enforcement officer, in reality: "It depends. If you [an informant] get pinched for drunk driving and it's not related to the homicide I'm investigating, I'm not going to go and get you off of a DUI. But does that really hurt me? No. Now, if he [an informant] goes in there and commits perjury on another similar case, I know I have no use for him." Central City investigator Miller explained what, in his experience, he has found to be the best approach: "If your informant went to jail for, say, a suspended license, you know you might be able to help them out a little bit if you go down and talk to the judge. But for felonies and stuff, no—not unless you have something big and so forth and the court is willing to work with it."

Others also explained that they would not necessarily jump to the defense and assistance of an informant in legal troubles but would remain in a position where they might be able to intervene at a later date. Some investigators felt that this approach provided them with the ability to maintain their non-involvement while also continuing to string along an informant with the promise of stepping in and intervening "later" or "at the right time." In this way, investigators gained the favor both of their colleagues (by not intervening in other officers' cases) and of their informants (by presenting an air of concern and suggesting the possibility of intervention). In some instances, some investigators would actually intervene on behalf of an informant, but when they did so, it tended to be later in the processing of a case, not at the time of or immediately following an arrest or citation. Sonny described the approach he takes when contacted by an informant who has been arrested:

> If the officer asks me if I know the guy, I will say I know them. Why would I lie? But the officer will also be told that he has to do what he has to do. The charges that need to be put on that person, he needs to charge those charges. Now, later on, we will see what happens, but at that point, the officer has all the rights in the world to arrest him if he needs to and to continue with his job and the process.

In the most direct way of anyone we encountered, Ranger admitted: "We will look the other way on a lot of misdemeanors. We've got a rule though that we will never look away on a felony, ever. Well, maybe some bullshit felony, but alright, yeah, we're not looking the other way on, like, homicide, robbery, aggravated assault, rape."

The idea of an informant getting a "free pass" to engage in criminal activities, then, seems to be more of a myth than a reality. While some officers will intervene on behalf of their informants (especially informants helping with very big cases) if they get into trouble with other law enforcement agents, these situations present officers with a balancing act in which they are challenged to please (or at least not displease) both their colleagues and their informants. To intervene on behalf of an informant can be costly for an officer. The costs are not necessarily financial or concrete but rather come in the form of becoming indebted to other officers. A trading of favors or being indebted to one's professional colleagues for some favorable or desired action is common in many professions and arenas of life, but for a law enforcement officer, going into debt when he or she realizes no concrete, personal payoff from doing so is a very big step.

Informants are generally not allowed free reign in regard to criminality, and when an officer does intervene on an informants' behalf, the officer is likely to be indebting him- or herself for a situation in which there is no promise of a positive payoff. Rather, an officer intervening for an informant is mortgaging his or her intended, hoped-for payoff. Without benefits accruing to the officer, interventions on behalf of informants should not be expected. However, identifying the range of benefits to be gained from such an intervention (beyond the obvious one of being assisted in stopping a known criminal) is a task that remains for both officers and observers. In the next chapter, we turn to these benefits of working with an informant.

SUMMARY

As we have seen throughout this chapter, the relationship between a law enforcement agent and an informant (or simple source of information) can take many forms, be structured in a variety of ways, and have differing consequences for the investigator, the investigation, and the informant. How an officer thinks about and interacts with an informant will establish expected patterns of communication and depth of information sharing, both of which can produce widely varying types of information and case outcomes for investigators.

One of the defining elements in an investigator's relationship with an informant is whether or not the investigator bothers to go through the appropriate bureaucratic and legal channels and tasks to register an informant with the agency. Some officers always adhere to this well-known policy, regardless of whether an informant wants to do so or not and regardless of whether doing so might introduce strain or obstacles to a relationship. But just as often, if not more frequently, officers will sidestep (or simply delay) the registration process so as to not scare off tentative potential informants. However, these individuals cannot technically be considered confidential informants and are rather, in the parlance and minds of investigators, referred to as "sources of information."

Once an officer has registered an informant (or made the decision not to do so), the informant's relationship with his or her managing officer can take a number of forms. For some informants, the experience is undoubtedly stressful, strained, and uncomfortable, and their indentured relationship with their officers is time consuming and dominant in their lives for a period of time. For others, the experience is only an occasional event and may be something that, with the passage of time, the informant will all but forget. In some instances, some officers, especially those who have a more laissez-faire approach to informant management and work in general, strike a deal with an individual to become an informant and then never (or rarely and only after an extended time period) actually work with the individual as an informant.

Some law enforcement officers see informants as "regular people" who "just had something go wrong in their lives" and believe that they should be approached and interacted with in a respectful, serious manner. In these cases, close personal relationships can emerge. Other officers feel there is no reason to see an informant as someone with whom they should interact personally or authentically or treat as anything more than a simple tool or piece of equipment. In these cases, the officer and informant have a cold, businesslike relationship. Still others choose a middle ground and develop shallow personal relationships with their informants in order to gain their trust and keep them providing quality intelligence. Officers who take the more humanistic approach to their informants tend to have informants for longer periods of time, get volunteered information from their informants, and have a more productive and less stressful experience with informants in general. In other words, those officers who approach their informants in this manner tend to have more positive and more productive informant relationships. These are the officers who are more likely to experience the many benefits of such a close personal relationship. It is the realization of benefits—especially the benefit of receiving information that leads to the clearance of an investigated criminal offense—that is the reason informants are cultivated and relied on. However, this is only the tip of the iceberg for investigators. As we will explore in chapter 7, there are numerous personal and professional benefits that can accrue from maintaining a good relationship with an informant.

SEVEN

Benefits of Working with Informants

There are numerous benefits for law enforcement investigators that follow from working with confidential informants. Some of the benefits are rather obvious, such as accessing information about clandestine criminal activity or uncovering evidence on open cases that can be used to tie up an investigation and effect an arrest. Other benefits may be less obvious but can serve equally, if not more, important roles to officers at certain times and in select situations. This is the case when an officer fosters a long-term, mutually respectful relationship with a neighborhood resident that, many years later, unexpectedly yields an unsolicited tip in a big case. As with all social activities and interactions, there are benefits that come to only some who are involved, and there are benefits that may not even be recognized or known as possibilities prior to their being realized.

In this chapter, we focus primarily on why police use confidential informants. Up to this point, we have used our fieldwork and interviews to explore what informants are, why they are interested or willing to work with the police, how officials recruit and work with informants, and where informants fit into the social scheme that guides the worldview and activities of law enforcement officers. We have argued that law enforcement agencies and their officers simultaneously value and marginalize individuals who function as informants, regardless of which avenue brought them to their informant role. Informants are viewed as useful tools of the workplace and, as we have seen, are more or less treated as equipment by most law enforcement officials. With the stresses and challenges of interacting and working with informants laid out, the question becomes, what is the payoff for officers expending the energy and focus necessary to manage a confidential informant? In this chapter, we move the discussion to what many may see as the most obvious question: why are officers and agencies so willing to cavort with members of the criminal subculture in order to bring to justice other members of that same subculture?

As we will see in this chapter, there are three primary areas of benefits that law enforcement officers report can be gained by working with informants. The first and most manifest purpose of working with an informant is to generate intelligence that will help solve open investigations or stimulate new ones, the end game of which is to remove specific offenders or groups of offenders from the community. But this is not the only benefit. A second benefit of working with informants is that it allows individual investigators as well as law enforcement in general to accrue the more long-term payoff of gaining a more informed understanding of community dynamics, the norms that underlie criminal and noncriminal behavior occurring in the community, and the nature of ever-evolving criminal enterprises. A third and similarly delayed benefit of working with informants is that it serves an important professional development and career advancement function within the organizational structure of the law enforcement community.

FACILITATING INVESTIGATIONS

The most obvious reason for an investigator to work with an informant is to facilitate the investigation process. The manifest purpose for informants to exist and for law enforcement to work with them is to gain intelligence—to learn about the who, what, where, when, and how of criminal activities, thus making the investigation process smoother and more efficient. Informants provide not only an additional set of eyes and ears on the ground, but because they are truly from inside the communities where the criminal activity actually occurs, they provide a different perspective for understanding the community, community members, norms, activity patterns, and so on. The fact that informants are truly *of* the community also means that they often provide a much easier and more efficient means of access into organizations, groups, and social circles, and sometimes, simply because of their presence, they are privy to information that would not normally be revealed in the presence of outsiders (such as police investigators). Sergeant Johnson, a seasoned Central City homicide supervisor, explained the basic value of working with informants:

The information is out there in the streets. You can't get people to trust the police, or they're afraid for retaliation from their own kind if they snitch. So you can't get the information that's out there on the street and, until it happens to their own or their own family or somebody that's really close to them, do they then understand they want somebody to help their family. But without them [informants], ... I mean, police don't solve crimes, communities solve crimes.

Informants provide a means of getting information from a group of people that may be reticent to provide information to outsiders. Informants, as people in and of a community, have an advantage in either eliciting information directly from people or being present while criminals openly engage in offenses or inadvertently or willingly disclose information about past crimes. Investigators who work to gather intelligence on their own (i.e., without the help of insiders) are likely to encounter communities where they are shut out, actively avoided, and/or purposely misled by community members. Woods, a veteran street-level narcotics and violent crime investigator from Central City, summarized his view on the importance of informants in many investigations by pointing to a group of neighborhood youth and making the following statement:

But, see, all of these people are from a particular area that is so tightly woven and tightly knit that they don't talk a lot, and ... nobody pimps each other out. It's bad to be a snitch, you know, and that's how they're brought up, and that's how they're taught, and that's how they are. So getting information from these folks is like pulling teeth. It's like having to literally hold somebody down and stand on their forehead and yank a tooth out with a pair of pliers. It's that hard.

Therefore, having someone who is truly from inside the community at an investigator's disposal can facilitate intelligence gathering and can accomplish more than the best trained, most experienced, hard-charging investigator may ever be able to accomplish on his or her own. Yet, while most investigators were willing to suggest that paid informants are highly valuable and important, they hesitated to name these entrepreneurial agents as pervasive in number or as a necessity for solving most cases. Mark, a street-level investigator with five years of experience on a metro police department followed by three years with a federal agency, commented: "I've probably closed 95 percent of my cases, 99 percent probably, without a paid informant. But I can guarantee you that 100 percent of those cases had at least someone in there supplying me a piece or two of information. You can't do it by yourself." Note that Mark puts emphasis on inside information but downplays money-for-information exchanges. It was a subtle but important pattern in the data that entrepreneurial informants were only one type of informant and that the other types discussed in chapter 3, namely civic-minded informants, police sources, and indentured informants, played a much more prominent—and frequently more respected—role in the overall accumulation of criminal intelligence.

That said, it is also important to acknowledge that investigations of crimes occurring in some communities and organizations may not be well suited for informant usage due to the tight-knit nature of the collective. Sometimes, the community, organization, or group in question is small and not conducive to being infiltrated by any new outside member for intelligence-gathering purposes. In other cases, community insiders are reluctant or unwilling to talk with law enforcement officials, regardless of the pressures or incentives being applied. While it is sometimes possible to recruit a reluctant informant from the existing members of such a community, doing so is highly challenging and difficult. If an investigator's attempts to recruit an informant from the existing group membership become known to the group, not only will the potential recruit likely be subject to reprisals but, moving forward, community members will be more attentive and alert to the possibility of someone else in the community being turned into an informant. Pedro, a twenty-year veteran of federal law enforcement, suggested that there are some communities or groups of people that, due to the small number of members and the intensity of their relationships, may not be penetrable by informants: "It is very difficult to get informants in small towns because, normally, the criminal element has such a stranglehold on that community that nobody is going to talk to you. So I can't use an informant there." Such situations are the exception, however, not the rule.

It is not only how tightly knit a community is that can inhibit or facilitate particular investigative approaches for cases. Sometimes, informants may be needed because law enforcement lacks "appropriate" people for making inroads to particular communities. In some instances, the characteristics and demographics of available law enforcement personnel may simply not be matched with the types of people that are at the center of an investigation. For example, some departments lack sufficient numbers of streetwise officers from the various racial and ethnic groups that comprise the majority of the criminal element within the community that constitutes their jurisdiction.

When there is an important divergence between the characteristics (especially the physical characteristics) of a community of focus and available law enforcement personnel, entrepreneurial or indentured informants can provide an important bridge over the gap. Kareem, explained this idea:

> There are certain field offices where we just don't have the personnel that represent where we're doing an investigation. So an Irish white guy may just not be able to go into a place, but someone who is from there and that area can penetrate it easy.... You know, for instance, there are segments of Boston where a white guy from New York couldn't necessarily easily penetrate South Boston, even if he's dealing with other white guys. Some, there are certain things that an informant could bring if they're already part of that culture. So that's the biggest advantage: they already know part of, or they've been part of, or they've just been around, the segment of people that you're trying to go after.

The use of informants is, of course, only one strategy and approach that an investigator will use to try to resolve a crime. Many times, informants provide the critical piece(s) of information for an investigation, but other times, they may be only a way to confirm information gathered via other means or simply serve as a pointer toward other intelligence. To say that investigators could not generate leads or close cases without the contributions of informants would be an overstatement, just like suggesting that we could not do our jobs without some key resource or tool (e.g., computer, cell phone, car). In short, informants improve the efficiency of most law enforcement work but are not essential to the criminal investigation process. Reflecting on his more than two decades of experience as a street-level officer in suburban Central City, Shawn surmised that, while he could do an effective job without the presence of any informants, it would be much more difficult:

> You could do it. It would be a little bit more difficult. You would have to get a little bit dirtier though. And by "dirty" I mean, you know, hitting the pavement more or get to know the bad guys more as opposed to letting the CIs do it.... It's not the fact that we can't do it or won't do it, it's the fact of work smarter not harder concept. Why do I need to go out there and get dirty when he's already dirty and can get me the information?

Similarly, Miller, a veteran of more than twenty years on the streets of Central City, believed that informants can be very useful but that they are not necessarily a necessity for solving crimes: "Informants do help. I mean, you're going to need them in detective work in drugs, narcotics, home invasions, robberies, burglaries, and all of those sorts of things. You're going to be able to solve, though—I don't know what percentage—but you're going to be able to solve some on your own. But certainly those informants are going to help."

An even stronger case for the immediate information-generating benefits of informants was made by Frank, a retired investigator with a lengthy history of work in narcotics. When asked what types of narcotics investigations would be best suited for using informants, he explained: "Every case is, and the level of involvement of the informant is what changes—their ability to take on risk, their fear, their involvement. . . . So it's not like every case will benefit from informants, but the level of informants is what changes and the level of involvement."

While informants can be useful in a wide range of types of investigations and can provide information on all types of crimes and criminals, they may be most useful in the realm of narcotics investigations. With narcotics investigations, the primary goal of investigators is usually to disrupt a clandestine criminal organization (sometimes sophisticated with several levels and sometimes small and relatively flat in its structure) and to destroy a social structure that provides drugs to a community. Moreover, vice crimes involve consensual criminal transactions between providers and consumers, where neither party sees him- or herself as an offender or victim. While an investigator may find it relatively easy to eliminate street-level dealers through simple surveillance, "street rips," or buy-bust operations, moving up the supply chain requires infiltrating an organization through protracted undercover work or gaining access through someone who is already infused in the organization—an informant. With other varieties of crimes (homicide, robbery, sex crimes, etc.), the goal of the police is typically to identify and apprehend a specific offender, not to disrupt a structured, organized entity. Therefore, while certainly valuable and useful in all varieties of criminal offenses, informants are especially valuable in addressing organized and victimless crime.

It is important to note, however, that for the detective, the lines are often blurred between the consensual victimless crimes and the traditional offender-victim type offenses that we associate with monikers such as violent crime and property crime. For example, Kareem, an investigator in a federal agency with a wide offense jurisdiction, noted the following:

Well, [cases] come in various formats. A lot of what happens with the guns and gangs is all of the guns, gangs, and drugs kind of run together. But we may start off doing a drug case, and it ends up being a drug and gun case. So usually, that combination brings a higher level of difficulty for the potential inform-ant, so we'll get some of them that way. So that way, if they are facing a more stringent [violent] charge, we'll tell them that we'll mention their cooperation and possibly reduce the charge—if there is any—to the US Attorney's office and for the US Attorney's office to give them whatever consideration they deem necessary or deem appropriate. After that, they can actually do some-thing in another arena [such as drugs or property crime] and generally tell us. And that's how informants are developed by way of them facing charges.

Learning about a community or a group of people via an informant is often a quicker, more time-efficient way to get information than through more traditional investigative techniques. Central City homicide investiga-tor Orlando summarized his valuing of informants as follows: "Informants know a lot quicker than police do about drug places and drug areas." Additionally, many times, investigations are conducted in neighborhoods and in social settings where law enforcement officers have little or no cultural competence or experience. In such situations, using someone from inside the community may be the best, if not only, way to gain access to certain indi-viduals, levels of organizations, or arenas of activities. So in the eyes of many investigators, good law enforcement involves constantly being vigilant with one's intelligence gathering in whatever way is productive (and legal). Referring to intelligence-gathering efforts, Frank, a retired officer with thirty years of metropolitan policing experience ranging from patrolman to the second highest rank in his department, noted:

It's not that there's an upside [to intelligence gathering], it's a given in police work. It's not an upside, it's a fact. If you're going to be a cop, a police officer, or investigator, you have to develop relationships with people where you keep them confidential. You want them to give you information, and it's a neces-sity. It's not negotiable like we talked about unless you want to be a police officer who is constantly only responding to events. If you intend to initiate investigations or develop leads that solve crimes, you've got to have the ability to create and manage and facilitate informants.

Similarly, federal agent Mark reacted very strongly when asked if using informants was really "real police work" and whether law enforcement could succeed without the existence of informants:

The guy who is actually doing his job is the one that talks to those people—sweet talks one of them, gets them to flip or agree to work with you for a couple of dollars. And they go and find the information somewhere you can't find it logistically. Because you're not welcome in the freaking ghetto at eleven o'clock at night. That's just not realistic. . . . I mean, there are neighborhoods in most cities that you can't roll up to—you just can't do it. So if that area just suddenly becomes completely off limits—off limits at times where you don't know what the fuck is going on there—[you need] the people in there. Really, the only way to find out all about it is with good sources. And if you get rid of that, those [neighborhoods] are suddenly going to become safe havens [for criminal activity]. I think you'll see more safe havens for very bad people pop up by taking that tool away from law enforcement.

Expanding further on this point, homicide investigator Orlando explained that informants can be highly valuable in some communities: "Are you going to go out there and get in the [criminal] organization? No, you ain't! No, you ain't! Are you going to be able to go out there and get that information you need to build up a search warrant? Are you going to be able to verify some of this stuff you're hearing [on the street]? No, you are not. So, yes, informants are necessary." However, investigators cannot rely solely on information provided by informants to solve cases. This type of information must be verified and corroborated. And usually, the information provided by an informant is only one piece of a set of necessary information for identifying and substantiating the who and how of a criminal act. As numerous law enforcement officers emphasized, and as we saw in the cases of nearly all informants we observed in our Central City and River City fieldwork, informants almost always provide just one or a few pieces of a puzzle or only one piece of information that contributes to the investigation of a case. Whereas popular assumptions and frequent media portrayals suggest that informants actually solve crimes and deliver a complete case to an investigator, such is the product of myths and gross exaggerations. Informants may comprise a big piece of the puzzle, but investigators noted that it is almost unheard of for a case to be built exclusively around the information provided by a single source. Federal agent Pedro articulated this idea most clearly: "Never have I had an informant come to me and say, 'Yeah, John committed the murder in the library with a candlestick.' Never do you get that, right? I mean, they may come to you and say, 'John owns a candlestick,' or, 'I saw John in the library.' Never do they give you everything together. It's just a piece of the puzzle."

Similarly, Central City retiree Frank related that his view has always been that informants provide officers with direction or suggestions of where to look and information that may be accessible only to those inside of a community: "So an informant might not solve a crime for you, [but] he might tell you that somebody showed up with a lot of money. So he didn't really tell you what crime they committed, he just told you they're flush this month, and you take that information and turn that into a criminal investigation. You can't think of informants as a choice. It's a choice of being effective or ineffective."

One underlying theme to nearly all of the discussions of how informants can benefit investigations is that informants go through the risks associated with providing information and/or access so that officers do not have to do so. In other words, informant use directly contributes to officer safety. If an informant is injured or killed while conducting their duties, it is a sad, frustrating, and paperwork-producing event for an investigator. But the investigator would be uninjured and alive. Few law enforcement officers at any level or type of agency mentioned this point explicitly. One of the few who did, Julius, whose work focuses on tracking down missing and wanted persons for a federal agency, claimed: "I think here's probably the biggest advantage I can think of: officer safety. You're not really putting yourself into that potentially volatile atmosphere. You know, if you've got someone that is maybe trusted within an organization, trusted within a neighborhood or a group, that is giving you information, then you're not putting an officer in undercover or otherwise exposing somebody to potentially being exposed." Informants not only provide information to law enforcement, but, by their presence and participation, they also actively contribute to the safety and well-being of individual law enforcement officers. This is harsh but true.

LEARNING ABOUT THE INTRICACIES OF COMMUNITIES

As an adjunct to facilitating investigations, working with informants provides the benefit of supplying investigators with knowledge about social networks in a community to which they would not otherwise be privy. The true benefit here is not necessarily information about a specific case that a particular informant works but rather an improvement in the long-term investigative capacities of the officer. One reason that informants are necessary is that some communities are closed and resistant to infiltration by outsiders, and learning about what is inside these communities can be a significant benefit for an investigator. Future investigations in and near these closed communities may benefit from investigators moving closer to gaining cultural competence of them. One way to develop such cultural competence is through learning from informants.

While driving through his old patrol beat, Alonzo, a homicide officer who had worked in the neighborhood ten years earlier, noted:

> I've used the friends-and-family approach more times than I can count because—let me tell you the truth—when we have a woman whose son gets killed, and the years go by, and you go out there and you find the killer, it's real. She's on the crack with cancer and AIDS and shit, and the DA's office is trying to get her to come in. I say, "I will go talk to her." I say, "Look, Boo. I remember when Little Ray Ray got shot in the forehead. We did all we could to get the killer, and we got him. He's gone [from the community]. It's your turn now, and if you want me to go out and tell everybody in the neighborhood you're with me, I will do that because it's just to me from homicide now." It's not even about having a fucking gun; that is the last tool you're going to use. Mine never comes out; I don't need it for what I do. I go down to these neighborhoods and get to know these people. Here's the thing, you don't have to be from a neighborhood to get these informants. What resonates more than anything is . . . See, this is my neighborhood we're in right now. I came out [here] in the summer of 1986. . . . This is where they sent me from eleven at night until seven in the morning. I stayed like that for ten years; it changed me. I was only twenty years old, and it changed me for the rest of my life because of those relationships. . . . I have good relationship[s] because I'm from [here]. . . . You've got to understand, I was twenty-one in this neighborhood in the eighties. It was New Jack City. You could date the girls in the projects then; I didn't know it was against the rules. . . . I'm taking her to fucking Godfather's Pizza. . . . Crime has changed so much that you can't just go in here having gone to college with your criminal justice degree or your master's in sociology—whatever the fuck these guys that come on have. They just don't have any people skills and everything that translates out here in the street. And it's really started to hurt the city. It's hurting all kinds of cities.

In the eyes of some investigators, one of the best benefits that a law enforcement officer can derive from working with an individual informant, or especially a set of informants, is learning about a community, including its residents, businesses, activities, and norms. By talking with and sometimes simply spending time with informants, Orlando said that he always felt as if he were investing in his future investigative capacities:

> You gain a lot more knowledge. I can't go and hang out in these neighborhoods, so if you got somebody that is hanging out, you're going to gain a lot

more information. I mean, to me, it's a big difference. . . . With informants, you get more knowledge of what's going on through an informant than you would having to go through all of the tiers of a group or community to get to where you want to go or get trusted to get in yourself.

This same idea extends not just to general knowledge about a community's people and structures but also to actual activities and behavioral norms in that community. As with any setting, when first entering into a new social world, we tend to bring with us our previous ways of doing things. Consider the typical American tourist in Europe. The vast majority of American tourists are instantly identifiable by their dress, how they act, how they speak, and how they simply go about a day's worth of activities. The same idea holds for a police officer newly entering a cultural world he is unfamiliar with. Shawn, a veteran suburban, street-level investigator, explained why he sees informants as especially beneficial: "We know how the bad guys work, but how do we learn how the bad guys work? It's through the use of confidential informants basically training us on how the bad guys do their stuff, and it changes all of the time. Bad guys change their tactics all of the time to stay ahead of us. So how are we going to know that if we don't talk to some of the bad guys?" Reiterating this view, federal agent Kareem explained that he feels one great benefit of working with informants is being taught how to act and simply be seen in a world that is new to him:

Say you're doing undercover with an informant, and you're driving your car. You come to a stop sign, and you don't fully stop before you turn the corner. And he nudges you and says, "Hey man, the way we do it around here is, you come to a complete stop and then you turn the corner. If you don't, people around here think you're the police." You know, so it's little things they observe from you like that. They might not wear jewelry. They may not wear a watch, or they might wear a watch a certain way. They don't necessarily carry their cell phone in a clip; it will be in their pockets. A good informant will tell you things like that.

Building on the idea of informants being able to educate officers about a community's structure, norms, and general information, federal agent Mark encouraged simply listening to informants and allowing them to offer up information that they believe is valuable to investigators. He observed that, while questioning is certainly appropriate and beneficial in such relationships, a great deal of (unanticipated) knowledge be learned from simply chatting with an informant:

A lot of times, the sources are going to know the neighborhood. They're going to know the whereabouts and know the people more than we're ever going to know. So if you continuously pound them with questions before they even finish what they're saying, that is foolish. You're going to get a lot more information by prompting them with an open-ended question, getting them to talk, and then eventually just guiding them here and there to the areas of interest that you need.

Because the members of different communities are involved in different activities to different degrees and the fact that cultural expectations can and will vary across communities, some criminal investigations will be more conducive to the use of informants. This does not simply mean that certain communities require an insider to collect information but rather that certain types of criminal activities occur within social contexts that are more amenable to intelligence gathering via informants. Specifically, when a hierarchical criminal organization is the focus of an investigation, and the goal of the investigation is to disrupt or dismantle such a structure, someone is needed on the inside of the organization above the entry-level set of roles. Kareem suggested which types of cases he believed were most likely to benefit from the use of informants:

> Gun and some drug cases, and here's why. There are some crimes that lend themselves to tight-knit communities, so an undercover agent can't just readily get in and penetrate those. And so we need to utilize an informant to do so. So those cases where the community network is tighter than generally, an informant would be in an ideal situation to actually gain access. The goal in most investigations that you are dealing with is to dismantle the organization, so the easiest way to do that is to penetrate as far as you can, dismantle from the inside.

Learning about a community benefits investigators not only by better situating them for future investigations but also by improving overall police-community relations. Informants can "teach" investigators about communities, help police remove offenders from communities, and provide an ongoing feedback loop to investigators regarding community sentiments, issues, evolving norms, and concerns related to crime, safety, and how policing is being conducted. Alonzo explained: "If people in a community believe they have access, if they think they have access, then when they have a voice, all of our results are [going to be] so much better."

There is also a potential reciprocal benefit for investigators who have good relationships with informants in a particular community. Although informants are not likely to identify themselves to other community members as such, they can reinforce positive views in the community of individual investigators. While recounting a story about working with an informant on one homicide case, Alonzo related that he also learned some information that benefitted him in a separate investigation: "I come to find out that those two guys knew people from other homicides that I dealt with, and my name recognition through them rang out as, 'Oh, he's cool; you can fuck with him.' So I cleaned up that homicide too, got me good witnesses, and to me, that's a good informant."

BENEFITS TO AN INVESTIGATOR'S CAREER

In addition to informants facilitating investigations and providing investigators with knowledge about particular communities, some investigators find that their own status and professional advancement are enhanced by their work with informants. This is because informants have a multifaceted impact on an officer's productivity. The repeated and fruitful use of informants can lead to an officer being seen as particularly active and valuable. Informants can provide officers with a quick way to generate a case and/or arrest, or with new lines of investigation that prove beneficial and may produce more intelligence than anticipated, or even open fresh cases. Such situations, give the investigator a reputation of being successful and of high quality, and this can set him or her up for promotion or transfers into highly sought-after assignments.

Informants can also provide a boost to an investigator who has been struggling with cases and not providing superiors with expected levels of productivity. This occurred in River City. George had been on what he called a "dry run" of cases for several weeks and was starting to feel depressed and frustrated at serving only in support roles for active investigations being led by fellow investigators Lucky and Justin. One day, George and Lucky were doing general surveillance in a neighborhood known for drugs and prostitution, and they performed a field interview with Tiger. In the course of the interview, Tiger mentioned some drug activity in the neighborhood. George saw an opportunity and began to question Tiger in more depth, eventually asking him if he thought he could make a buy at the house in question. After a short negotiation, Tiger agreed to do a series of buys over the next week in exchange for a cash payment. The buys led to a search warrant, arrests of three people, and seizure of a small amount of marijuana and prescription painkillers. George was very pleased to "be back in the saddle," and when he paid Tiger, he asked if he might have anything else. From this chance meeting, Tiger came to be an at least weekly informant who provided George with information that led to more than a dozen search warrants over a period of a few months.

As George's cases grew in number and significance, so too did his stature both in the unit and in the department. George was soon deemed a "high producer" and accordingly received benefits for his efforts, including more and better overtime details, positive considerations for requested time off, and public praise from his fellow unit members and supervisors. George was soon being mentioned as a likely candidate for promotion. In this case, Tiger provided George with the opportunities to shine in the eyes of his peers and superiors.

The fieldwork and interviews that shaped this book clearly demonstrated that officers afford an elevated status to their peers who are adept at nurturing and using informants to generate new cases and close old ones. This was captured in the words of Kareem, who worked extensively with other agents in his own agency as well as in numerous taskforces staffed by investigators from various metropolitan police departments: "Generally speaking, some of the most successful agents and officers in the streets have good informants, and it's not because they're lazy; it's because those people are already involved in the criminal element that you're seeking to penetrate, and that's what makes it beneficial to utilize them. So the more successful ones will have informants." Kareem associates informant usage with being a productive and proactive investigator, traits that are highly valued by other investigators. In short, investigators with a high acumen for informant usage are valuable members of a unit or taskforce, as they are an integral cog in the production of good cases and arrests.

Others also acknowledged that cases built on informants' contributions can professionally benefit individual officers. Ranger, reflecting on his more than a dozen years of experience in street-level narcotics work, admitted early in his interview: "I'd be lying to say that those cases did not bring a whole lot of prestige when you make a big bust and they make it big in the press. So, you know, your career is going to be boosted by that." As discussed above, providing information that will lead to the clearance of crime(s) and removal of offenders from the community should lead to accolades for the responsible investigator. Therefore, an indirectly recognized benefit of working with informants is the longer-term payoff, the second-stage reward that follows and is dependent on the first stage success (e.g., solving the crime). This benefit is not restricted to straight-line promotions through a single unit or unified command. Off audio, Percy, the commander of the Central City homicide unit, noted that he looks for a track record of informant usage when sizing up a street-level narcotics investigator for an opening in the homicide unit. To him, the proactive and repeated use of informants is the sign of a savvy detective who sees the value of short- and long-term intelligence building. He went on to recount the diverse prior assignments of several of the homicide detectives in the unit, in each case noting that they were well versed in informant usage and well connected to the streets. It was clear that Percy valued these qualities just as much as, if not more than, an officer's supervisory references, felony arrest record, formal training, or proficiency in assembling investigative files.

Additionally, in a world of accountability, performance standards, and never-ending pushing for departments to quantify productivity, some law enforcement investigators believe that the mere act of identifying, recruiting, and registering a larger number of informants is a professional benefit. Vic succinctly stated: "Well, the more informants you have, the better police officer you have." While this is not a commonly encountered perspective, it does build on the idea that officers with more (and more high-quality) informants do tend to look better to superior officers, as they make more arrests; seize more drugs, weapons, and so forth; and fulfill quantified performance standards more efficiently. In some departments, and with some supervisors and administrations, building one's count of any positive achievement—including the number of registered informants—is an indication of success. So to have informants is to demonstrate success in one aspect of the law enforcement job.

In the end, informants are almost always seen as important contributors to investigations, especially in narcotics cases, but also in cases dealing with other forms of crime, including property crimes, violent crimes, and even white-collar crimes. Summing up his view in a concise and straightforward way, Pedro responded to a question about whether law enforcement could be effectively done without the use of informants: "I think it would be very difficult to do my job without informants at all. . . . I've solved many more cases without informants than I have with informants, but [in] the cases I have used them on, they've been very useful."

All things considered, there are three primary benefits that come from law enforcement, especially investigators focused on drug crimes, working with confidential informants. Not all of the benefits are universally realized, not all of the benefits will be realized by all officers and in all cases, and not all of the benefits are always (at least initially) recognized as benefits. But there is a wide range of positive outcomes that can be, and frequently are, realized by using informants in the investigative process.

The most obvious and intended benefit of using informants is the gathering of intelligence that leads to the clearance of active criminal cases or generates new case possibilities. This is most often why informants are used. This is also the cornerstone of the mission of law enforcement agencies. So when a tool such as a confidential informant becomes available, it would seem logical and sensible for an agency and its representatives to make use of such a tool.

The additional two benefits that are commonly experienced by both individual officers and, at least on occasion, the community of law enforcement agencies and officials are an enhanced knowledge of communities and professional advancement and/or prestige. For officers, knowing more about the communities in which they work can only be beneficial. Community policing, problem-solving policing, and numerous other strategies and approaches that have been instituted in recent decades are all dependent (at some level) on having intelligence about communities. Therefore, the idea of working with community members, whether through official channels such as citizen advisory boards or more informal approaches such as those involved in cultivating informants, is central to the mission and vision of nearly all American law enforcement agencies. And for officers that realize success in their work with informants, there are clear professional benefits.

EIGHT

Pitfalls of Working with Informants

Just as there are benefits to be derived by law enforcement investigators and investigations working with confidential informants, so too are there negative products that accompany such practices. Most investigators believe that the benefits of working with confidential informants outweigh—sometimes significantly and sometimes only marginally—the potential costs and pitfalls. Some officers, even some of those assigned to investigative functions, consider the pitfalls of working with informants to outweighing the benefits of doing so and thus choose not to use informants, except in tandem with others or only in extreme circumstances. But even for those who do see the value of the practice and who have personally realized benefits from it in the form of multiple case closures and/or promotions, costs and pitfalls remain. Therefore, it is important to identify and understand the ground-level negative consequences of working with confidential informants, as these may discourage investigators from using informants. At a minimum, the costs need to be managed so as to be tolerable and worth the accompanying benefits.

In this chapter, we break the costs or pitfalls of officers' reliance on confidential informants down into three broad categories: personal, professional, and highly individualized (to particular investigators, informants, or cases). The personal costs are mainly the time and attention that an officer must invest when managing informants. Such costs are commonly conceived of as the job "invading" investigators' personal lives and disrupting their conventional life activities. Also experienced as a potential personal cost is the possibility of an investigator's relationship with an informant becoming too close, resulting in something more than an impersonal, exchange-based interaction. Professional costs and pitfalls include the reliability of informants' information, the dependability of informants (including as interaction partners), the veracity of (and need to verify) information that comes from informants, informants' inability or incompetence at following through on actions and information gathering, and the possibility of being deceived or double-crossed by an informant who concurrently provides information and engages in criminal activities. In short, reliance on confidential informants can place a case or career in undue jeopardy. Finally, individual costs shape officers' future approaches and views of confidential informant usage in general.

It is important to note that, on weighing the range of costs as well as the benefits that can be derived from using informants, most investigators that we interviewed and observed expressed a sense of resignation about working with them. The use of informants was seen more or less as a "necessary evil," and investigators described how they sought to actively manage their relationships with informants, with an eye toward minimizing the potential costs of such relationships. Two investigators, Sonny and Frank, one a veteran officer in a state government agency and the other a career officer in a metro police department, illustrate this general compromise position. Sonny suggested: "Informants are a good source of information, but they can also cause a lot of trouble for an agent. Either you can get to know that person, or they get to know too much of your personal information, and that could be a problem." Frank surmised: "The downside of working with informants is its messy. They lie, they cheat, they manipulate, they want something, and there are so many games. And a big part of investigator training is how not to be caught in the trap of being manipulated or used by an informant."

It was consistently noted that learning to not be manipulated or used by an informant is important, and it often seemed to be a lesson that investigators learned only once they had been used or manipulated by an informant. Regardless of if and when such a lesson is learned, it is evident that working with confidential informants will be stressful, will likely intrude on officers' personal time and after-work activities, and will introduce, at the minimum, concerns about veracity, trustworthiness, and being double-crossed.

PERSONAL PITFALLS OF WORKING WITH INFORMANTS

The personal costs borne by law enforcement investigators who choose to work with informants center on the unpredictable, often untimely, and intrusive contacts that characterize interactions with most informants. These are costs that are directly experienced by investigators as well as their loved ones and members of their social circles. Relationships of all forms are a challenge to manage and nurture, but relationships with individuals with whom one interacts not out of desire and mutual attraction but out of "necessity" and a wish to access resources held only by the other are predictably more stressful and fatiguing than other forms of relationships. This is especially the case when the informant-agent relationship is driven by duress, as is the case when officers are working with indentured informants.

Impositions on One's Time

Kareem acknowledged and at least grudgingly accepted the cost of having to be available even at hours that were far beyond the bound of his normal work day: "Informants generally don't keep normal business hours, so you've got to be accessible. And that may mean three or four o'clock in the morning phone calls." The time demands, and the fact that these demands often seem to come at unwelcome times, are the most commonly voiced cost and frustration of law enforcement investigators who work with informants. Not only are telephone calls, requested meetings, and other necessary tasks unpredictable, they are also perceived (whether accurately or not) as coming at "the most inconvenient" times. Shawn, the suburban narcotics investigator, said that he makes an effort to be accessible as much as he can and that this has not infrequently meant that he has been interrupted or drawn away from other personal, family, or outside commitments. In response, he noted that he finds it necessary to consciously decide to be inaccessible at some times, simply so he can manage and fulfill his other life obligations:

> The calls come at two o'clock in the morning or five o'clock in the morning, or at your daughter's birthday party. You know, calls all of the time. These guys, some of them, you never hear from them until they've got a deal. But some of them just call and call just because they want to talk to somebody. . . . Sometimes you've just got to say, "Not today; it ain't happening." You know, its Sunday morning and you're trying to go to church when out of nowhere you get a call from a CI. You might be on the phone for an hour, and it might be the guy that calls you all of the time with nothing [of investigative value] at the end of the conversation.

Keeping in mind that informants are typically from neighborhoods that are significantly different from the neighborhoods in which investigators live and interact on a daily basis, investigators know that the "action times" for informants, which are likely to also be times they either come across information or find themselves in need of help, are likely quite different from the busiest times in their own lives. As a married man without the time demands of young children, Miller expressed that he did not encounter significant intrusions on his family time, but he did find it frustrating and taxing to be called by informants when they needed him rather than merely when he needed them: "They'll call all of the time. They're getting arrested all of the time, getting pulled over, their license has been suspended—you name it. Maybe they were in a house and a search warrant was hit. And the shit just goes on and on, and your name will be dropped in a heartbeat." Just because an informant he manages drops his name does not mean that Miller is necessarily going to do anything to help out the individual, but it does mean that he will have to have several conversations, whether in person or electronically, if for no reason other than to let the informant and any other involved law enforcement officials know that he is not looking to be involved. Ironically, even "doing nothing" can be taxing on an officer's time and emotions.

Investigators believe that some entrepreneurial informants who are trading information for cash or some civic-minded informants in the form of police wannabes can come to see their managing officers as more than simply employers or work partners. These select informants can become dependent on their handling officers as a primary source of social support. These informants may be inclined to look up to their officers, seek their officers' advice and intervention on problems, and treat their officers as both role models and friends with whom they can interact informally and socially. But without exception, investigators rejected the idea of socializing with informants. Even Justin, who would regularly provide his informants with money, food, or other necessities and items, did so because he believed that it was important for nurturing his relationship with informants, not because he viewed his informants as friends. Similarly, Alonzo, the Central City homicide detective who recalled cavorting with women on his beat back in the 1980s, steadfastly noted that he would not dream of doing anything like that now that he was a seasoned investigator who has come to appreciate the pitfalls that can follow such behavior. For most law enforcement personnel, the recognition of the cultural differences between themselves and their informants is enough to suggest that, if they were to meet in any other arena of life, they would be highly unlikely to become friends or acquaintances. The idea of being friends with individuals that one cultivates as confidential informants is essentially beyond the scope of possibility in the minds of law enforcement investigators. As Pedro explained: "It's always a business relationship, right? You're never going to call me on my personal phone, and you're never going to show up at my house. I mean, it's very businesslike throughout, the whole way. Anytime you see police officers or agents get in trouble with CIs, it's because they've crossed that line somewhere along the way."

However, officers acknowledge that somewhat of a relationship does need to be cultivated, and informants need to believe that they are valued as human beings and as sources of intelligence. Communicating that informants are valued is largely contingent on officers demonstrating to them that they are important. One of the most expedient ways investigators can accomplish this is to answer the phone calls or text messages that come in from informants and to make time for informants when they request it or make contact. This is the source of the personal costs experienced by investigators. Police focused on drug crimes need informants, and these informants need to feel wanted and appreciated. In order to receive the information they want from an informant, investigators need to demonstrate their appreciation of their informants. This is done by making time for them, talking with them (sometimes even about completely irrelevant topics), and simply being accessible. Miller explained how he handles this: "When they call you, you're going to have to answer those calls, because if you don't over a short period of time, they'll quit calling you. So even though you might not want to talk to them, you've got to talk to them and see what's going on. And a lot of times it's nothing, and then a lot of times it's going to be some good information."

Somewhat similarly, Frank noted that he encountered a number of informants over his career who could or would have become overbearing demands on his time if he had not found a way to divert their attention and redirect their attempts to befriend him. He reflected on how he had seen and experienced "clingy" informants throughout his career: "They try to befriend you. They want to because being a snitch is lonely. They can't talk to their friends about what they're doing. So it's the fact that they're lonely—they want to talk to you, and they want to make you their friend. They want to borrow money from you, they're going to have emergencies, their car's going to get impounded, they're going to be arrested." But regardless of the degree of respect, familiarity, or personal attraction that an investigator may have for an informant, it was consistently noted that the line between personal and professional interactions and contacts is not to be broken. In some— albeit probably rare—instances, the actions investigators take to maintain the line between personal and professional can themselves be stressful. But the investigators that we encountered in our fieldwork and interviews were all of the opinion that the distinction between "friend," "buddy," or even "fairly nice guy I don't mind being around" and confidential informant must always be respected and maintained.

The officers who took part in this study consistently described a negotiation process that underlies the informant-agent relationship, in which the agent makes it clear when he or she will be accessible to informants but remains open to exceptions under exigent circumstances. Individual investigators negotiate the placement of this line differently, and where the line is drawn is influenced by personalities (both of the investigator and the informant), experience, current life situations, the stage and status of an investigation, and a host of other idiosyncratic variables. This sentiment was captured well by Orlando: "Depending on the informant, you're going to get called all of the time. I've been woke up in the middle of the night thousands of times with my informants calling. So yeah, it gets to where sometimes you want to tell them, but you can't tell them not to call you or you miss opportunities."

While Orlando said that he never tells informants to call less frequently or not to call at all, other investigators did recall situations when they needed to curtail contacts with informants and cut down on the amount of time that was consumed in the working relationship. Doing so can be difficult and can require active steps beyond simply telling an informant to cut down on frequent contacts. Manny, a federal law enforcement agent with more than twenty years of experience, explained:

> You get them to where they start blowing your phone up for silly shit. Not just that they want to give up a body or give up guns and drugs. I mean, they're calling for everything. They've got a problem with a girlfriend, so they want to call you. They've got a problem paying their rent, they want to call you. You know, we've had guys who had to change their phone numbers because snitches are just burning it up, and it's just not worth it to me.

Inherent to most calls from informants is the fact that the officer does not know where the conversation is headed. The officer always has the option of cutting the informant off to ask about the exact point of the call, but doing so can come across as offensive or insensitive to the risks being shouldered by the informant. As such, the safe route is to let the informant dictate the conversation to a certain degree. After all, this is a person with inside information of criminal activity, and anything he or she says might have intelligence value. The challenge for the officer is to show respect and patience while keeping the conversation focused on pertinent topics.

Getting Too Close to an Informant

It was acknowledged that, despite the best of intentions and repeated warnings in training and from colleagues, some investigators do in fact become too close to an informant, sometimes without even realizing it is happening. While none of the investigators interviewed or observed in this study admitted to having done so themselves, we were told numerous stories of others who had inadvertently or perhaps even consciously crossed the line with informants. Some of these recollections focused on investigators who discovered personal similarities with informants that led to small social engagements, which slowly built to more intense and more frequent interactions that eventually became more social than work-oriented. In other cases, stories of fellow investigators getting "too close" to informants centered on inappropriate sexual relations. Stories abound in the law enforcement community about male officers getting sexually involved with (primarily) female informants—or females associated with informants—who seduced investigators specifically so as to gain a powerful upper hand over the investigator. In such situations, the goal of the temptress is seemingly to neutralize any (or some) power that the investigator may hold over her (such as criminal charges) or to negotiate a better, more lucrative, or less demanding deal with the investigator.

Because they had witnessed things "go wrong" in the past in others' informant relationships, the subjects in our study universally warned against getting too close to informants, saying things like, "Never think of them as a friend," "Don't let yourself get sucked in," and, "Never, never forget who they are and why you're dealing with them." In those instances in which others had neglected such advice, it was emphatically noted that the "weak officer" had suffered as result, both personally and professionally. Typically, such relationships carried the price of a job loss, or at absolute minimum, a demotion and transfer to a less desirable position within the organization. Regardless of what actual prices were paid, it was common knowledge that getting too close to an informant is a bad thing with serious personal and professional repercussions.

It was consistently noted in our observations that, once investigators had crossed the line of a professional relationship with an informant, they found themselves subject to official complaints, being double-crossed by informants, or even being blackmailed by informants. All of this typically arises as a result of an informant seeking to get out of his or her negotiated obligation to the investigator. As Miller succinctly summarized: "You've got to be very careful, and you can sometimes get too close to those informants and trust them too much. So you've got to back off on that sometimes so you can be careful." Or, in the cautionary words of Shawn: "If you start to befriend them and are becoming really good friends and pals or whatever with these guys, [you need to] remember they're bad guys, they're criminals. They're going to exploit you the best they can, and they might be trying to befriend you and, the next thing you know, they're turning on you, making false complaints, saying, 'He did this,' or, 'He did that.' Then your job is in jeopardy."

It was suggested that officers and agents, both those who do work with informants and those who do not, must be on guard for informants or their close associates trying to manipulate them into either a sexual relationship or a sexually compromising position in order to get the upper hand in the informant-agent relationship. Richardson, a homicide detective in Central City with prior time on a street-level narcotics unit, summarized this sex-related setup as follows: "If it's a female informant, it might be [sex] with her. If it's a male informant, it might be [sex] with a stripper girlfriend of his or a stripper friend. Or he'll create a scenario where there's him and his girlfriend, and [he'll say], 'Look, Tiffany is here with us.' And they know if they can ever get you to compromise yourself with drugs, alcohol, or women, then no longer are you working them. Now they're working you."

As a result of their awareness of this possible setup, as noted briefly in chapter 4, male investigators typically view female informants as warranting some additional precautions. These include only meeting in the presence of at least one other officer or only meeting in public places. Some officers, however, especially those who had limited or no experience with seeing other officers "learn the hard way," the idea of getting "too close" to an informant was an inconceivable proposition. These investigators considered informants to be tools of the job or a form of property. Although these officers certainly acknowledged that informants were people, they engaged informants only as entities that could provide a service. In the words of federal agent Manny: "For me to catch a bad guy, I'm old school. I do what I have to do, and if I have to use an informant, I will. But when that case is done, I cut them loose. End of story." While this may seem unfriendly or unappreciative, Manny is unapologetic and focused on his informant relationships as business relationships—nothing more, nothing less.

The professional pitfalls and costs of working with informants center on the character of informants and how investigators can ensure receipt of valuable, valid, reliable, and truly useful information. The investigator-informant relationship exists (in the eyes of the investigator) for one purpose and one purpose only: to make cases. When the costs or threats to fulfilling that goal become larger than the balanced weight of the information to be gained, or when the validity and reliability of received information is too questionable, difficult, or expensive to verify, then the costs outweigh the benefits and the informant becomes expendable.

Almost without exception, investigators defined informants as, at the core, unreliable, manipulative individuals from whom absolutely nothing should be believed or trusted until independently verified. Just below the surface, in the minds of most investigators who participated in this study, was a sense of apprehension that informants may try to double-cross them or set them up for attack or blackmail. Mark, a seasoned federal investigator based in Central City, surmised the situation as follows:

> Honestly, they are a pain in the ass. You know, you just don't know the reliability of them.... How much can you rely on them? That varies. And there are safety concerns too. I mean, recently I was riding in the back of a car with my partner sitting in the front, and the source was in the passenger seat. Before the guy gets in, my partner turns to me and says, "If he does anything, fucking blow his brains out." And you know, that was only half-joking.

While framed in a joking manner, the seriousness of his comment was readily apparent. Informants typically come from the seedier segments of the community and bring with them values, norms, expectations, and behaviors that are fundamentally contrary to those being espoused and enforced by the majority of law enforcement officers. While law enforcement officers encounter criminal offenders on a near-daily basis, it is only with informants that law enforcement officers find themselves in protracted and repeated interactions with "the same enemy." Typically, interactions with known habitual offenders are adversarial and based on the display and execution of power (and for those informants recruited through an arrest, such a start to a relationship is adversarial and power-based). But once an informant is recruited and a deal is closed (e.g., when an officer is "partnering" with an informant), these interactions need to be modified, even if the officer's basic beliefs about the informant are not modified. The following two comments from investigators do well to illustrate this point. First, as Vic stated in simple terms: "They are crooks. The majority of them are crooks. I mean, 100 percent crooks.... It's a dirty deal working with informants because they're dirty people." Second, and a bit more explicit and foreboding, Kareem stated the obvious: "First and foremost, they're criminal, so that is a huge disadvantage. They've been involved in that [criminal] element, they've probably hustled somebody before, so there is a great chance that everything they are telling you is not true. So probably one of the biggest disadvantages is that you're dealing with someone who is involved in that element, and it could come back to bite you."

The majority of informants are from less privileged backgrounds than most investigators and often have rougher lifestyles than them, which means that investigators have to get their own hands dirty (both figuratively and literally) when interacting with informants. Much of the contact and work investigators engage in with informants is not in "nice" areas of a community. Instead, as Mark explained, this work often exposes officers to a culture that is distinctively different from what they know in their own lives:

It's the ones that live in the shittier areas that are usually better. I mean, it can be as general as possible because those are the ones that know how to handle themselves. Those are the ones that know how to play the game, and those are the ones that are exposed to the stuff that you need. So those are the ones that are in the right places. I would say you want the guy that has some dirt; you want the guy that has done some stupid shit before. Those are the ones you want. You don't want the guy that just walked up at the wrong place at the wrong time. That's not the guy you want; you know that guy is worthless to you.

Critical to Mark's assessment is the fact that the "dirt" is a desired facet of the interaction. If the officer does not feel a little uncomfortable or put off by the environment or disposition of a prospective informant, then that informant is not likely to be a marquee intelligence asset. Investigators are interested in informants because they are privileged insiders who can provide them with information and access that investigators cannot (easily) access on their own. Therefore, it is essential for investigators to find and be with people who differ from themselves in order to identify individuals who can serve their informational needs.

While investigators recognize that the character of most informants is less than stellar, that most informants have at least some degree of criminal background, and that many informants come from different cultural backgrounds than they do, it is not just the overall background and personality of informants that make investigators circumspect. Some of the actions of informants reinforce their label as unreliable. Central City narcotics investigator Miller punctuated his warnings about informants' lack of reliability and the need to "stay on top of them" by pointing to something simple but important: "A lot of the problems with an informant is for him to return calls in a timely manner, you know, to where a lot of them are just busier doing whatever else is in their life, and that makes it a little more difficult." Even simple tasks can be frustrating to the investigator, and these get framed as further evidence of an informant's lack of reliability. Investigators complain about issues such as an informant not being able to follow explicit directions about how to do a drug buy, not remembering where to meet his or her handling officer, not paying attention to the prearranged paths to traverse between leaving his or her handling officer and the site of a drug buy, not remembering details (or not remembering them accurately), and failing to be punctual, honest on all points of information, and simply able to remember, process, and act on directions. When an informant cannot, or simply does not, follow instructions and do as he or she is instructed, he or she is likely to have a short tenure as an informant. In his typical straightforward way, Miller explained: "You can't work with them if they don't follow directions."

Compromising Case Integrity

When informants "freelance," or do things differently than instructed, they are considered by investigators to be a liability, as they are said to pose a major risk to safety or case integrity. By not following directions or not reporting accurate and complete information, an informant renders the planning and precautions that officers put into planning a drug buy, bust, or any other investigative activity irrelevant. In short, they compromise the viability of the case and, in some cases, can pose a threat to their own safety or the safety of law enforcement officers. Consequently, if an informant does not perform precisely in the ways investigators instruct and expect, he or she is typically abandoned and will not receive the negotiated payment, leniency, or whatever benefit he or she was due to gain from the arrangement. In the words of Stan, a seasoned investigator with a federal agency: "I never trust them in the sense that I wouldn't put my life in their hands. I only trust the information they provide if I can corroborate in some way and I can use that in a sense for further information. But there's always a line you won't cross."

The primary concern of investigators regarding the reliability of informants is not their work ethic, ability to complete simple tasks, or overall character. Rather, what they consider to be most important and to trump other issues, problems, or challenges is that informants are reliable in providing accurate, desired information in a timely manner. According to Duffy, a Central City homicide sergeant, a good informant "can give you what you need. Do I need a body? Do I need information? Do I need a piece of evidence? Do I need to know a conspirator? If they can give you what you want them to give you, then they're a good informant." If an informant can provide this type of information when needed, an officer may overlook or accept other transgressions, as long as they are not related to safety. However, if an informant demonstrates a pattern of providing unreliable information, it is likely that he or she will be dropped, any negotiated deal will be canceled, and he or she will be considered as no different from all other offenders. Whether the information provided by an informant is believed to be simply wrong or an investigator suspects that he or she is being set up by the informant, the intelligence that the informant provides will be subject to a more thorough vetting process. It is quite rare for an informant not to be dropped by their handling officer if it is determined that the informant provided "bad information" for a second time.

All of this is not to say that investigators do not know, and even expect, that informants will lie to them. Lying is perceived by investigators as "just what people do," especially criminals. If lying is expected from most offenders, the police know that those with whom they have contentious relationships are even more likely to provide them false information. Investigators do not see this as a reason to not work with informants but rather see it as a primary reason for why all information gained from informants must be verified independently.

One core contradiction in the structure and operation of the informant world is that investigators consider informants to be valued and beneficial (because they provide information that allows crimes to be solved) while simultaneously concluding that all informants lie. Recall that informants are motivated by either self-advancement or self-preservation, and some informants believe that the most efficient or effective means of achieving these ends is by providing false information to law enforcement or anyone else.

Investigators recognize this. For most investigators who have worked with informants, knowing that informants will lie is little different from knowing and stating that informants will breathe. As Vic simply stated: "They're liars. They are unreliable, and they lie a lot." Frank took the point further: "The biggest challenge for me is the fact that informants lie, and unless you really understand their motivation, you don't know which direction they're going to be lying or how they're going to skew the information." As most investigators reminded us in interviews: "You're working with criminals. By nature, they're going to lie; they're going to try to get one over on you." This is simply part of the landscape of the job. Perhaps frustrating to some degree, but not nearly as frustrating as other aspects of investigators' work, lying informants are seen as something that just happens.

Dishonesty is recognized as being normative in many communities and in many forms of business that the police spend time investigating and trying to curtail. This means that many informants are used to lying frequently and may even do so without realizing what they are doing. However, it is not only people in the lower echelons of society that lie frequently and lie to the police. As Pedro pointed out with resignation: "I've had guys lie to me who were million-dollar CEOs, and I've had crackheads in the street lie to me. It's no different."

Informants Not Fulfilling Their Role

Not everyone who performs a task is necessarily very good at it. This is true of the various tasks requested of confidential informants, as there exist varying degrees of competency in general and in relation to specific tasks. For some informants, this may well be a consequence of educational development and problem-solving skills, as most informants are low-level drug dealers or other career criminals who are likely to have dropped out of school and are therefore often more prone to using physical modes of problem solving over verbal ones. Other informants come from more traditional backgrounds and may be generally reliable and easily managed by their overseeing officers, but due to limited connections or knowledge, they may not be well suited or skilled for certain operations. Some informants, due to their intricate familiarity with the ways of the street, are especially skilled at conversation and observation in settings where the police cannot go. Some are particularly good at making drug buys, while others are not. Sometimes, informants have the access along with the raw observational and conversational skills but lack the motivation or follow-through. In short, investigators accept the fact that every informant has his or her strengths and weaknesses, and the challenge is to find those with the skills and predilections that meet the needs of the job at hand or of the personal preferences of the officers involved. The investigators involved in the fieldwork and interviews of this project were unanimous in the view that one should nurture ongoing relationships with those select informants that excel in the role and minimize exposure to those who do not. More often than not, informants are like the tools in a craftsman's toolbox; ideally, you reach in and pull out the perfect tool for the job at hand, but sometimes you find yourself pressed for time and out of patience and pull out the first blunt object you can find (usually a hammer) and start pounding away in hopes that it will fixe everything.

It is also important to respect that, sometimes, an informant will have the total package of access, skill set, and motivation but may simply consciously elect to not follow through on negotiated tasks. Such a decision may be a passive-aggressive tactic used to respond to an investigator that is disliked, or it may be a way of testing an officer to see whether his or her promises and threats are real or not. Some informants, usually those who are indentured and find themselves working off charges, will promise to make a deal, provide information, or carry out some other task and then simply not contact the officer or perform any activities related to informing. Often, the informant has every intention to follow through but decides at the last minute not to do so because some aspect of street life intervened. These individuals recognize the ire that this produces and will typically try to avoid the officer and any other law enforcement personnel known to be affiliated with the officer or investigative unit or agency. It seems that informants may expect to get paid or be given leniency even though they fail to live up to their end of the negotiated agreement. Such "rip offs" or "burns" are not uncommon in the criminal community and may actually be normative behavior for some informants. However, investigators made it clear that decisive action must be taken in these situations to avoid a repeat occurrence.

A failure to come through and fulfill negotiated tasks is likely to be responded to in one of two ways. First, an officer may track down the supposed informant and remind him or her of their agreement and the threatened outcome if he or she does not come through. In this scenario, the officer will then either act on the threat or, if it is the informant's first transgression, afford the informant one more chance to make it right. Second, the officer may simply write the individual off and move forward with other investigative options. The first of these methods is what we most commonly witnessed in River City. Justin kept his file of informants, and on occasion, especially when weather precluded unit activities or on days when several other unit members were off duty, he would track down informants that had not yet followed through and completed their tasks. Typically, Justin would cajole and gently push a first time violator, telling them: "Come through in the next week, or I'm gonna cut you free." Invariably, these potential informants reiterated their commitment to find and report information or to arrange a meeting or a buy (whatever had initially been requested of them). The responses of these individuals at this time were very similar to when they had first been arrested and offered the opportunity to work off charges in exchange for information. However, in a majority of cases, even after this reminder visit or phone call, these individuals were never heard from again. Consequently, the next time Justin reviewed his files, he removed these individuals from his list of active informants and sent their cases sent forward into the court system.

Other officers recounted how some informants would deliver on their prescribed information-gathering tasks but then attempt to renegotiate the agreed-on remuneration plan. Officers consistently characterized this as an example of informants not fulfilling their obligations. Most officers argue that it is important to have an explicit agreement (or "contract") with an informant that specifically spells out what each party will do for the other. In some instances, even when a formal agreement was in place, it was possible that an informant would try to get more than had originally been agreed on. Informants would try to renegotiate by simply asking for or demanding something additional, attempting to guilt officers into more payment by saying things like, "I did so good for you," or other means. Stan, a federal agent, noted:

> [I have had] a few different people where everything is all straightened out, there is the agreement that you are going to do this for us, and this is what we're going to do for you. In my mind, no question, on the backside of everything maybe we've made our arrest, all of the sudden those extrications have changes on their side: "Now, wait a minute. I want this, I want that." And then you just never hear the end of it: "Well, I'm not going to work with you again, blah, blah, blah." . . . It's just like, whatever you said you were going to do, it's like ten times more. Or whatever carrot you put in front of them, there's a much bigger carrot than they thought they were going to get, which is pretty obnoxious.

Stan's experience appears to be the exception. However, it should not be surprising that individuals from the criminal underworld, who are ready, willing, and able to deceive and turn on their colleagues, friends, and even family, would try to renegotiate their arrangements.

The failure of these potential informants to come through was seen as a negative reflection on the officer managing them. Being unable to "control" or "deliver" one's informants is a notable and important deficiency for an investigator. Ironically, such negative sentiments were directed at the managing officer not only by fellow officers who were well versed in informant development but also by those officers who chose not to work with informants or were unskilled in informant usage. Therefore, when an informant does not come through or does not do things correctly, properly, or as instructed, the handling officer is often embarrassed, angry, and more than happy to let the informant go to court "and just see what they get."

While working with confidential informants presents numerous opportunities for an investigator to enhance his or her standing within an organization or bolster his or her professional reputation, this investigative approach also presents potential professional pitfalls. In general, the personal and professional pitfalls associated with informant usage are commonly identifiable by seasoned investigators and come with predictable response strategies. Next, we discuss a less predictable type of pitfall, "getting burned."

INDIVIDUAL PITFALLS OF WORKING WITH INFORMANTS

An officer gets "burned" when an informant offers inaccurate, bad, or misleading information that leads to a failed, flawed, or misdirected investigation. During our fieldwork and interviews, we were told numerous stories of investigators getting burned while engaged with an informant. In most every instance, the story was recounted in a third person format and involved the unfortunate experiences of another officer. It was not uncommon for multiple officers from the same department to reflect on another particular officer's misfortune in this regard. Only in rare instances did investigators admit to getting burned themselves, and in these cases, there was always a sense of relief expressed that the severity and fallout of the situation had been manageable. It became clear to us that others were not so lucky. Most of the stories ended with the involved officer being fired from the force or transferred out of a desirable investigative unit. In other instances, the circumstances were said to have scarred the officer personally and resulted in a voluntary career redirection, either inside of law enforcement or outside of it. While the concept of getting burned occupies a known space in the world of undercover police work, the same cannot be said about the details that comprise the individual cases. In short, while it is predictable that select investigators will be burned while working with informants and that such events will yield predictable and significant personal and career outcomes for the persons involved, there does not appear to be a discernable pattern to the confluence of events that bring about the burn. For this reason, we ascribe an individualized aspect to this category of pitfall.

At its core, getting burned involves getting set up or double-crossed by an informant. For starters, it is important to note that investigators consider it more problematic, more dangerous, and more anger inspiring to get burned by an informant than to be disappointed by an informant who does not fulfill his or her negotiated deal or who fails to follow instructions. This was commonly considered to be one of the biggest pitfalls to informant-based police work. An informant can double-cross the police in three basic ways. First, an informant can provide information he or she knows is false. Second, an informant can share information about an investigator or investigation with those being targeted by the investigation. Both of these instances are potentially very dangerous for the police. Third, an informant can use the information gained from being with and around the police to more safely or effectively advance his or her own criminal acts or the acts of other seasoned criminals. This, while usually not yielding immediate personal danger to others, does set the stage for law enforcement officials to be deemed complicit in the production of crime, an outcome that runs contrary to the main charge of the profession. Beyond these common categories, we noted a wide variation in the sophistication and severity of outcomes that followed from the rogue actions of an informant. Moreover, it was apparent that the individual investigators played a varying and unpredictable role in exposing themselves to being double-crossed and also reacted to the situation in varying ways, ranging from passive acceptance to active retaliation.

Informants Intentionally Providing False Information to the Police

The officers we interacted with during our fieldwork commonly described informants as liars. Simply put, it is accepted that police and criminals are natural adversaries and that even the most compliant informant, be they motivated by elf-preservation or self-advancement, may withhold information or misrepresent criminal behavior that they are involved in. In most cases, these lies have few consequences, as handling officers are often adept at verifying information or sniffing out lack of authenticity as a conversation unfolds. Officers surmised that they are able to do this because they tend to be more careful and invested in the outcome of information exchanges than are confidential informants. In most cases, this is true. In some cases, however, informants are careful and more cunning than their managing officers and are able to exploit their control over privileged information and their officers' ability to double-check its veracity. In these cases, the informant seizes the upper hand over the officer in the power struggle that underlies the officer-citizen information exchange. Luckily for officers, most of the lies that slip by have few repercussions; perhaps an officer will miss his or her criminal target or waste his or her investigative time on a bad lead. In other cases, especially when an informant is seeking to do harm to an officer, a carefully constructed and strategically placed lie can have significant consequences for the handling officer, the criminal investigation in question, or others involved in the matter. For example, Vic recounted an incident in which he inadvertently burned an informant and almost got her killed. He was using a female prostitute informant to do a buy-bust on an outlaw biker who was selling drugs. The plan called for the informant to set up a deal to buy marijuana. After she had done this, Vic would return to the location and seek to make a buy himself in an undercover role, thus protecting the identity of the prostitute and removing her from harm's way. However, the prostitute chose to freelance and solicit cocaine as well as marijuana from the dealer. This lie allowed the biker to figure out that Vic was law enforcement and that the prostitute was an informant. Luckily, Vic was able to make the arrest without incurring any harm to himself or other team members. However, on arresting the biker, the dealer revealed that the prostitute's lie inadvertently revealed her identity and said that this would not go without reprisal. Vic had to act swiftly and creatively to extricate the prostitute from harm's way and disincentivize the biker from acting on his violent inclination. This required Vic expending a great deal of time and social capital.

Accounts of the officers we interviewed suggest that most informant lies are transparent and can easily be diffused by a savvy investigator. In some cases, however, a precisely placed lie by a foolish or maliciously motivated informant can create big problems for a case or the individuals involved.

Interestingly, very few of the investigators we encountered during our fieldwork admitted to ever having been "burned" by an informant. All of them, however, did recount instances of fellow officers having experienced an informant either purposely trying to misdirect an investigation or setting up an officer for possible harm from other offenders. It was made clear that getting burned is a natural hazard of working with confidential informants. Kareem, although he swore that he had never had an informant double-cross him in his nearly twenty years of investigation experience, warned:

> You always have to make sure that you're doing everything above board because remember you're dealing with a criminal who's doing what? Setting other people up. You could be one of those people. I mean, this could be one of those setups. I mean, hey, if you get, you know, a law enforcement officer. . . . So you always have to assume when you're talking on the phone that you're being recorded, or [when] you're meeting with an informant, especially a female informant, you know, as a man, you don't want to do that alone because you don't want anything to be inferred, implied, or whatever that could put you in a trick bag.

Similarly, Shawn claimed that he had not had any serious problems with his informants trying to double-cross him in the past, but warned:

> They can always set you up. I mean, you never know what they've told the dealer, you never know what they're doing; they might be trying to set you up. You know, "I'm going to come by tonight, but the guy that's going to be with me is a cop. Let's take him out." You know, you have a huge officer safety issue there. That's why, a majority of the time, I have them go do the buys, or put wires on them, or whatever.

One difficult-to-avoid potential problem for law enforcement agencies is that informants will come to know (by sight, name, vehicle, and personality) at least some of the investigators involved in their case. This can be a detriment to law enforcement in that officers could be identified to other offenders. Additionally, informants who have worked with the police will know that particular persons are law enforcement investigators and therefore know to be careful with their own illegal activities in the presence of such persons. In the worst case scenario, an informant will identify a street-level undercover agent as being a police officer and expose that individual to physical harm at the hand of others out on the streets. Shawn explained this cost of working with informants: "CIs are going to know us. They're going to meet my undercovers [officers posing as offenders], and they're gathering information on us just as much as we're gathering information on them and who they know. So you know, they see me driving away in whatever car. They might go back and tell all of their buddies, 'Hey, watch out for this car because that's a cop.' So you know they're going to get information on us."

Unwittingly Contributing to Criminal Behavior

The inside information that informants can gain about the goings on of law enforcement or criminal competitors can be especially valuable for informants who continue with their own criminal activities either during and after actively working as an informant. For example, Vic recounted the following story about his unfortunate experience with a savvy confidential informant seeking to advance his own criminal endeavors:

> So the informant's name was Stubs [because he had] no fingers, just the stubs. He set it up, so we arrested the drug dealers, and we pretended we arrested Stubs too because we had another case with him too. So we brought him on this paddy wagon to jail. Then we'd separate them, and then we let Stubs go. Well, I kind of said to myself, me and another detective, that the drug house wasn't very secure; we better go back down to that house and secure it better. Well, we go back in the house and who's in the house? Stubs! He's burglarizing it [taking stash money and drugs out of a hiding place in the wall that he knew of but didn't disclose to police]. And it turns out that's not the first time it happened, but that's the first time we learned how low down they are. He was working cases off, so we usually say [that informants work] until we bust a group—four or five good cases. Well, Stubs was working alright! We threw him in jail. That's the kind of people you're dealing with.

All formal, and most informal, agreements between law enforcement investigators and informants prohibit informants from engaging in any illegal activities (unless directed to do so as part of an investigation). However, these prohibitions (just like laws in general) are often violated. After all, nearly all informants have criminal backgrounds and have engaged in some level of criminal activity for lengthy periods of time. For some, abandoning all illegal activities would represent a major change in life, and such changes are hard to maintain. Nearly universally, officers observed and interviewed for this project said that they do not tolerate their informants committing crime while working with them, and as discussed earlier in chapter 6, the idea of an informant essentially having immunity from arrest and prosecution is a myth. Officers also know that, if one of their informants is continuing with crime, the credibility of that informant may be questioned. Therefore, if an informant were required to testify in a case, the case could be significantly weakened. So while the criminal nature of informants is a platform on which an informant's activities are built, that criminal nature is also a liability for officers and their cases.

SUMMARY

Working with confidential informants can be a blessing and a curse for law enforcement agencies and officers. The blessing comes in the form of the information that facilitates investigations and apprehension of offenders. As we have shown throughout this book, the information provided by informants is often information that either is impossible for law enforcement to access on their own or would take extremely long and diligent work to access. However, while the payoffs of working in tandem with a confidential informant are significant, the drawbacks of doing so can also be considerable.

The negative aspects of working with informants come at the personal, professional, and individualized levels. Personal costs have to do with the time and attention that are required to manage informants. We see these costs realized in the form of the job "invading" investigators' personal lives and disrupting their conventional life activities. Also experienced as a potential personal cost of working with informants is the possibility of an investigator's relationship with an informant becoming too personal, resulting in something more than an impersonal, exchange-based interaction. Professional costs and pitfalls involve the reliability of informants' information, the dependability of informants (including as interaction partners), the veracity of (and need to verify) information that comes from informants, informants' inability or incompetence at following through on actions and information gathering, and the possibility of being deceived and double-crossed by informants who concurrently provide information and engage in criminal activities. Individual costs vary, but they all shape an officer's future approach and view of confidential informants.

The value that confidential informants bring to an investigator can be huge, but the costs of such a partnership can also be substantial. Whether the benefits outweigh the costs is a decision that individual investigators must make for themselves. Most investigators appear to believe that the costs, while perceived as bothersome, intrusive, and potentially danger producing, are worth it, although frequently only "just barely." Use of informants is commonly perceived to be a necessary part of police work, although it is an often disliked aspect of the job that is approached with apprehension, skepticism, and (hopefully) eyes that are wide open to potential backlash and negative consequences.

NINE

Summary and Implications

The preceding chapters describe and theorize the relationship that exists between law enforcement officers and members of the public as they interact within the context of criminal investigations. In this context, police serve as the active consumers of criminal intelligence and citizens as the purveyors of this privileged information. We employ the term "police-citizen information exchange" to characterize this fluid and multidimensional relationship dynamic. We observed that law enforcement officers from almost every job assignment (from beat officers to specialized investigators) and in all sorts of agencies (local, state, and federal) routinely looked to cajole criminal intelligence from members of the public who had firsthand knowledge of past wrongdoing and/or access to perpetrators and thus could facilitate future criminal transactions. Admittedly, the general phenomenon of confidential informant usage has been around since the earliest days of organized policing and has been subject to a number of systematic inquiries. We revisit the phenomenon, providing an updated description of its inner workings with an eye toward providing a series of theoretical and policy implications to inform the path forward.

THEORETICAL IMPLICATIONS

The police-citizen information exchange spans a vast set of circumstances and arrangements. In most cases, the law enforcement agents serve as the driving force in the information exchange process. Not surprisingly, then, most of the extant literature places police in the foreground of the discussion. There exists a sizable and longstanding literature—primarily geared toward law enforcement officials—that describes in depth the mechanics of developing confidential sources, managing them, and putting the resulting criminal intelligence to work within the context of criminal casework. Several scholars have gained access to law enforcement officers and sought to theorize the dynamics of confidential informant usage. Far fewer have drawn on the information providers or members of the criminal underworld to shed light on this phenomenon.

Through the existing literature, keen insights have been gained into the policy landscape that shapes police operations, the common steps that officers follow when developing informants, the everyday lived experiences of agents that manage confidential informants, the perceived motives and behaviors of informants, and the personal and bureaucratic benefits and pitfalls that can follow working with informants. The preceding chapters revisit and further elaborate on many of these topics in an effort to provide a contemporary thick description of the officer's vantage point in the police-citizen information exchange. Drawing on copious field notes and face-to-face interviews with a diverse sample of law enforcement officers, we pay particular attention to the human side of working with informants. We seek to detail the complex relationship dynamics at play and the tenuous trust and case management issues inherent in this sort of work. We also try to add to the existing knowledge base by contextualizing the use of confidential informants within the modern urban landscape. Referred to as "the game," the criminal subculture and corresponding normative tapestry provide a vexing backdrop for the police-citizen information exchange. Deep-seated legitimacy issues and competing interests both within and across the police and community subcultures are relevant factors that must be considered if one seeks to fully appreciate how clandestine information is exchanged.

We apply a creative twist to the study of confidential informants. Namely, we conceptualize the confidential informant phenomenon as an information exchange involving three entities: (1) the citizens who provide the information, (2) the law enforcement officers who consume it, and (3) the at-large offenders who stand to have their criminal conduct exposed and interrupted by such information. Considering all three of these perspectives privileges the information and the exchange relationship. This represents an important conceptual shift from the status quo wherein researchers and practitioners adopt a mechanistic approach to the topic, emphasizing outcomes over processes. For example, most of the practitioner literature is explicitly instructional in nature and serves to situate the informant phenomenon within the unchallenged and simplified bureaucratic realities of modern law enforcement. The goal of those works is to describe the various ways in which confidential informants can advance existing police priorities (i.e., solve open cases or access clandestine operations to make new cases) and provide a blueprint on best practices and pitfall avoidance where confidential informants are concerned. Works such as those by Billingsley, Nemitz, and Bean (2001), Fitzgerald (2007), Gardiner (2002), and Grimes (2009) privilege existing law enforcement priorities and confidential informant roles within the context of said priorities. In doing so, they emphasize bureaucratic realities over the perceptions and behaviors of the officers that do the work. Largely absent from this practitioner literature is systematic consideration of the lived experiences of informants and at-large offenders.

Much of the scholarly work on the topic problematizes the confidential informant phenomenon within the context of modern law enforcement. In doing so, details of the information exchange process get blurred in favor of critical questions about the utility of clandestine information gathering practices or broader policing priorities (i.e., the war on drugs or vice enforcement). Monographs such as those by Marx (1988) and Natapoff (2009) challenge the ethical and normative underpinnings associated with law enforcement agencies using covert intelligence practices to advance their investigative efforts. Such a vantage point captures how the existing policies and practices of the policing agencies compromise the legitimacy of the institution and the individual rights of citizens. Again, little emphasis is placed on individual officer's perspectives or the exchange dynamic that exists between the parties in the information exchange.

The scholarly work of Manning (2004), Wilson (1978), Innes (2000), Ericson (1981), and others does well to illustrate the role of confidential informant practices within a broader organizational context. These works are less critical of the goals of law enforcement and instead seek to articulate organizational processes and culture. In emphasizing organizational culture over individual agency, they provide thick description of the work that officers do but spend little effort emphasizing the perceptions and behaviors of officers specific to the informant exchange.

Like most other work on the topic, our project draws on data derived exclusively from law enforcement actors to shed light on the confidential informant phenomenon. Absent is data from offenders or citizens who provide the information. However, we spend considerable effort trying to privilege the information exchange in addition to individual officers' lived experience within the exchange. In chapter 3, we operationalize the police-citizen information exchange using a four-part typology. The framework is presented as a 2 × 2 matrix with the motives of the providers (citizens) and the consumers (officers) of the information serving to organize the conceptual categories. While we recognize that at-large offenders suffer the consequences of the information generated through the police-citizen exchange, they generally have no direct role in the exchange and are thus excluded from our discussion in chapter 3. On the consumer side, we differentiate between police officers engaging street-level sources in order to solve existing cases and those engaging sources in order to generate new cases. On the citizen side, we differentiate between citizens who provide information out of a sense of self-preservation and those who act out of self-advancement. We find this approach useful in distinguishing between the various types of information exchanges and how the intent of the actors shapes the relational and power dynamics. The police-source scenario is characterized by those situations in which a fearful or morally righteous citizen engages the police in an effort to bring an offender to justice. Here, the citizen possesses considerable power in the relationship dynamic, and the officer must contend with factors such as a fear of reprisals or overzealous emotions on the part of the citizen as he or she seeks to discern the veracity of the claims and reactively situate them within an ongoing (or at times newly emerging) investigation. Often, the officer will stumble across a potential police source while canvassing the area around an active crime scene or interviewing known witnesses or involved parties to a crime. Here again, the citizen enters the interaction holding all of the initial power as he or she decides if and what to reveal to the police officer.

In other instances, an officer will find him- or herself working an open case when confronted by a motivated citizen who comes forward to actively advance an open investigation. Unlike the more passive police source, the civic-minded citizen informer usually perceives him- or herself to be a valuable asset in the crime-fighting equation. We frame this as an instance of a citizen motivated by self-advancement (i.e., a cop wannabe). We also include in this category anonymous tipsters who engage the Crime Stoppers program. In this case, a citizen provides information to police anonymously with the promise of a financial reward if the information proves central to solving the crime. As with the police source exchanges, those exchanges falling under the rubric of the civic-minded citizen informer category involve an active provider of information and a passive recipient. Police officers recognize that this situation requires a special set of management strategies and operational tactics to assess, aggregate, and validate the information and put it to good use.

When one hears the term "confidential informant," the tendency is to think of those instances in which the police officer occupies a position of power and can more proactively manage the information exchange. In most cases, the officer is motivated to generate new cases or set up additional case outcomes beyond what he or she currently has on the work docket. The most common conception of this case-making approach is the indentured inform-ant information exchange, wherein a savvy and initiative-filled police officer apprehends an individual in the act of committing a crime and then leverages the threat of judicial processing and punishment to get the accused person to begrudgingly provide information about criminal activity or even exploit contacts in the criminal underworld to generate subsequent criminal trans-actions. Like trying to tame a wild horse that is none too happy about the imposition, the indentured informant scenario presents a whole host of chal-lenges and power dynamics not observed in the other types of information exchanges. The officer seeks to leverage cooperation as long as possible, while the coerced information provider seeks to put an end to the relationship as soon as possible. There is generally no love lost on either side of the equation in this sort of information exchange.

The last variant of the police-citizen information exchange that we opera-tionalize is the entrepreneurial informant type. This is when a "freelance" operator within the criminal underworld chooses to augment his or her activities and income by collaborating with police in exchange for some sort of personal remuneration. Here, the power dynamic is much more even, as both actors (the officer and the informant) possess a high degree of agency in the relationship. These sorts of relationships are often repetitive in nature, with the same officer and informant partnering in multiple transactions over time. Such a situation poses a unique set of challenges for both parties, not the least of which have to do with the maintenance of a mutually skeptical relationship.

We submit that it is theoretically fruitful to engage the confidential informant phenomenon from a vantage point that situates the actions of police officers and citizens within the context of the information exchange. For sure, we draw on the motivations and behaviors of the two parties, but we do so as they relate specifically to the information exchange. In doing so, we seek to make the point that no one party in the equation monopolizes the human agency of the moment. Both the officer and the citizen bring important intentions and predilections to the table, and the resulting relationship dynamic has important standalone qualities to it that should be carefully considered.

Many aspects of police work manifest themselves as interactional dynamics between officers and other constituents. These run the gamut from officers engaging citizens, offenders, coworkers, and other members of the criminal justice system. Too often, researchers lose sight of the fact that the motives and behaviors of officers are shaped by the structure and function of the interactional exchange within which they are engaged. In other words, it is easy to privilege individual agency over interactional context. On the other hand, researchers studying organizational culture or bureaucratic structures often deemphasize the role of individual agency and the manner in which officers seek to tailor their motives and behaviors to fit within the organizational context of the task at hand. By placing an emphasis on the informational exchange, we intend for readers to better appreciate the give and take that occurs not only between individuals and the organizational culture but also between various individuals that engage one another within the context of a recognizable interactional dynamic.

What we have striven to illustrate is that the officer-informant relationship is often a complex, multidimensional, emotionally laden, and mutually suspicious relationship. Much more than a mere economic exchange, the relationship requires management and attention from both or all parties involved. These relationships do typically reflect a sense of counterfeit intimacy—in which the involved parties actively strive for a presentation that is perceived as trustworthy, caring, and legitimately motivated. However, many times, these presentations are merely managed presentations that are done for the purposes of maintaining and/or advancing a sense of trust from one's interaction partner(s). It is with the ongoing, reciprocal moves, twists, and plays by each party that the interactions are directed, resisted, shaped, reshaped, and ultimately brought to the point of fruition and payoff. The power that each party brings to the interaction ebbs and flows; it is the goal of each party—officer and informant—to find a way maintain his or her superior, power-yielding position and to extract the biggest benefit from the interaction. Understanding individual motives and behaviors within this sort of context requires a researcher to be in tune with the work of Erving Goffman (1959) and others who stress the importance of impression management and presentation of self as they relate to structured human interaction.

The extant literature and our original research with active members of law enforcement establish that police have long relied on sources, informers, and informants to shed light on criminal conduct. Previous monograph-length treatises by Manning (1980), Marx (1988), and Natapoff (2009) both chart the historical development of confidential informant usage in this country and make predictions about the future of this approach to law enforcement. It is instructive to step back at this point and reflect on these earlier works to inform the takeaway messages of the current project.

Peter Manning (1980) drew on his extensive fieldwork in two metropolitan police departments to situate informant use within the gathering storm that we have come to know as the American war on drugs. As an organizational ethnography, Manning's work theorizes the interface between street-level narcotics officers and the bureaucratic structure within which they operate as it relates to "doing" drug policing. Manning emphasizes the discretionary nature of officers' decision-making and the myriad of investigative techniques that they can employ as they go about searching for and responding to illegal narcotics offenses. He honed in on the case as the organizational unit of analysis that structured officer actions and records of their narcotics work. Moreover, he stressed how the ritualized nature of making and solving cases fueled officer productivity and accolades. Manning observed that police officers must navigate competing organizational interests as they go about their daily activities. He did well to deconstruct many of these interests as they relate to the narcotics enforcement efforts of the officers and agencies that he was studying. We highlighted a host of competing interests that officers had to navigate as they enlisted the aid of informants to advance cases. We touched on many of these competing interests in our research. This is particularly relevant as it applies to contemporary narcotics enforcement. Increased prioritization and corresponding resource reallocation has resulted in more officers dedicating more of their time to drug interdiction efforts. Individual officers seeking promotion or accolades recognize the value associated with making drug busts. They also recognize the utility of confidential informant usage within this context. Everyone in law enforcement, from the generic patrol officer to the dedicated narcotics detective, comes to recognize the importance of the police-citizen information exchange. This can lead officers to gravitate toward narcotics enforcement in general and confidential informant use in particular as they strive to refine their craft and advance up through the organizational hierarchy. There is a risk for officers to outpace the training or bureaucratic capacities dedicated to the police-citizen information exchange. Police organizations need to recognize that individual officers are likely to initiate or expand their involvement in the information exchange and proactively implement policies, procedures, and training to address this situation. In this day and age, police supervisors are wise to assume that all street-level officers, regardless of their title or scope of duties, are frequent participants in the police-citizen information exchange. Such a shift in thinking will not come easy for commanders who choose to adopt a reactive, as opposed to proactive, mindset about the work at hand. Nonetheless, it is an important realization, given the potential fallout that can result from ill-prepared or undersupervised officers getting involved in the information exchange.

At the organizational level, it is now common for metropolitan police departments, such as the ones included in this study, to assemble multiple specialty units charged with narcotics enforcement. This yields competition for resources and results. For example, we observed that narcotics units routinely rely on one or more detectives to refine and expand their skills in the area of confidential informant cultivation. This can result in multiple officers tapping the same habitual drug offenders as indentured informants or the same street-savvy operators as entrepreneurial informants. It is unwise to have one individual too deeply immersed in the police-citizen information exchange as a provider of criminal intelligence. Many police departments have operationalized deconfliction systems* and other bureaucratic mechanisms designed to strike a balance between secrecy and officer safety to assure that fellow officers do not encroach on one another's investigation targets. Given the likelihood that multiple officers will engage the same confidential informant, it would be wise for departments to entertain similar mechanisms designed to head off potential problems that follow.

Also published at the beginning of the war on drugs, although cast much more in a negative and conspiratorial tone, Gary Marx's (1988) monograph

---

*Event deconfliction systems rely on databases or secure hotlines shared between multiple, overlapping undercover units to enhance officer safety and the pursuit of shared tactical goals. Units submit information to the system about planned events such as surveillance operations, buy-bust operations, or the execution of search and seizure warrants. Other units check the system before engaging in their own tactical operations. The system is designed to reduce the likelihood of multiple units focusing on a single target or unknowingly conducting undercover transactions against one another. See www.ncirc.gov/deconfliction/ for details.

depicted widespread use of surreptitious police operations targeting every-thing from street-level drug offenders to national security threats abroad. While highlighting the intent behind undercover police operations, Marx spotlighted the techniques of covert intelligence gathering. He warned of how technological advances and quick results might serve to expand under-cover police operations in a host of new directions. Recent scholarship by Manning (2008) and Haggerty and Ericson (2006) speaks to the expansion across law enforcement of crime mapping, crime analysis, and a whole host of technologies being used in the realm of intelligence gathering and resource deployment. These run the gamut from proactive innovations, such as drones and CCTV used to conduct covert intelligence gathering, to reactive strate-gies, such as predictive policing software designed to strategically deploy police resources. Interestingly, Manning (2008) observed that technologies have been adapted to existing police practices and conventions more so than police practices have been altered by technological advancements. Following this logic, one would expect that the current rush to deploy body cameras as a means of transforming police-citizen legitimacy would result in more sys-tem improvement than system redesign, as it applies to police-citizen use-of-force incidents. The same applies to technology's potential impact on the police-citizen information exchange. Technology has not had a transforma-tive effect on the logic and processes that underlie covert intelligence gather-ing by police agencies. Instead of using technology to substantively alter the fundamental need and use for confidential informants, departments have committed themselves to using technological advances to refine existing protocols and routines. As new technologies become available, as they undoubtedly will, police leaders will be wise to think carefully about the unintended consequences that lie around the corner should they cut their officers loose with an eye toward enhancing what represents already delicate covert intelligence-gathering efforts.

More recently, Alexandra Natapoff (2009) provided a critical treatise on the use of confidential informants, focused largely on narcotics enforcement. Like Marx, she is highly critical of the moral compromises that underlie vari-ous covert operations, including the use of confidential informants. She identifies a host of civil rights and justice ideals that suffer as a consequence of informant-based policing and provides various remedies for consideration. Nearly two-and-a-half decades after originally publishing *The Narc's Game*, Manning (2004) takes time in the second edition of the book to acknowl-edge that he underestimated the sprawling and protracted nature of the war on drugs and how seemingly never-ending resource allocations would come to define the routinized interplay between drug offenders and members of law enforcement in "the game." Modern police agencies have been largely remiss in confronting the realities of the modern code of the streets and growing normative gap that it represents in comparison to predominant middle-class ideals. The increased reliance on confidential informants across all realms of the criminal investigation infrastructure further increases the gap between police and most inner-city communities. Inner-city residents grow increasingly frustrated with the war on drugs and the corresponding consequences that its punitive orientation has on their communities. Rolling up low-level drug users in street-level enforcement actions and pressing them to provide intelligence to assist in accessing higher echelons of the illicit drug market is not viewed as fair play by most persons living in drug-sieged neighborhoods (Gau and Brunson 2015). Moreover, the routine use of confidential informants has spawned a "stop-snitching movement" among the criminal element at the center of the street-level drug trade (Rosenfeld, Jacobs, and Wright 2003). Drug dealers and other habitual offenders warn against citizens cooperating with the police and, where practical, mete out violence against those suspected of doing so. Collectively, the use of confidential informants serves to enhance, not weaken, the code of the streets. Most law enforcement officers do not come from impoverished inner-city neighborhoods and thus do not readily relate to the normative intricacies faced by the offenders and citizens who reside in these drug-torn communities.

Certainly, police represent a core actor in the inner-city drug and crime dynamic commonly referred to as "the game." However, they approach and participate in the game from a decidedly different perspective from others involved in it. Simply stated, police do not readily relate to the motives and behaviors of the people they engage on the streets within high-crime areas. Deliberate policy initiatives are needed to narrow this gap of understanding. This applies broadly to the daily interactions that occur but should also be tailored specifically to the interactional dynamic of the police-citizen information exchange. Structured efforts that help officers appreciate the motives and behaviors of the citizens and offenders that are coparticipants in the information exchange have the potential to pay significant and long-term dividends. One possibility in this regard would be to borrow from David Kennedy's (2011) focused deterrence model of street-crime intervention. Kennedy endorses an approach wherein criminal justice authorities, from local and federal law enforcement officers to their prosecutorial counterparts, come together with law-abiding members of the community, service providers, and members of faith groups to develop a unified voice against a specific type of criminal wrongdoing, usually drug dealing or gun violence. Doing so would require open and honest communication designed to coalesce the diverse interests and behaviors of a diverse set of actors. "Call-in" sessions would then be used to confront active gang members and drug dealers about the harm they do to the community and to detail the unified message and intervention efforts that would be brought to bear on those who continue to engage in the negative behavior. A similar model might prove useful applied to the police-citizen information exchange. Namely, law enforcement authorities could engage in structured communication sessions designed to educate the citizens and known offenders about the dynamics of the information exchange. Doing so would potentially reduce the unknown for all entities and produce a higher level of empathy and shared understanding among all participants in the game.

It is interesting to note that the bulk of academic scholarship on confidential informant use was published during two time periods: at the start of the war on drugs in the 1980s, when drug dealers and their law enforcement counterparts operated with reckless abandon, and in the early twenty-first century, when the war on drugs had settled into a grind, with battle lines drawn and very little change being effected by either set of combatants. Of course, criminals and police have put in much "work" over the interceding quarter century. Both sides jockeyed for position, navigating the complex system of culture, economics, bureaucracy, and justice. While these years have seen much turnover in human capital on both sides of the equation, there have emerged some important developments that we need to set forward as food for thought.

First and foremost, we submit that, by focusing narrowly on the use of confidential informants within the narcotics-enforcement context, scholars have largely overlooked that narcotics-specific confidential informant usage has spread into all aspects of criminal investigation work. It is widely acknowledged that relying on inside sources to shine light on clandestine criminal markets or to identify perpetrators is a centuries-old practice for police. While perhaps most pervasive within vice crime enforcement, where the transactional nature of criminal exchanges breeds established criminal markets, confidential informant use has also long occupied a place in the criminal investigation of predatory crimes, such as murder, robbery, and burglary. We sense a subtle but important transformation, however, in the nature of the roles of confidential informants in modern law enforcement operations. Armed with threats of disproportionate and mandatory drug-related sanctions, which are often meted out at the federal as opposed to state level, police seem to have routinized the use of confidential informants to solve more and more cases. For example, if faced with an uncooperative murder witness who is unwilling to identify a shooter, a savvy homicide detective will lay back and wait for the individual to get arrested as part of the widespread narcotics-enforcement effort. When this arrest takes place, the homicide investigator can swoop in and leverage weighty drug-related sanctions to coerce the individual into cooperating in the murder investigation. This practice has seemingly spread widely across metropolitan policing, with everyone from street-level general investigators to detectives within the major crimes units increasingly leveraging narcotics offenses to gain traction in hard-to-crack cases. Law enforcement authorities would be wise to exercise restraint when it comes to the proliferation of and over-reliance on confidential informants. Commanders should stress the utility of other investigative practices, with an eye toward diversifying the investigative portfolio of the organization.

The increasing centrality of narcotics enforcement represents an important development within law enforcement. Recent years have seen growing momentum to roll back the punitive approach to drugs in this country. Many jurisdictions have begun to decrease or abandon mandatory sentencing options for low- and mid-level drug offenses. Decriminalization and legalization propositions are being entertained at all levels of government. At the same time, the leveraging of narcotics enforcement to advance investigations of violent and property crimes shows no signs of relenting. In short, investigators are as dependent as ever on indentured and entrepreneurial informants to make and solve cases of all shapes and sizes. These forces exist within law enforcement organizations that are fixated on productivity measures that stress case closures as much as or more than prevention efforts. This fixation on case outcomes is directly acknowledged in the epilogue to Peter Manning's (2004) second edition of *The Narc's Game*. If the policy and legislative trajectory away from a punitive war on drugs continues without a concomitant recalibration in criminal investigation strategies, law enforcement authorities might unwittingly find themselves facing decreasing clearance rates and a reduced ability to bring criminals to justice. As a result, the legitimacy, and perhaps even the authority, of law enforcement would likely be called into question. When "success" is reduced, the public is likely to see less value in policing, less of a reason to collaborate and cooperate with police, and more reasons to either ignore or individually respond to the threats in their environment. In this way, if current practices continue unabated, the realization of positive policing outcomes is sure to decrease, and this will subsequently create environments in which future successes are yet more difficult to achieve.

Our research also confirms an important organizational insight raised by earlier researchers. Namely, we found scant evidence of systematic and thorough training for officers who engage in the use of confidential informants. The stakes are very high when dealing with informants. News reports routinely surface of transgressions regarding the use of confidential informants seriously jeopardizing case legitimacy (both isolated instances and whole dockets of cases worked by a guilty officer or unit) or the personal safety of officers, informants, and bystanders. Given these high stakes, there needs to be enhanced vigilance applied to the training and oversight of the police officers who develop and use confidential informants. Our research suggests that officers see the strategic development of criminal intelligence as part and parcel to good police work. This sentiment applies to nurturing information to close open cases and generate new ones. It applies to all ranks and types of job assignment. Given this situation, departments need to develop more wide-ranging and deliberate methods of training and retraining officers on the mechanics of the police-citizen information exchange. Training should expose officers to dynamics of the four different manifestations of the police-citizen information exchange detailed in chapter 3. In particular, officers need to appreciate how their own motivations and priorities shape their approach to situations that allow for confidential informant usage. Moreover, it would behoove officers to understand the corresponding motives and behaviors associated with the different types of information providers. Doing so would allow them to better navigate the complex and fluid situations that they may encounter.

Training efforts should not be limited to law enforcement authorities. As noted above, agencies would be wise to engage community groups on the topic of the police-citizen information exchange. Doing so would decrease the likelihood of community members harboring negative sentiments about the police and potentially increase the likelihood of citizens coming forward with criminal intelligence. We uncovered evidence of this approach being used by select officers who have grown to appreciate its utility, but we found nothing to suggest that departments are systematically implementing such efforts. Prosecutors are also in need of training. Law enforcement agents and prosecutors are inextricably linked in the fight against crime, and given the primacy of confidential informant usage, both groups should do as much as they can to assure a common understanding and approach.

The police-citizen information exchange is central to police-community relations, the effectiveness of crime-fighting, and just about every other aspect of modern-day policing. To treat it otherwise is naïve. Police administrators should be actively engaging the process, seeking to wrestle with the unique challenges posed by it, and creatively formulating solutions where practical. Once training is in place, effective oversight and policy formulation must follow to assure that the intentions become routine practice throughout the organization. This is particularly the case in the current era as the nature of policing is actively evolving from a more proactive model of engagement to a more active and strategic one. Add in the uncertainties that lay ahead with the war on drugs, and departments should see that the police-citizen information exchange needs be placed front and center and considered in great detail.

Our last set of implications applies to the researchers and practitioners who seek to systematically understand the police-citizen information exchange. We view the phenomenon of informant usage to be central to modern-day policing. The use of confidential informants has so saturated the realm of criminal investigation efforts that it needs to be subject to more systematic inquiry. There is a need for creative and expanded research efforts aimed at peeling back the layers of this proverbial onion. There exist only a few small-scale studies of this phenomenon that have been conducted over the recent quarter century. Given the significance of the issues involved, there is a need for more broadly based work, ideally supported by federal or foundation funding, to explore the intricacies of the phenomenon and provide targeted recommendations on how to proactively move forward.

With the exception of Mitch Miller's 2011 article based on interviews with eighty-four former informants spread across five states, we are unaware of any scholarly works that privilege the information providers' perspective in undercover police operations. This should not come as a surprise, given the reputational and physical risks that come with serving as a confidential informant in an age in which stop-snitching movements and their corresponding threats of reprisals are alive and well within the criminal subculture. These very access issues inhibited our ability to draw on a sample of individuals with personal experience as confidential informants. This is unfortunate, given our focus on the interactional dynamics of the police-citizen information exchange. We made efforts to have officers theorize the citizen perspective based on their personal experiences with said individuals, but obviously, officers are limited in their ability to effectively do this. Therefore, researchers should explore creative means of accessing the informants' perspective on the topic. Replication and extension of the design and substantive focus used by Miller would be useful. However, we would urge researchers to pursue a more complete sampling strategy that includes both officers and informants in order to fully articulate the interactional dynamic. We submit that a focus on the police-citizen information exchange would be particularly fruitful in this regard.

As noted above, police officers occupy the consumer role in the police-citizen information exchange, and citizens from various points on the citizen-criminal continuum, who are compelled by a range of motives, constitute the providers of the privileged information. However, both of these constituencies direct attention toward the criminal wrongdoing of at-large offenders. Thus, additional research is needed to better appreciate the way offenders perceive the use of confidential informants within the context of criminal enterprise (the game) that plays itself out on a daily basis across the urban landscape of this country. For example, much has been proffered about the stop-snitching movement that is orchestrated and promulgated by the criminal element that thrives within urban communities.

Many scholars have observed that race plays a central role in America's war on drugs as well as in systematic efforts to reduce urban violence. Scholars such as Natapoff (2009) have directly implicated the use of confidential informants as a contributing factor to the disproportionate racial outcomes of the criminal justice system. Additional research is needed to further explore the role that race plays in the process and outcomes of the police-citizen information exchange.

To our knowledge, the extant research into the confidential informant phenomenon has been qualitative in nature. No efforts have been made to access official records of confidential informant involvement in criminal investigations or to systematically explore policies or practices across agencies or over time. Clearly, complicated ethical issues litter this research landscape, but select researchers have developed solid trust relationships with law enforcement agencies and conceivably could design and execute such studies. Doing so would create a valuable building block to aid us in our understanding of the confidential informant phenomenon. Alternatively, researchers might pursue survey research efforts that draw on representative samples of law enforcement agents who have experience working with confidential informants to more fully articulate the perceptions and experiences in this regard.

In this book, we have sought to provide an initial step forward in this understanding. It is only through enhanced understandings of the ways, means, and motivations of all involved in the police-citizen information exchange that we can expect a more productive, fair, and civilized approach to the control and prevention of crime. Confidential informants are no doubt here to stay. How we see them, cultivate them, manage them, and work with them is central to the goals, and often the fulfillment of the goals, of law enforcement.

REFERENCES

Alvarez, T. 1993. *Undercover Operations: Survival in Narcotics Investigations.* Springfield, IL: Charles C. Thomas.

Anderson, E. 1999. *Code of the Streets.* New York: Norton.

Berg, B. L. 2007. *Qualitative Research Methods for the Social Sciences.* 6th ed. Boston: Allyn and Bacon.

Billingsley, R. 2001a. "Informers' Careers: Motivations and Change." In *Informers: Policing, Policy, Practice*, edited by R. Billingsley, T. Nemitz, and P. Bean, 81–97. Portland, OR: Willan Publishing.

————. 2001b. "An Examination of the Relationship between Informers and Their Handlers within the Police Service in England." MPhil diss., Loughborough University, UK.

————. 2003. "The Police Informer/Handler Relationship: Is It Really Unique?" *International Journal of Police Science and Management* 5: 50–62.

————. 2009. *Covert Human Intelligence Sources: The 'Unlovely' Face of Police Work.* Hampshire, UK: Waterside Press.

Billingsley, R., T. Nemitz, and P. Bean. 2001. *Informers: Policing, Policy, Practice.* Portland, OR: Willan Publishing.

Blan, P., and R. Billingsley, 2001. "Drugs, Crime and Informers." In *Informers: Policing, Policy, Practice*, edited by R. Billingsley, T. Nemitz, and P. Bean, 25–37. Portland, OR: Willan Publishing.

Bloom, R. 2002. *Ratting: The Use and Abuse of Informants in the American Justice System.* Westport, CT: Praeger.

Brown, E. 2007. *SNITCH: Informants, Cooperators, and the Corruption of Justice.* New York: Public Affairs Books.

Brown, M. F. 1985. "Criminal Informants: Some Observations on Use, Abuse and Control." *Journal of Police Science and Administration* 13: 251–256.

Chalk, P. 2011. *The Latin American Drug Trade: Scope, Dimensions, Impact and Response.* Santa Monica, CA: Rand.

Charmaz, K. 1983. "The Grounded Theory Method: An Explication and Interpretation." In *Contemporary Field Research,* edited by R. Emerson, 109–126. Boston: Little and Brown.

———. 2006. *Constructing Grounded Theory: A Practical Guide through Qualitative Analysis.* London: Sage.

Cloyd, J. 1982. *Drugs and Information Control: The Role of Men and Manipulation in Control of Drug Trafficking.* Westport, CT: Greenwood.

Clark, R. 2001. "Informers and Corruption." In *Informers: Policing, Policy, Practice,* edited by R. Billingsley, T. Nemitz, and P. Bean, 38–49. Portland, OR: Willan Publishing.

Cooper, P., and Murphy, J. 1997. "Ethical Approaches for Police Officers When Working with Informants in the Development of Criminal Intelligence in the United Kingdom." *Journal of Social Policy* 26: 1–20.

Dabney, D. A. 2010. "Observations Regarding Key Operational Realities in a Compstat Model of Policing." *Justice Quarterly* 27: 28–51.

Davies, P. 2004. "Systematic Reviews and the Campbell Collaboration." In *Evidence-Based Practice in Education,* edited by G. Thomas and R. Pring, 21–33. New York: Open University Press.

Dodge, M. 2006. "Juvenile Police Informers: Friendship, Persuasion, and Pretense." *Youth Violence and Juvenile Justice* 4: 234–246.

Dorn, N., M. Karim, and N. South. 1992. *Traffickers: Drug Markets and Law Enforcement.* London: Routledge.

Dunningham, C., and C. Norris. 1999. "The Detective, the Snout, and the Audit Commission: The Real Costs in Using Informers." *Howard Journal of Criminal Justice* 38: 67–86.

Ericson, R. 1981. *Making Crime: A Study of Detective Work.* Toronto: Butterworth.

Federal Bureau of Investigations. 2005. *The Federal Bureau of Investigation's Compliance with the Attorney General's Investigative Guidelines.* Washington, DC: U.S. Department of Justice, Office of the Inspector General.

Fijnaut, C., and G. Marx, eds. 1996. *Undercover: Police Surveillance in Comparative Perspective.* The Hague: Kluwer Law International.

Fitzgerald, D. G. 2007. *Informants and Undercover Investigations: A Practical Guide to Law, Policy, and Procedures.* Boca Raton, FL: CRC Press.

Fleisher, M. S. 1995. *Beggars and Thieves: Lives of Urban Street Criminals.* Madison, WI: University of Wisconsin Press.

Gardiner, P. A. 2002. *Criminal Investigation's Use of Confidential Funds for Undercover Operations is Appropriate; However, Certain Aspects of Undercover Operations Need Improvement.* Washington, DC: U.S. Department of Justice.

Gau, J. M., and R. K. Brunson. 2015. "Procedural Injustice, Lost Legitimacy, and Self-Help: Young Males' Adaptations to Perceived Unfairness in Urban Policing Tactics." *Journal of Contemporary Criminal Justice* 31: 132–150.

Geberth, V. J. 1979. "Confidential Informant." *Law and Order* 27 (6): 38–41.

Geertz, C. 1973. "Thick Description: Toward an Interpretive Theory of Culture." In *The Interpretation of Cultures: Selected Essays,* edited by C. Geertz, 3–30. New York: Basic Books.

Girodo, M. 1984. "Entry and Re-Entry Strain in Undercover Agents." In *Role Transitions,* edited by V. L. Allen and E. van de Vliert, 169–179. New York: Plenum Press.

———. 1985. "Health and Legal Issues in Undercover Narcotics Investigations: Misrepresented Evidence." *Behavioral Sciences and the Law* 3: 299–308.

———. 1991. "Drug Corruption in Undercover Agents: Measuring the Risk." *Behavioral Science and the Law* 9: 361–370.

Glover, P. R. 2001. "Re-Defining Friendship: Employment of Informants by Police." *University of Colorado Law Review* 72: 749–777.

Goddard, D. 1988. *Undercover: The Secret Lives of a Federal Agent.* New York: Times Books.

Goffman, E. 1959. *The Presentation of Self in Everyday Life.* New York: Anchor Books.

Greenwood, P. W., J. M. Chaiken, J. R. Petersilia. 1975. *The Criminal Investigation Process.* Santa Monica, CA: Rand.

Greer, S. 1995. "Towards a Sociological Model of the Police Informant." *British Journal of Sociology* 46: 509–527.

Grieve, J. 1992. "The Police Contribution to Drugs Education: A Role for the 1990s." In *Drug Abuse and Misuse: Developing Educational Strategies in Partnership,* edited by R. Evans and L. O'Connor, 53–64. London: Fulton.

Grimes, M. E. 2009. *Informants: A Guide for Developing and Controlling Informants.* New York: LawTech Publishing Co.

Haggerty, K. D., R. V. Ericson. 2006. *The New Politics of Surveillance and Visibility.* Toronto: University of Toronto Press.

Hamilton, H., and J. O. Smykla. 1994. "Guidelines for Police Undercover Work: New Questions about Accreditation and the Emphasis of Procedure over Authorization." *Justice Quarterly* 11: 135.

Hanvey, P. 1995. *Identifying, Recruiting and Handling informers.* London: Police Research Group.

Harney, M. L., and J. C. Cross. 1960. *The Informer in Law Enforcement.* Springfield, IL: Charles C. Thomas.

Herbert, D. L., and L. Sinclair. 1977. "The Use of Minors as Undercover Agents or Informants: Some Legal Problems." *Journal of Police Science and Administration* 5: 185–192.

Hess, A., and M. Amir. 2002. "The Program of Criminal Justice Undercover Agents Sources in the Drug Trades." *Substance Use and Misuse* 37: 997–1034.

Hight, J. E. 1998. "Avoiding the Informant Trap: A Blueprint for Control." *FBI Law Enforcement Bulletin* 67 (11): 1+.

Innes, M. 2000. "Professionalizing the Role of the Police Informant: The British Experience." *Policing and Society* 9: 357–383.

International Association of Chiefs of Police. 1990. *Confidential Informants, Concepts and Issues Paper.* Washington, DC: IACP National Law Enforcement Policy Center.

Jacobs, B. A. 1992. "Undercover Deception: Reconsidering Presentations of Self." *Journal of Contemporary Ethnography* 21: 200–225.

———. 1993a. "Undercover Deception Clues: A Case of Restrictive Deterrence." *Criminology* 31: 281–299.

———. 1993b. "Getting Narced: Neutralization of Undercover Identity Discredita-
tion." *Deviant Behavior* 14: 187–208.

———. 1994. "Undercover Social-Distancing Technique." *Symbolic Interaction* 17:
395–410.

———. 1996. "Cognitive Bridges: The Case of High School Undercover Officers."
Sociological Quarterly 37: 391–412.

———. 1997. "Contingent Ties: Undercover Drug Officers' Use of Informants."
British Journal of Sociology 48: 35–53.

———. 1999. *Dealing Crack: The Social World of Streetcorner Selling.* Boston:
Northeastern University Press.

Janzen, S. 1990. *Asset Forfeiture: Informants and Undercover Investigations.* Washington, DC: Police Executive Research Forum.

Katz, H. A. 1990. *Developing and Using Underworld Police Informants.* Washington,
DC: National Institute of Justice.

Katz, J. 1988. *Seductions of Crime: Moral and Sensual Attractions of Doing Evil.* New
York: Basic Books.

Kennedy, D. M. 2011. *Don't Shoot: One Man, a Street Fellowship, and the End of
Violence in Inner-City America.* New York: Bloomsbury.

Kleinman, D. M. 1980. "Out of the Shadows and into the Files: Who Should Control Informants?" *Police Magazine* 3 (6): 36–44.

Kraska, P. B. 2001. *Militarizing the American Criminal Justice System: The Changing
Roles of the Armed Forces and the Police.* Boston: Northeastern University
Press.

Langworthy, R. H., 1989. "Do Stings Control Crime?: An Evaluation of a Police
Fencing Operation." *Justice Quarterly* 6: 27–45.

Laskey, J. A. 1997. "The Snitch Profile." *Journal of Gang Research* 4: 1–16.

Lee, G. 1981. "Drug Informants: Motives, Methods and Management." *FBI Law
Enforcement Bulletin* 50 (9): 10–15.

Leo, R. A. 2008. *Police Interrogation and American Justice.* Cambridge, MA: Harvard University Press.

Leson, I. 2012. "Toward Efficiency and Equity in Law Enforcement: 'Rachel's Law'
and the Protection of Drug Informants." *Boston College Journal of Law and Social
Science* 32: 391–419.

Levine, M. 2009. "The Weakest Link: The Dire Consequences of a Weak Link in
the Informant Handling and Covert Operations Chain-of-Command." *Law
Enforcement Executive Forum* 9 (2): 21–46.

Lyman, M. D. 1987. *Narcotics and Crime Control.* Springfield, IL: Charles C.
Thomas.

Madinger, J. 1999. *Confidential Informant: Law Enforcement's Most Valuable Tool.*
Boca Raton, FL: CRC Press.

Mallory, S. L. 2000. *Informants: Development and Management.* Incline Village,
NV: Copperhouse.

Manning, P. 1980. *The Narcs' Game: Organizational and Informational Limits on
Drug Law Enforcement.* Cambridge, MA: MIT Press.

———. 2004. *The Narcs' Game: Organizational and Informational Limits on Drug Law Enforcement.* 2nd ed. Prospects Heights, IL: Waveland.

———. 2008. *The Technology of Policing: Crime Mapping, Information Technology, and the Rationality of Crime Control.* New York: New York University Press.

Marx, G. T. 1974. "Thoughts on a Neglected Category of Social Movement Participant: The Agent Provocateur and the Informant." *American Journal of Sociology* 80: 402–442.

———. 1981. "Ironies of Social Control." *Social Problems* 28: 221–233.

———. 1985. "Who Really Gets Stung?: Some Issues Raised by the New Police Undercover Work." In *Moral Issues in Police Work,* edited by F. A. Elliston & M. Feldberg, 99–128. Totowa, NJ: Rowman and Allanheld.

———. 1988. *Undercover: Police Surveillance in America.* Berkeley: University of California Press.

Mastrofski, S., and R. B. Parks. 1990. "Improving Observational Studies of Policy." *Criminology* 28: 465–496.

Mauet, T. 1995. "Informant Disclosure and Production: A Second Look at Paid Informants." *Arizona Law Review* 37: 563–576.

Mericle, J. G. 1994. "Countersurveillance: Exploring Local Level Deepcover Narcotics Enforcement." Unpublished dissertation, Florida State University.

Miller, G. I. 1987. "Observations on Police Undercover Work." *Criminology* 25: 27–46.

Miller, J. M. 2011. "Becoming an Informant." *Justice Quarterly* 28: 203–220.

Morton, J. 1995. *Supergrasses and Informers: An Informal History of Undercover Police Work.* London: Warner Books.

Motto, C. J., and D. L. June. 2000. *Undercover.* 2nd ed. Boca Raton, FL: Charles C. Thomas.

Mount, H. A., Jr. 1991. "Criminal Informants: An Administrator's Dream or Nightmare." *Prosecutor* 24 (4): 23–26.

Murphy, S., D. Waldorf, and C. Reinarman. 1990. Drifting into Dealing: Becoming a Cocaine Seller. *Qualitative Sociology* 3: 321–343.

Natapoff, A. 2004. "Snitching: The Institutional and Communal Consequences." *University of Cincinnati Law Review* 73: 645–652.

———. 2006. "Beyond Unreliable: How Snitches Contribute to Wrongful Convictions." *Golden Gate University Law Review* 37: 107–116.

———. 2009. *Snitching: Criminal Informants and the Erosion of American Justice.* New York: NYU Press.

Niederhoffer, A. 1969. *Behind the Shield: The Police in Urban Society.* New York: Doubleday.

Newburn, T., and S. Merry. 1990. *Keeping in Touch: Police-Victim Communication in Two Areas.* Home Office Research Study 116. London: HMSO.

Neyroud, P., and A. Beckley. 2001. "Regulating Informers: The Regulation of the Investigatory Powers Act, Covert Policing and Human Rights." In *Informers: Policing, Policy, Practice,* edited by R. Billingsley, T. Nemitz, and P. Bean, 164–175. Portland, OR: Willan Publishing.

Nugent, H., F.J. Leahy Jr., and E.F. Connors. 1991. *Managing Confidential Inform-ants*. Washington, DC: Bureau of Justice Assistance.

Office of National Drug Control Policy. 2015. "Drug Control Funding Priorities in the FY 2016 President's Budget." Accessed June 30, 2015. www.whitehouse.gov /sites/default/files/ondcp/press-releases/ondcp_fy16_budget_fact_sheet.pdf.

Osther, D.G. 1999. "Juvenile Informants: A Necessary Evil?" *Washburn Law Jour-nal* 39: 106–127.

Palmiotto, M. 1984. *Confidential Informant: Management and Control*. Cincinnati, OH: Anderson.

Pfuhl, E.H., Jr. 1992. "Crimestoppers: The Legitimation of Snitching." *Justice Quar-terly* 9: 505–528.

Pogrebin, M.R., and E.D. Poole. 1993. "Vice Isn't Nice: A Look at the Effects of Working Undercover." *Journal of Criminal Justice* 21: 383–394.

Rees, J.T. 1980. "Motivations of Criminal Informants." *FBI Law Enforcement Bul-letin* 49 (5): 23–28.

Reuter, P. 1982. *Licensing Criminals: Police and Informants*. Washington, DC: Rand.

Rich, M.L. 2010. "Coerced Informants and Thirteenth Amendment Limitations on the Police-Informant Relationship." *Santa Clara Law Review* 50: 681–745.

Rosenbaum, D.P. 1989. "Enhancing Citizen Participation and Solving Serious Crime: A National Evaluation of Crime Stoppers Programs." *Crime and Delin-quency* 35: 401–420.

Rosenfeld, R., B. Jacobs, and R. Wright. 2003. "Snitching and the Code of the Street." *British Journal of Criminology* 43: 291–309.

Schoeman, F. 1986. "Undercover Operations: Some Moral Questions about S.108." *Criminal Justice Ethics* 5: 16–22.

Schreiber, A.J. 2001. "Dealing with the Devil: An Examination of the FBI's Trou-bled Relationship with its Confidential Informants." *Columbia Journal of Law and Social Problems* 34: 301–368.

Settle, R. 1995. *Police Informers: Negotiation and Power*. Annandale, New South Wales: Federation Press.

Shover, N., and D. Honaker. 1992. "The Socially Bounded Decision Making of Per-sistent Property Offenders." *Howard Journal of Criminal Justice* 31: 276–293.

Skolnick, J.H. 1966. *Justice without Trial: Law Enforcement in a Democratic Society*. New York: John Wiley and Sons.

———. 1982. "Deception by Police." *Criminal Justice Ethics* 1: 40–54.

Sobczak, T. 2009. "The Consent-Once-Removed Doctrine: The Constitutionality of Passing Consent from an Informant to Law Enforcement." *Florida Law Review* 62: 491–518.

Tewksbury, R., and E.E. Mustaine. 1998. "Lifestyles of the Wheelers and Dealers: Drug Dealing among American College Students." *Journal of Crime and Justice* 21: 37–56.

Tewksbury, R., and P. Gagne. 2002. "Looking for Love in All the Wrong Places: Men Who Patronize Prostitutes." In *Contemporary Perspectives on Sex Crimes*, edited by R.M. Holmes & S. Holmes, 85–98. Thousand Oaks, CA: Sage.

Topalli, V. 2005. "When Being Good Is Bad: An Expansion of Neutralization Theory." *Criminology* 43: 797–836.

Tunnell, K. D. 1992. *Choosing Crime: The Criminal Calculus of Property Offenders.* Chicago: Nelson-Hall.

U.S. Department of Justice. 2005. *The Drug Enforcement Administration's Payments to Confidential Sources.* Washington, DC: U.S. Department of Justice.

Vasquez, J., and S. Kelly. 1980. "Management's Commitment to the Undercover Operative." *FBI Law Enforcement Bulletin* 49 (2): 3–12.

Weinstein, I. 1999. "Regulating the Market for Snitches." *Buffalo Law Review* 47: 563–644.

Weisburd, D., S. D. Mastrofski, R. Greenspan, and J. J. Willis. 2004. *The Growth of Compstat in American Policing.* Washington, DC: Police Foundation.

Westmarland, L. 2013. "'Snitches get stitches': US Homicide Detectives' Ethics and Morals in Action." *Policing and Society* 23: 311–327.

Westley, W. A. 1956. Secrecy and the police. *Social Forces,* 34: 254–257.

Williams, J. R., and L. L. Guess. 1981. "The Informant: A Narcotics Enforcement Dilemma." *Journal of Psychoactive Drugs* 13: 235–245.

Williamson, T., and P. Bagshaw. 2001. "The Ethics of Informer Handling." In *Informers: Policing, Policy, Practice,* edited by R. Billingsley, T. Nemitz, and P. Bean, 50–66. Portland, OR: Willan Publishing.

Wilson, J. Q. 1968. *Varieties of Police Behavior.* Cambridge, MA: Harvard University Press.

———. 1978. *The Investigators.* New York: Basic Books.

Wisotsky, S. 1986. *Breaking the Impasse in the War on Drugs.* Westport, CN: Greenwood Press.

Worden, R. 1986. "The Premises of Police Work: What Policemen Believe and What Difference It Makes." Unpublished doctoral dissertation, University of North Carolina.

Worrall, J. L. 2001. "Addicted to the Drug War: The Role of Civil Asset Forfeiture as a Budgetary Necessity in Contemporary Law Enforcement." *Journal of Criminal Justice* 29: 171–187.

Wright, R. T., and S. H. Decker. 1996. *Burglars on the Job: Streetlife and Residential Break-Ins.* Boston: Northeastern University Press.

Yin, R. 1989. *Case Study Research Design and Methods.* Newbury Park, CA: Sage.

Zimmerman, C. 1994. "Toward a New Vision of Informants: A History of Abuses and Suggestions for Reform." *Hastings Constitutional Law Quarterly* 22: 81–178.

INDEX

prostitutes, 69, 89–90, 91, 92, 117–18, 123–24, 183; fear of disease, 94–97; "hos," 87, 89–90, 106
protection, informant, 8, 131–32, 136–44

rapport, 52, 73–75, 111–12
recruitment, informant, 67–78, 107, 153, 164; background stage, 70–73; closing stage, 76–78; construction stage, 75–76; foundation stage, 73–75; of indentured informants, 45–49
registration, informant, 108–114, 164
respect, 52–53, 73, 99, 115, 121, 149, 150; among specialty units, 103–5, 137
Rich, Michael, 8
ride-along sessions, 19, 20, 22–24

self-advancement (motive), 31, 33, 35, 36, 39, 62, 67, 191. See also confidential informant, entrepreneurial
self-preservation (motive), 31, 33, 38, 62, 191
sell-busts, 12. See also buy-busts
Skolnick, Jerome, 10–11
snitch/snitching, 4, 10, 15, 16, 18, 50, 52, 59, 132, 137, 141, 152; "stop-snitching" movement, 41, 197, 201–2
snowball sampling technique, 25, 37
Sobczak, Tim, 8
"sources," 5, 31, 34, 109–112, 148–49, 167; cooperating, 40–42; unwitting, 42–43, 67

standard operating procedure (SOP), 58–59, 110, 111
street credibility, 28

thick description, 17
Thirteenth Amendment ban, 8
"thugs" ("corner boys," "dope boys," "perps"), 87–88, 90–91, 106, 145
"troublemakers," 87
trust, 15, 40, 71–72, 73–75, 94, 110–12, 115–24, 131–32, 167, 193. See also rapport; respect
"turning" informants, 56, 68, 71, 77, 94, 107, 111, 143, 153; approaches to, 45, 46, 51–53, 91; literature on, 4, 37
typology, 17–18, 30–40, 31 fig., 191

U.S. Department of Justice (DOJ), 7, 108
U.S. Drug Enforcement Administration (DEA), 11

vice crimes, 14, 65–66, 155

waiver of liability, 108
"wannabe," 35, 44–45, 169, 191. See also "civic-minded citizen informant"; police buffs
Wilson, James Q., 10, 11, 190
Wisotsky, Steven, 14

Zimmerman, Clifford, 4–5, 8, 9